Y0-BQE-383

THE CATHOLIC PRIEST IN THE MODERN WORLD

THE
CATHOLIC
PRIEST

BX
1912
.M22

IN THE
MODERN
WORLD

93221

JAMES A. MAGNER

ST. JOSEPH'S UNIVERSITY   STX
BTQ 2931 .M19
The Catholic priest in the modern world.

3 9353 00012 3487

THE BRUCE PUBLISHING COMPANY
MILWAUKEE

NIHIL OSBTAT:

    John A. McMahon
    Censor librorum

IMPRIMATUR:

    ✠ Samuel Cardinal Stritch
    February 18, 1956

BX 1912
M 19 C

Rosary College Dewey Classification Number: 253

Library of Congress Catalog Card Number: 57–6319

© 1957 BY THE BRUCE PUBLISHING COMPANY
MADE IN THE UNITED STATES OF AMERICA

Dedicated
in grateful memory to my brother
a great priest, pastor, and bishop
the Most Reverend Francis J. Magner, Ph.D., S.T.D.

CONTENTS

FOREWORD

THERE is a large, rich literature on the priest from the *Lex Levitarum* to this latest book by Dr. Magner. Through all this literature the fundamentals are the same and only adaptations of these principles to changing conditions vary. There really can be nothing new on this subject more than picturing the priest in changing conditions. Our blessed Saviour gave us the perfect model of the priest and ever since writers have been studying this model in all its details and presenting it to priests. The sanctity of the priest, which St. Pius X said must be as different from that of the pious layman as the heavens are from the earth, flows from the very nature of the priesthood. The ordered zeal of the priest must take its inspiration from the love of the Sacred Heart of Jesus. The diligence and industry of the priest are inseparably related to his mission. His love of learning comes from his office in the Magisterium of the Church. The Fathers of the Church aptly summed up the priest in the scriptural phrase, *Lux Mundi*.

Still, there is a twofold need of more books on priests for priests. Despite what is contained in our libraries, it is practically helpful to gather together in brief summaries what has been written for the convenience of priests and it is necessary to picture the priest in changing social and world conditions. The priest in the medieval village culture was not different from the priest of a large urban parish of today and still we must understand the priesthood as it shines forth in a world of modern industry, commerce and transportation. To tell the priest in the colors and hues of our world is to picture the unchanging priesthood, which knows no age or era and is the perpetuation of the Mystery of our Redemption.

Dr. Magner in this book, in simple language, without pretensions of profound erudition, speaks of the priest in our country today. He has repeated very much which has been said by saints and scholars and added his own observations from his experience and learning. Perhaps the best achievement of this book is that it will stimulate deep thinking and meditation. Some things in it will provoke discussion, in which there will be disagreements with the author. If so, since the basic principles are so well stated, these very discussions will achieve the purpose for the writing of the book.

A particular emphasis of the author has been the danger of what some have called actionism in the life of a priest, that is, so overstressing active labors as to fail to give a proper place to vigorous personal living in the Mystic Body of Christ. This emphasis is opportune and happy at a time when so many new demands are made on the priest in his pastoral labors. To appear before men as if he had just left the conscious presence of God is the sequel of much prayer and penance and yet it is the secret of the great, good priest of Christ.

We are sure that many, familiar with the other writings of Dr. Magner, will read this book in which a priest talks almost familiarly with priests about their one great concern.

✠ SAMUEL CARDINAL STRITCH
Archbishop of Chicago

October 15, 1956

THE CATHOLIC PRIEST IN THE MODERN WORLD

"Being mindful of the work of your faith and labor and charity: and of the enduring of the hope of our Lord Jesus Christ before God and our Father" (1 Thess. 1:3).

CHAPTER I

THE PERSONALITY OF THE PRIEST

I

IN HIS beautiful Exhortation on the Priestly Life, Pope Pius XII has written a description of this sublime calling, its significance, and its responsibilities, which may well serve as the text for all who would understand the Catholic priesthood. "The priesthood," he writes, "is a great gift of the Divine Redeemer, Who, in order to perpetuate the work of redemption of the human race which He completed on the Cross, confided His powers to the Church which He wished to be a participator in His unique and ever-lasting Priesthood. The priest is like 'another Christ' because he is marked with an indelible character making him, as it were, a living image of our Saviour. The priest represents Christ Who said, 'As the Father has sent Me, I also send you'; 'he who hears you, hears Me.' Admitted to this most sublime ministry by a call from heaven, 'he is appointed for men in the things pertaining to God, that he may offer gifts and sacrifices for sins.' "[1]

The purpose of the Catholic priesthood, as instituted by Christ is, therefore, to distribute the merits of the Saviour to succeeding generations and to assist in securing the salvation of men through this ministry. One of the first responsibilities of this mission is to

[1] *Menti Nostrae* Apostolic Exhortation of Pope Pius XII (Washington, D. C.: National Catholic Welfare Conference, 1950), par. 7.

preach the Gospel of Christ with all the teachings of the divine Master and of the revealed word of God in both the Old and the New Testament. In addition to this, the priest conveys the mind and the legislation of the Church to the faithful as an authorized officer of the Institution. But the distinctive mark and power of the Catholic priesthood as separate from the laity and as categorically different from the conception of the Protestant ministry is its sacramental power.

The Catholic priest is ordained with the power to say the Mass, to forgive sins, to give Extreme Unction to the dying, to administer the sacrament of Confirmation under special circumstances, and to engage as the official representative of the Church in the administration of the other sacraments, by virtue of the power conferred by Christ upon His Apostles and their successors, the bishops of the Church. The priesthood itself is a sacrament of Christ, which confers an indelible mark upon the soul, similar to that of Baptism and Confirmation. It is not simply a call to preach the Gospel or an appointment to an ecclesiastical post. Its validity and power stem directly from an unbroken transmission of the sacrament of Holy Orders from Christ through the bishops of the Church. It is, in the strict sense, a supernatural state and office, which no natural power or acceptance can produce or substitute for.

In the administration of the sacraments, the priest or the bishop, who possesses the fullness of the priesthood including the power of ordaining priests, acts as the agent of Christ. The validity of the sacraments does not depend upon the state of grace or soul of the person giving or receiving the sacrament. A sacrament of Christ remains such even if it is given or received unworthily. But from the standpoint of truly and effectively representing Christ in any phase of the ministry, there is no substitute for personal sanctity in the priest himself.

If the sublimity of the Catholic priesthood arises from its institution by Christ and its special sacramental powers, its effective power stems from the personal example of the priest himself. The first task of the priest is, therefore, that of his own sanctification. As "another Christ" showing forth in his own life and works the personality of the divine Master, he can sincerely proceed to the sanctification of others. In the words of Pope Pius XII, "This lofty dignity demands from priests that they react to their exalted office with the strictest fidelity. Since they are destined to promote the glory of God on earth and to cherish and increase the Mystical Body of Christ, they must be outstanding by the sanctity of their lives in order that through them the 'fragrance of Christ' may be spread everywhere."[2]

These considerations apply to all priests, whether they live in a religious community or labor in the world. But the priest who is called to the active ministry, where force of example may be as important in its way as his sacramental power, in gaining souls, is under special stress to bring his natural personality into conformity with his supernatural character.

Every man is subject to two great natural forces in attitude and action. One is his own inner, congenital character and temperament, built from the spiritual and physical heritage of his ancestors and formed anew in his own personality. The other is the force of education. This ranges from personal experience, which begets conclusions about life and its values, to formal study and external training or discipline. In some men, these two forces are closely welded, to produce a well-integrated personality, settled convictions, and singleness of purpose. In others, there is never more than a superficial connection between the two. And in still others, there remains an underlying uncertainty and shifting of values, depending on external influences or opportunities.

As a man, notwithstanding his supernatural character, the priest must recognize and come to grips with these forces in his own mind and personality. Unless he is basically at one with himself and his life purpose, he cannot develop constructively as a man or as a priest. Much less can he make personal progress as a spiritual leader and mature guide of others. A priest whose outlook on life is divided into separate compartments, one of

---

[2] *Ibid.,* par. 9.

Christian teaching which he learned in the seminary and which serves for his sermons, and others of shifting practical expediency, cannot be said to have a priestly personality in the full, integrated sense of the word.

The desire for moral excellence and the following of Christ, which are basic to the priesthood, must be reduced to definite terms and objectives along which progress can be made and the whole personality developed. Moreover, it will be found that the following of Christ in the priesthood involves far more than moral rectitude and blamelessness of life. The priest, particularly if engaged in pastoral, administrative, or teaching work, will find that natural prudence and affability come by practice as much as by prayer. It is possible for a priest to pursue all the prescribed spiritual exercises at the same time as he is developing an insular mentality and antisocial eccentricities. It was undoubtedly with this danger under consideration that St. Paul penned his admonition about "being mindful of the work of your faith and labor and charity."

The process of sanctification, which follows an intellectual pattern as well as discipline of the will, must be a constant one. It should manifest itself in the broadening and deepening of the priest's spirit and perceptions, on both supernatural and natural levels, as well as in his observance of the Commandments. This process requires the courage of self-examination as well as the study and exhortation of others, in the light of Christian principles.

2

The very conception of the Catholic priesthood, as the public consecrated service of God and the ministry of the sacraments, is based upon faith. Faith, however, like idealism, requires careful analysis and evaluation by the individual, a gradual bringing into focus, and a real identification with the principles and purposes of Christ, if it is to be fruitful.

In these times, the word "faith" has been broadened out to signify hardly more than an optimistic state of mind or expectancy. With many Protestant groups, "faith" means only the "acceptance" of God by the individual, who thereupon becomes convinced of his salvation. It is possible that some Catholics entertain an idea that, with the profession of Catholic faith in general, it is not necessary to go into the particulars of belief. The Catholic definition of faith, whether as a theological virtue or as a human act relative to the truths of divine revelation, points directly to an intellectual acceptance of or assent to these truths, for the reason that they have been revealed by God, who is incapable of error or deceit. For this reason, it is entirely reasonable that the individual Catholic, and above all the priest, should be acquainted with the specific objects of his Catholic faith.

The acceptance of the divinity of Christ, the adoption of His teachings, and recognition of the divine teaching authority of the Catholic Church as founded by Christ are, consequently, basic to the personal formation as well as to the social mission of the priest. His faith is the foundation of his whole priestly outlook and career. To the extent that it is deep and constant, with the force of conviction as well as of voluntary discipline, it will be an unfailing source of strength and inspiration throughout the priest's life and shine as a powerful beacon for him to guide and direct the lives of others. A mere surface acceptance of the truths of religion is easily punctured by personal disappointment, temptation, and difficulty of fulfillment.

For this reason, the Church has insisted upon a thorough education for her priests, in philosophy and theology — dogmatic, moral, and ascetic. In this training, which represents a tremendous body of knowledge and commentary by the Fathers, Doctors, and theologians of the Church through the centuries, there is no effort to conceal the element of mystery and partial understanding of divine revelation. It is understood that many natural truths, such as freedom of the will and the existence of evil, and many revealed truths, such as the existence of the Holy Trinity, will never be fully understood, for the reason that they surpass human comprehension. Even the advance of natural science and the interpretation of the Holy Scriptures in the light of current discoveries are a slow and often tedious process. But such difficulties and human limitations should never disturb the faith of the priest, no matter how profound his studies, if he retains the spirit of humility and prayer.

A living, active, and growing faith is, moreover, the source of zeal and enthusiasm in the priest for his work. In the words of St. James, "Some man will say: Thou hast faith, and I have works; show me thy faith without works, and I will show thee by works my faith."[3] The Apostle goes so far as to make good works a test of faith. "What doth it profit, my brethren," he asks, "if a man say he hath faith, but hath not works? Shall faith be able to save him? . . . So faith also, if it have not works, is dead in itself."[4]

This principle is indeed one of the basic points of difference with the Protestant position that faith alone, as the acceptance of God and confidence or trust in Him, is sufficient for salvation. The Catholic teaching on this point is that keeping the Commandments is also necessary for salvation.[5] A lively faith will certainly assist one in keeping the Commandments; but there are times when it may be necessary to stir one to an act of contrition after a fall. Moreover, the Commandments are not kept simply by avoiding sin, but also in the positive fulfillment of the laws of justice and charity, as embodied in Christ's injunction: "Thou shalt love the Lord thy God with thy whole heart and with thy whole soul and with thy whole mind and with thy whole strength. This is the first commandment. And the second is like to it: Thou shall love thy neighbor as thyself. There is no other commandment greater than these."[6] For the priest, as the Apostle of Christ, this love must show itself in the active preaching of the Gospel and in an exemplification of the works of social charity.

In his Exhortation on the Priestly Life, already referred to, Pope Pius XII warns priests against allowing the whirl of external activity to lead to the neglect of their primary duty, namely, their own sanctification. He refers to what has been called "the heresy

---

[3] James 2:18.
[4] James 2:14–17.
[5] Mt. 19:17.
[6] Mk. 12:30–31.

of action," which is a sheerly secular program of social, cultural, or athletic activities without reference to grace or the means of sanctification appointed by Jesus Christ. But at the same time, he points out that the Catholic faith must not become stagnant or shrouded in the mere repetition of dogmatic principles. Its implications must be reduced to the practical order of daily living.

"In the same way," he writes, "we have deemed it timely to stimulate to the activities of the ministry those who, shut up in themselves and almost diffident of the efficacy of divine aid, do not labor to the best of their ability to make the spirit of Christianity penetrate daily life in all those ways demanded by our times."[7] He mentions specifically as the chief activities of the apostolate the enlightening of men's minds with divine truth, guiding their consciences in righteousness, and strengthening and comforting souls torn with doubt or suffering. "To these forms of apostolate," he notes, "add also those others which the needs of the times demand."

3

In determining the activities in which they will engage, priests should use as a criterion the fact that their entire lives are dedicated to spiritual service. As the lawyer directs his attention and energies to the practice of law, and the doctor to the practice of medicine, the priest devotes himself to the salvation of souls. The spiritual conception of his life work should dominate and penetrate all his labors and not represent simply one phase or aspect of his interests. There ought to be a relationship of everything that he does, even his hobbies, to this objective. Even his recreational activities should be co-ordinated in some way toward the development of his talents or the recuperation of his powers for the service of God. The sense of priesthood should give him a professional, serious outlook on his career and a constant awareness of his responsibility as the ambassador of Christ.

So that they may devote themselves exclusively to the apostolate, the Church endeavors to free its priests from the necessity of

----

[7] *Op. cit.,* par. 60–61.

worldly, gainful pursuits. The priest is normally dependent for his livelihood upon the offerings of the faithful, even though this may take the form of a salary; and corresponding moral obligation is placed upon the laity by law of the Church. "Therefore," says the Holy Father, "instruct the faithful under your care on their obligation to help their priests in want. Our Lord's words always hold true: 'The laborer deserves his wages.' How can you expect fervent and energetic work from priests when they lack the necessities of life?"[8]

Even the celibacy of the Catholic clergy has, as one of its purposes, the liberation of the priest from the cares and responsibilities of family life, so that he may devote his full attention to the needs of his spiritual flock. The thoughtful priest should ponder on this fact and direct his steps accordingly.

The priest who has entered a contemplative religious order and devotes his life to meditation, prayer, and silent labor among his brethren is not, of course, involved in the challenge and problems of a social mission. But the parish priest and the priest engaged in teaching or administration of any kind, requiring contact with people and an active ministry, must gear himself for an unselfish public service. He must be ready to serve. He cannot withhold himself, whether from shyness or temperament. He must learn to sacrifice his personal preferences, and plunge into the hard toil that pastoral work involves and make up his mind that he will put in a good eight-hour day and more, if need requires.

Every priest in active work should develop the ability to mix freely and easily with people. The priest who is ill at ease with people or who shrinks from daily and familiar contact with the laity can easily develop eccentricities of outlook and manner that increase with the years and render him something of a museum piece rather than a second Christ. It is important to remember that Christ was not a recluse. He drew his Apostles around Him from the people, and He lived for the people and partook of their life. He visited His friends and extended His ministrations to all classes of people, even at the risk of being accused of con-

[8] *Ibid.*, par. 132.

sorting with sinners, of being a "wine bibber," and of violating the Sabbath. His sermons and parables were those of a man who knew the meaning of labor, understood the community in which He lived — the farmer, the fisherman, the shopkeeper, the tax collector, the governor — as well as the joys and sorrows of real people; and He spoke their language. The priest who is engaged in pastoral work cannot do less if he wishes to fulfill his mission.

The pastor and guide of souls must keep in close touch with people, men and women, if he is to understand their problems and be understood by them. He should be acquainted with the familiar aspects of their life, the details of home activities that may call for sympathy and adjustment, the problems of business ethics, and the temptations and particular situations that people in the world have to face. Without this knowledge and understanding, the priest may become so removed from realities that he has no genuine contribution to make to his flock, no perceptible influence in the community, no ability to apply supernatural principles to concrete existence. His thinking becomes sterile, his advice meaningless, and his sermons without relation to life.

Particularly since the pontificate of Leo XIII, with the rising challenge of materialistic socialism and communism, the popes have emphasized the role of the Church in solving the social, economic problems of the age and, through numerous encyclicals and other communications, have urged bishops and clergy to co-operate in applying the principles of Christ to both Capital and Labor. The evils of communism, the abuses of capitalism, writes Pope Pius XII, "must persuade everyone, especially priests, to remain faithful to the social teaching of the Church, to spread the knowledge of it, and, to the extent of their power, to reduce it to practical application."[9]

With this objective in mind, it would seem appropriate for every priest in the active ministry to be informed, from his seminary days, not only of the basic principles, but also of the social conditions and economic problems of the diocese or fields

[9] *Ibid.*, par. 123.

of labor in which he will work. Without this preparation, it is possible for a young priest to emerge into his field of activity with little more preparation than a knowledge of his own neighborhood, his innate intelligence, and the assumption that all problems can be solved by the application of a syllogism. Throughout his active ministry, the alert priest will continue his study of the conditions and mentalities, the needs and temptations of various classes in different areas. He will endeavor to face realistically such problems as the living wage, marital breakdown, juvenile delinquency, civic and commercial corruption, cultural needs, and trends in religious attitudes.

In all of this work, an important part of the mission of the priesthood is precisely to lift the view of the world from sheerly material considerations and the turmoil of material details into a larger and spiritual perspective. To achieve this, the priest must always remember that while he is in the world, he is not of it. When he allows himself to be pulled down into the morass, he not only loses the respect of the world with which he must deal but also weakens his grasp of his own essential personality, purpose, and outlook. Christ Himself was tempted by the devil to barter His spiritual mission for material gain, worldly power, and the worship of evil. The priest who follows in His footsteps is not exempt from the same blandishments.

A ready evidence of false and materialistic evaluation that may tempt the priest is preoccupation with money. This may take the form of obsession in the material administration of the parish or it may enter the field of personal enrichment. Careful and businesslike attention to the material aspects of one's charge is essential for successful administration; but where this becomes practically an exclusive concern and "money raising" seems to dominate over all other considerations, spiritual poverty in the priest and disgust in the jaded parishioners are the result.

When a priest begins to devote his best thought and energy to the accumulation of a fortune for himself, he has lost the reason for his vocation. There is such a thing as prudence in making provision for the contingencies of sickness, old age, and various obligations of justice and charity. But it is hard to see the justification for turning this into a reason for amassing a fortune, to the neglect of genuinely priestly concerns and possibly to the scandal of the faithful. The priest who finds himself constantly preoccupied and worried about money may do well to renew his confidence in Divine Providence and recall the words of the Master: "Behold the birds of the air, for they neither sow, nor do they reap nor gather into barns: and your heavenly Father feedeth them. Are not you of much more value than they?"[10]

Another temptation against which the priest should be on his guard is an inordinate ambition for honors. St. Paul refers to the episcopacy as a *bonum opus* — a good work — and indeed every priest of the required qualifications should be willing to accept advancement to posts of responsibility within the Church if the appointment is given. Temptation, however, comes in the form of an overweening desire for preferment as a personal honor and for power, which is distinct from the conception of spiritual service. A man who succumbs to this temptation undergoes a kind of psychological sickness. Every change or move within the Church becomes like a morbid checker or chess game. If his personal expectations are not fulfilled, he lapses into a sour and disappointed outlook on his ministry and on life in general, as though he had lost against an unworthy adversary.

What such men often forget is that high office within the Church, or elsewhere, calls for much more than ceremonial qualifications or good intentions. To step into boots that are too large may be as painful as to walk in those which appear to be too small. The purple robes, the pectoral cross, and the ceremony that surrounds the bishop are quite as much a rigorous discipline upon the man to whom they are given as they are an evidence of honor to others who behold them. These are but the externals of an office whose cares are at least equal to the glory and whose problems are seldom revealed to innocent but ambitious aspirants for the honor. The Apostles asked Christ: "Grant to us that we may sit, one on thy right hand and the other on thy left hand,

---

[10] Mt. 6:26.

in thy glory. And Jesus said to them: You know not what you ask. Can you drink of the chalice that I drink of or be baptized with the baptism wherewith I am baptized?"[11]

Even when the wing of imagination does not fly so high, care must be taken to guard against envy for the posts and promotions of others. The spirit of cynicism, small talk, belittling attitudes, and parlor intrigues can render a man unhappy and make his ministry sterile. Mistakes of judgment, of course, are within the realm of possibility in ecclesiastical appointments: but this is no reason why anyone should allow his attention to be diverted from the primary purposes for which he has been ordained to the priesthood. Even when a man feels that, naturally speaking, he has every reason for resentment, he cannot do better than to recognize the providence of God working in the Church with a far greater wisdom than appears on the surface or at the moment.

The priest who bases his values on what he can give, not what he can get, and finds the rewards of life, not in external recognition, but in honest devotion to the cause which he serves, is not likely to become the victim of a gnawing ambition for honors. This does not mean that a man of God should despise legitimate honor or affect scorn for appreciation and recognition of merit. But he will do well to acknowledge that true success is identified with the humble, zealous pursuit of duty and not with the proud possession of external badges of distinction.

It is rare indeed that a priest is subjected to the third type of temptation which confronted Christ, when the devil asked Him to fall down and adore him. But it appears in the modified form of a worship of creature comforts and pleasures and a general spirit of worldliness. While preaching the doctrines of penance, self-denial, and self-discipline, the priest may be personally demanding of every form of comfort and service for himself and become extremely irritated if he is not provided with the very best available.

It is entirely reasonable and desirable that a priest should live in decency of surroundings and maintain a standard of living

---

[11] Mk. 10:37, 38.

that will provide for his physical health and cultural needs, as well as command respect from others. Moreover, as a man of culture there is no valid reason why he should not, within the limitations proper to his state of life and without ostentation, enjoy and even possess those objects of convenience and beauty that make his life a joy and inspiration. But when a man becomes engrossed in material considerations, to the point where he is unhappy unless surrounded with luxury, always critical and complaining about minor discomforts, and unable to adapt himself to his surroundings, he has lost the sense of spiritual values which justifies his existence as a priest. Out of touch with the realities of existence, unaware of the hardships that people must normally put up with, and of the inconveniences that are a part of ordinary life, he comes to live in a tower of ivory. Such a priest has little comprehension of the human problems with which he is supposed to deal, and only stirs resentment and disaffection in the flock which he has been appointed to protect and aid.

The spirit of worldliness is a creeping and persistent thing which no priest can afford to dismiss or ignore as not pertaining to himself. It may come in the form of overindulgence in eating and drinking, too much time for recreation, excessive attachment to social life, too free an association with the opposite sex, or sheer laziness and the evasion of duty. No one need be surprised to find these tendencies in himself. But the priest who would advance in wisdom and grace should daily recall the words of St. Paul: "I therefore so run, not as at an uncertainty; I so fight, not as one beating the air. But I chastise my body and bring it into subjection; lest perhaps, when I have preached to others, I myself should become a castaway."[12]

Every priest engaged in the active ministry should take time out regularly for an appraisal of his spiritual condition and orientation. He may find it necessary to apply brakes to some of his activities and to redirect his course on others, if he is to follow in the footsteps of Christ.

---

[12] 1 Cor. 9:26, 27.

4

The third ingredient in the personality of the priest, constantly stressed by St. Paul and in many ways the distinctive contribution of Christianity, is charity. The holiness of the priest, the flame ignited by his faith, is the love of God. This love is communicated and further demonstrated in his kindness, helpfulness, and love for all mankind. The essential element of charity is more than the correct fulfillment of duty; it is more than faith in God and the observance of the Commandments. It is the spirit of love, which warms the act of divine faith with recognition, appreciation, and gratitude. In human relations, it is the reflection of this love, which brings the glow of understanding and sympathy and of human, personal cordiality into the act of service.

"If I speak with the tongues of men and of angels," writes St. Paul, "and have not charity, I am become as sounding brass or a tinkling cymbal. And if I should have prophecy, and should know all mysteries and all knowledge, and if I should have all faith, so that I could move mountains, and have not charity, I am nothing. And if I should distribute all my goods to feed the poor, and if I should deliver my body to be burned, and have not charity, it profiteth me nothing."[13]

From the standpoint of effectiveness in parochial work and in winning friends for the Church, there is nothing to compare with a functioning charity. The priest who has only mediocre intellectual ability, but possesses a pleasing personality and a real desire to help everyone, can do far more to attract souls than the gifted individual who hands out his services with a cold formality.

It is sometimes said that Father So-and-So is a very pious man or a very brilliant person, but extremely difficult to get along with. While meditating on the higher things of the spirit, he may lose sight of the problems of earth and of practical psychology. Instead of radiating the warmth of Christ's personality, he may develop a scolding and demanding attitude toward the flock entrusted to his care. He may be impeccable in his own life, but

---

[13] I Cor. 13:1-3.

put up so severe a front that people fear to approach him or, having dared to do so, leave with their problems untouched or unsolved. Under these circumstances, a priest who is a perfectly good man in himself may come to occupy the position of a recluse in his community, with marked peculiarities. Apart from the celebration of Mass on Sunday, it cannot be said that he has any positive influence or exerts a real leadership.

There is no doubt that dullness of routine, contact with stupid and cantankerous people, frequent misunderstanding, and lack of appreciation tend to make one lose his patience and withdraw into himself. Moreover, the position of the priest in an established parish is such that he can put up a wall around himself and still not lack for the necessities of life. As a celibate, he does not have a wife or family to stir him from his aloofness or inspire him to a more human outlook. These possibilities are all the greater reason why every priest, who is aware of his responsibilities and desirous of fulfilling his mission, should deliberately cultivate the art of winning friends and influencing people.

He should make it a point to be gracious, approachable, cordial, thoughtful, and considerate. If he has cause to be firm, he should never lose his good manners. He should remember the injunction not to let the sun go down upon his anger and should strenuously avoid the harboring of resentment. He should cultivate the virtue of patience and learn to be a good listener. His approach to problems, whether in private counseling or in the pulpit, should be positive and friendly. A word of appreciation and thanks pays richer dividends than a torrent of invective and sarcasm. The priest who endeavors to pattern his personality upon that of Christ will never forget that he is a priest for all alike — the rich and poor, the interesting and the dull, the co-operative and the hostile, the virtuous who need not penance and the sheep that are lost. He will spread the radiance of divine grace with a gracious hand, whether he be appointed to the finest parish in the diocese or to the last outpost and least desirable task.

"May your apostolic zeal," writes Pope Pius XII, "be animated by that divine charity which bears everything with peace of mind, which does not let itself be overcome by adversity, and which embraces all, rich and poor, friends and enemies, faithful and unfaithful. . . . How much good have the saints not done, how many admirable deeds have they not performed by their kindness even in circumstances and in environments penetrated by lies and degraded by vice."[14]

Basic to this exercise of charity is the virtue of humility. "Learn of me," said Jesus, "for I am meek and humble of heart."[15] The priest should always be mindful of the sublimity and dignity of his priesthood. At the same time, he should never forget that this great privilege has been conferred upon him by divine favor, not by any special merit of his own. In this realization, his humility will be his strength.

"Genuine humility," writes Cardinal Gibbons, "consists not in disclaiming any good in ourselves, but in ascribing all our gifts of nature and grace to the Author of our being. This idea is admirably expressed by the Apostle when he says: 'Such confidence we have, through Christ towards God. Not that we are sufficient to think anything of ourselves, as of ourselves; but our sufficiency is from God.' "[16]

Because of his special character, the priest commands the rightful reverence and deference of the laity. But the considerate priest must guard against the development of a feeling of caste superiority or of exemption from the normal rules of social observance. The priest who assumes an overbearing attitude toward the laity, entertains an extralegal, superprivileged conception of himself, and imagines that he may ignore the ordinary amenities of life, is simply abusing his position and heading for trouble. The priest who enjoys a position of respect in his community should never forget that he is the beneficiary of predecessors who had prepared his way by gracious dealing and generous service in the community. All of this can be lost, if the priest exhibits a spirit of snobbery, boorishness, or tyranny.

---

[14] *Menti Nostrae,* par. 62–63.

[15] Mt. 11:29.

[16] James Cardinal Gibbons, *The Ambassador of Christ* (New York: John Murphy and Company, 1896), p. 144; 2 Cor. 3:4, 5.

The spirit of humility and gentlemanliness, it should be remembered, is never at variance with genuine leadership. Christ spoke as one having power. The priest should quietly insist on his unique position and his rights and maintain a reasonable urbanity and formality in his dealings with others. He should never feel inferior to anyone in his community, but should inspire confidence in all with whom he deals — civic leaders, business and professional men and women, the high and mighty as well as the poor and lowly. By virtue of his sacred ordination and appointment, he is in a position of leadership. He should never allow himself to become just a good fellow to be familiarly greeted by his first name, or a *tertium quid,* without sex or acceptance among those who command public opinion and influence.

"I may add," writes Cardinal Gibbons, "that a minister of the Gospel may, without prejudice to humility, earnestly assert and vindicate his patriotism and his civil and political rights when they are unjustly assailed, as St. Paul did when he protested against the indignity of being scourged, because he was a Roman citizen. It is, I think, likewise an imperative duty to defend himself from false and injurious aspersions on his character, whenever his humiliation and disgrace affect not only his own good name, but also the interests of religion, of which he is an acknowledged minister."[17]

5

There is an old saying that before one can command, he must learn to obey. The humble priest need never be exhorted or urged to obedience of his legitimate authorities. For him the word of the bishop is law. While, at times, he may have divergent ideas of his own, he recognizes the fact that his position is that of an integral member of an organization — the Holy Catholic Church. He may offer his ideas and special services or express his preferences; but in the last analysis, his duty is that of co-operation, obedience, and compliance with official policy and decisions.

Any other attitude, begotten of mistaken pride and stubborn-

[17] *Op. cit.,* pp. 159, 160.

ness, results in cynicism, self-pity, and a fruitless ministry. Alcoholism, defections from the faith, and unhappiness in the priesthood can nearly all be traced in one way or the other to the sin by which the angels fell—a pride that ruined their perspective and blinded them to the right order of things.

The Holy Father comments specifically on the virtue of obedience and quotes St. Ignatius of Antioch: "Obey ye all the bishop as Jesus Christ obeyed the Father."[18] "He who honors the bishop is honored by God."[19] "Do nothing without the bishop, keep your body like the temple of God, love union, flee discord, be an imitator of Jesus Christ as He was an imitator of His Father."[20]

The priest who would make his life and ministry a success must not, on the other hand, remain in a state of passive obedience, simply exhibiting a childlike faith and awaiting orders from above. He should be inspired by a dynamic appreciation of his opportunities and continue to grow intellectually as well as spiritually, in judgment as well as in experience. Every day should witness greater maturity and wisdom. No day should pass without a deeper understanding of the truths which he learned, perhaps in capsule form, in the seminary and of the scope of his mission which he beheld as in a dream during his formative years.

It is easy for a perfectly good priest to go to seed soon after his ordination, if he emerges from the seminary with the idea that he knows everything there is to know and can solve all problems by the flip of a syllogism. In such stale atmosphere no progress is made, no fresh conception of old truths is possible. Such a mind spurns the investigation of facts and their relationship to principles. The humanizing effects of the Gospels are lost. Sermons from such a source become little more than a repetition of the catechism; and stones, not bread, are passed out for the substance of spiritual and moral counsel.

"Industrious zeal," Pope Pius XII reminds us, "must be illuminated by the light of wisdom and discipline and inflamed by the

---

[18] Quoted from *Menti Nostrae*, par. 98. *Ad Smyrnaeos*, viii, 1.
[19] *Ad Smyrnaeos*, ix, 1.
[20] *Loc. cit. Ad Philadelphienses*, vii, 2.

fire of charity. Whoever sets before himself his own sanctification and that of other people must be equipped with solid learning that comprises not only theology but also the results of modern science and discovery."[21] This relationship of learning to sanctity in the priest, as noted by the Holy Father, is of particular significance. While it is true that learning by itself does not produce virtue, it should, if cultivated in the spirit of prayerful dedication to Almighty God, result in a deepening of all the spiritual perceptions and thus serve to strengthen self-discipline and a sense of personal responsibility.

The Catholic Church owes an incalculable debt to the illustrious line of saintly men and women whose studies and writings have kept bright the torch of truth and advanced the frontiers of knowledge in the light of divine revelation. Every priest should share in this apostolate of learning and make his own contribution, however small and humble, to this work. And he should be ready, in the spirit of obedience, to devote his talents to any field to which he may be appointed.

6

One of the most critical problems which the candidate for the priesthood must face is the maintenance of celibacy and chastity as a state of life, under vows, whether expressed or implicit, as in the case of the secular clergy. "Every care and solicitude must be used," writes the Pope, "to have the young soldiers of the sacred army appreciate, love, and preserve chastity, because the choice of the priestly state and perseverance in it depend in great part on this virtue."[22]

Some men are obviously unfitted for the life of the priesthood, simply because of a constitutional disposition, whether physical or emotional, which makes the requirements of celibacy beyond their steady power. One of the reasons for the years of training for the priesthood and for the discipline imposed upon seminarians is to allow the candidates ample time in which to test their capacities

---

[21] *Op. cit.*, par. 66.
[22] *Ibid.*, par. 99.

in this regard before taking the final step. The seminarian who goes on to take the final orders of priesthood must develop those outlooks and habits of chastity which make the assumption of the vows an easy and natural transience into a permanent and natural state of life. But it must be remembered that, notwithstanding this voluntary and well-considered choice, the priest remains every inch a man, with the same human nature and natural proclivities as his lay contemporaries who are eligible for the married state.

In wise recognition of the weakness and passions of mankind, the Church has emphasized the virginity and purity of the Blessed Virgin Mary, Mother of the Saviour, and has glorified the virtues of clean, disciplined living as a distinctively Christian ideal throughout the centuries. Much of the effectiveness of the Catholic priesthood has arisen precisely from its practice of celibacy, after the example of Christ; and there can be no doubt that the devotion of priests to the Blessed Mother of Christ has been one of the greatest sources of strength in preserving a strong, virtuous clergy within the Church.

Besides the devotional and sacramental aids which should be the daily protection of the priest, there are various subtle but nevertheless effective safeguards of a social nature which the prudent priest cannot fail to notice. In this as well as in other fields where human appetites are involved, for example in the use of alcoholic beverages, the priest must keep a wise perspective on himself and exercise a strict self-discipline. Human nature has a way of playing strange tricks and of breaking out, like water in a dam, in ways and places where least expected.

There are certain rules of social behavior and restraint which cannot be ignored without setting into motion a whole series of physiological and psychological forces which may sweep the unguarded individual far beyond his original ideas and intentions. However attractive the prospect or strong the impulse, if the object or the results are beyond the pale of the priesthood or out of harmony with its dignity and character, the prudent and self-respecting priest can utter only one sentiment: "This is not for me.'

It is, as a matter of fact, in the combination of faithful, earnest prayer and honest self-discipline that the priest finds his protection and his strength. His success and the joy of his life arise from the practice of virtue and the communication of this spirit to others. In striving for these objectives, with God's help, he develops his whole personality, unmistakable before the world, in the virile, commanding, yet lovely pattern of that of his Teacher, Master, and Ideal — Jesus Christ. From the fulfillment of this work of "faith and labor and charity" he finds his enduring hope. And with St. Paul, he can say at the close of his career: "I have fought the good fight: I have finished my course: I have kept the faith. As to the rest, there is laid up for me a crown of justice which the Lord the just judge will render to me in that day: and not only to me, but to them also that love his coming."[23]

---

[23] 2 Tim. 2:7, 8.

"And having brought their ships to land
leaving all things they followed him
(Lk. 5:1, 2).

CHAPTER II

THE SPIRITUAL LIFE OF THE PRIEST

I

MANY elements may enter into the effectiveness of the ministry of the Catholic priest. The ability to preach well brings prestige to the Church, as well as inspiration to the congregation. A kind and wise confessor can bring souls back to God when all others have failed. A loving and devoted care of the sick in itself may be regarded as justifying a priest's best energies. A prudent and gracious social sense — the ability to "mix" with people — opens many opportunities for the priest to touch the lives of men and women. But, however useful these various talents may be, they are in the second rank of importance when compared with the most basic of all priestly requisites, namely, that of personal sanctity.

Without a profound sense of the spiritual life and a high standard of personal sanctification, the priest lacks the moving force and reason for his calling. His life, however active, is more or less a surface activity, and the one element that should distinguish and characterize his vocation is lacking. But with a keen grasp of the principle that the salvation of souls begins with oneself and with a determination to grow in grace and in the love of God, the priest achieves success, even with the most meager and humble of talents. He communicates sanctity to others from his own treasure. The force of his own example possesses a persuasive

22

power far greater than that of the preacher's eloquence. There is a consistency in what he says with what he does, which is the surest proof of conviction and sincerity. His place and influence in the world as a man of God are readily recognized and respected by others, without explanation or apology, for the simple reason that they follow the basic recognition of the priest himself.

These considerations are perfectly obvious upon reflection. The first call to the priesthood is felt in the desire to serve God as a career. The primary object of seminary training is to develop the spiritual man. The life of the priest is a kind of contradiction in terms unless it holds up this objective and pursues this goal. The same shining truth is apparent in the fact that the priest represents himself as "another Christ," preaching the doctrines of Christ and endeavoring to persuade others that here is "the way, the truth, and the life."

I have heard it said in missionary countries that if the living example of the Christian or so-called Christian laity is at variance with the teachings of the good padres to the prospective native converts, then the missionaries had better pack their bags and go back home. If the example of the laity is so important, how much more under observation are the lives and examples of the priests themselves. Whether they swing the tide one way or the other will depend in large part on whether, with God's help, they follow up their words with deeds of service, of sacrifice, and of sanctity. This is applicable everywhere.

Recognition, however, is one thing; perseverance and fulfillment are another. Unfortunately, as human nature is full of weakness and contradictions, no one can ever say that he has reached that state of perfection in this life where virtue proceeds on its own momentum. There is an ancient saying to the effect that, if one does not go ahead, he will fall back; if one does not swim against the stream, he will be carried down with the current. Our Lord gave practical expression to this when He declared: "No man putting his hand to the plough, and looking back, is fit for the kingdom of God."[1]

---

[1] Lk. 9:62.

In other words, even for the priest — and perhaps especially for him — there is no assurance of continuance or growth in sanctity or of salvation itself, without the application of constant strenuous effort and systematic practice. In this respect, sanctity is far more than a bundle of good intentions. It represents a cultivated proficiency and, like other skills, requires regular attention. We recognize that sanctity is a gift of God, associated with the supernatural grace which comes from heaven, without being strictly merited, as such, by any individual. Nevertheless, the whole teaching of Scripture, as well as the indications of natural reason point to the importance of co-operation with grace and personal effort toward spiritual growth and perfection. "Draw nigh to God," says St. James, "and he will draw nigh to you."[2] The spiritual life, sanctification, and the possession of divine grace are not a static condition, but beckon to a dynamic progress and enlargement of one's powers. In the words of the Apocalypse "He that is just, let him be justified still; and he that is holy, let him be sanctified still."[3]

2

Perhaps the first question one should ask in this connection is "What is the spiritual life?" And second, "What is sanctity?" Undoubtedly there is a wide diversity of conceptions on this subject, even among the masters of the spiritual life. A great variety of pursuits and practices, even among the clergy and the religious, both by rule and recommendation, as well as personal preference and temperament, appear to complicate the question. The matter assumes even another aspect when one compares the pursuit of the spiritual life by the laity and by persons under religious vows. Between the market and the monastery, there is a great distance. Yet all men are called to develop their spiritual life and grow in sanctity.

The truth of the matter is that the spiritual life embraces the entire conscious activity of man. For this reason, we point to the

[2] James 4:8.
[3] Apoc. 22:11.

home life of the Blessed Virgin and the professional carpentry of St. Joseph as offering an ideal example of doing the will of God and growing in grace. The idea that the spiritual life is a kind of exotic thing, reserved for saints, or for special days, like Sundays or times when one is alone and at prayer is quite false and mischievous. I have heard persons say that they must take time out to save their souls. While there is an element of truth in this observation, insofar as everyone needs to pause from time to time for analysis and reappraisal of where he is going, the salvation of one's soul is an everyday business, as extensive as one's powers of intelligence and free will.

Essentially, the spiritual life is identified with the existence and faculties of one's immortal soul. In this life, the soul functions as substantially united with the body and tied into a material universe. Virtue, as we understand it, indicates the right relation of one's actions to God's law in every area. One can honor God in the most simple and humble of acts as well as in the most elaborate ceremonials. God is honored in His sunsets as well as in stained cathedral glass. The spiritual life is the life of recognition and motivation. Hence the importance of tying virtue in with the doing of one's work, whatever it may be, and the sublimation of one's daily tasks through the motive of divine love and service to God.

I recall some years ago a young lady who did some secretarial work for me, saying that she wished she could die. Asking the reason of this unusual desire, I learned that she felt her work was somehow alien to the spiritual life and, in her piety, she felt that everything was a waste of time until she could be with God. This desire to hasten the union with God in the next life has been expressed by the mystics, from St. Augustine to St. Teresa of Ávila and down to our own time. Even St. Paul declared: "For we know, if our earthly house of this habitation be dissolved, that we have a building of God, a house not made with hands, eternal in heaven. For in this also we groan, desiring to be clothed upon with our habitation that is from heaven."[4]

---

[4] 2 Cor. 5:1, 2.

Notwithstanding the sublimity of her desire, I felt constrained to remind my secretary that it was more important that she should do her work well as a typist and secretary than that she should die. I assured her that, so far as I could see, I represented the will of God at that moment as her employer and that God would take her home in His own good time. Meanwhile, she could behold God everywhere in this world through His creation, and she could live with God here and now by developing all of her talents and energies to their fullest extent for His service.

These considerations may seem rather trite to the priest, who has been trained in the art of spiritual motivation and who recognizes the fact that sanctity is to be preached as a goal for all men, whatever their station or calling. On the other hand, one may unwittingly slip into the ancient error, from which St. Augustine emerged, of regarding this world as an evil place, human instincts as somehow corrupt in themselves, and ambition to perfect oneself in natural skills and expression, to achieve success and pre-eminence in this life, as inconsonant with sanctity and salvation. It is easy to slip into the notion that saving one's soul is a kind of negative process, filled with danger signs, and studded with "thou shalt not's." Thus the prudent man becomes the man who does nothing, like the servant in the Gospel, who buried his talents in the napkin for fear that he might lose them by investment. From this jaundiced view, men, whether of the clergy or laity, who take a genuine interest in their work and forge ahead to leadership and action, are regarded as animated with selfish motives and not truly representative of the spiritual ideal.

This same narrow view may find comfort in the delusion that the spiritual life consists in certain formulae of prayer or action which have a justifying effect. Thus life becomes separated into two separate compartments. In one, the individual lives a normal, comfortable, possibly lazy, selfish, and even vicious existence. In the other, he lifts his heart to God by a certain routine at a certain time or performs some cleansing act, such as a monetary donation to a worthy cause, and emerges with a respectable feeling of satisfaction that the spiritual side of the ledger is in good condition.

The spiritual life thus is reduced to a static condition in which there is hardly more than an act of faith. Or it becomes an external mechanical thing tied up in mechanical gestures with only the appearance of natural virtue. Of the first error, St. James has written: "So faith also, if it have not works, is dead in itself."[5] Of the other distortion, he comments: "And if any man think himself to be religious, not bridling his tongue but deceiving his own heart, this man's religion is vain. Religion clean and undefiled is this: to visit the fatherless and widows in their tribulation and to keep one's self unspotted from this world."[6]

The spiritual life of the priest, therefore, like the spiritual life of any other person, embraces his *whole* life. In his moral life, it means keeping the Commandments and cultivating virtue. In his social life, it means the exercise of justice and charity, kindness, consideration, and good manners. In his professional life, it means the exact and devoted discharge of his duties. In his intellectual life, it means an awareness of what is going on in the world, at least so far as it affects the care of souls; and this is indeed a broad field of interest. In his cultural life, it means the development of his powers of appreciation, for literature, art, music, and nature — the ability, like that of St. Francis, to see God and to love Him in all of His marvelous handiwork and expression.

The pursuit of sanctity means the urging of all of one's faculties, talents, and energies in line with their natural aptitudes, which are God-given, with the great life purpose of giving glory to God, not only through prayer, but also through appreciation of one's fellow man. In its fullest and most legitimate sense, therefore, saving one's soul is a dynamic thing, an enlargement of all the gifts of nature and grace that God may vouchsafe.

Wondrous stories are told of unusual practices of prayer and forms of penance practiced by some of the saints. Each of these must be examined in its proper context and with all the facts and circumstances in focus, if any significance or practical application is to be derived. In some cases possibly, a strenuous exercise or line

---

[5] James 2:17.
[6] James 1:26, 27.

of conduct was necessary to meet an extraordinary situation. In others, the special temperament of the individual must be considered. In still other instances, one may seriously question whether the pious biographer may not have been drawing upon an over-zealous and not altogether balanced imagination. There is nothing exotic about the spiritual life, nothing eccentric about genuine sanctity, nothing abnormal about the development or manifestation of virtue.

The holy priest, the man of God, is always a sane and sensible person, with nothing of the fanatic in his character. He strives for normal, healthy living, and is suspicious of anything that smacks of the weird in religious life or practice. He is always on guard against the growth of erratic attitudes and habits on his part. He is not afraid of criticism and always retains a good sense of humor, which he can apply to himself as well as to others. He cultivates a positive outlook on life, stressing the motives of love, of service, and of solution of life's problems, rather than of fear, of caution, of worry, and of complaint.

In a word, as "another Christ," following the example of the Master, he is a humble but confident man among men. His sanctity rests upon his friendship with God, a sanctity which he communicates to others, with God's grace, by the action of normal living and high motivation. His acceptability and personal influence, like that of Christ, proceed from the greatness and goodness of his inner personality. His sincerity and integrity are apparent from his clear thinking, upright living, and power of decision. His leadership is founded upon supernatural faith and personal conviction, not upon show, calculated effect, or affectation; and he is not afraid to walk in the path of duty, even when deviation, compromise, or servile side-stepping might make life easier.

3

It is obvious, however, that as this conception and program of activity proceed from the inner personality of the priest, his inner spiritual life itself must be nourished, replenished, strengthened, repaired, and even corrected on a planned and systematic basis. In many ways, the human personality is like a machine. It has component parts, even in its spiritual faculties. In this life, human nature is composed of a sustantial union of the soul with body. The body is subject to wear and tear. It breaks down and wears out. The soul is subject to its moments of exuberance and its periods of exhaustion. Personal experience and nervous excitement produce emotional reactions which must be disciplined by both the intellect and the will. And both mind and body need interludes of pause, of repose, and refreshment if they are to function normally in their separate ways and as a team.

The Church recognizes these factors in human personality and in the spiritual life of the faithful. It makes certain demands in the external practice of faith such as the obligation of hearing Mass on Sundays and specified holydays. It requires an annual Confession and Holy Communion. It encourages the frequent, even daily, hearing of Mass and receiving of Holy Communion, and urges frequent Confession, even beyond that demanded for the forgiveness of mortal sin. It imposes certain disciplines, such as Friday abstinence and the Lenten fast; and it repeats Christ's recommendation of various forms of penance and self-denial in expiation of sin and the development of virtue. It constantly preaches the necessity of prayer, and by the cultivation of the holy liturgy and of artistic forms of external worship, through beautiful churches, stained glass, pictures, and statues, assists the faithful to achieve the fullest possible union of all the faculties with Almighty God. Missions, retreats, days of recollection, and a wide variety of special devotions are all provided to maintain a steady spiritual life within the Church and to point out to all the importance of a constant personal and community effort to keep alive the religious conception of life and to save one's soul.

What applies to the maintenance and strengthening of the spiritual life of the laity is true *a fortiori* for the clergy. "To keep oneself unspotted from this world," in the words of St. James, requires a constant process of soul searching and prayer. Laziness, desire for ease, and ready acceptance of material standards can all creep into the life of a priest, unless he exercises an eternal vigilance through spiritual exercise. Purity of motive can become sadly tarnished, even in the performance of the sacred functions of the priesthood — through desire for display and notoriety, greed for gain, seeking for praise, or envy and jealousy — imperceptibly and without deliberate intention. Vigorous, regular spiritual house cleaning and discipline are necessary for every priest. There is nothing haphazard or erratic about spiritual health and growth. It is true that divine grace is a gift freely given by God; but normally and regularly, we are taught by Holy Scripture, it is given to those who have disposed themselves to receive it and who persevere in this disposition.

I have always recalled the wise words of advice given me by my Archbishop upon being given a new assignment of responsibility where I should be thrown more or less on my own routine. "Keep up your regular spiritual exercises," he said, "your daily Mass, your prayers, Confession, and spiritual recollection; and God will be with you." At the time perhaps I did not fully appreciate the significance and the experience underlying his injunctions; but with the passage of the years, I have come to understand that the "spiritual machine," so to speak, does not run by itself with a kind of perpetual motion. It needs regular refueling, cleaning, overhauling, and care. The wise priest recognizes this and sets up for himself a program and routine of spiritual observances and exercise which keep him in direct contact with God and the flow of supernatural grace.

The idea that one should pray only when he feels like it or go to church only when he has a heart overflowing for God is quite false. It has served, however, to cloak the religious irregularity of both laity and clergy who profess a great fear of hypocrisy and lip service in religion. It may well be that one should pray most when he least feels like it, and discharge his religious obligations most of all when his heart is not in it. Faith and obedience are virtues most needed in times of weakness, confusion, and crisis.

To maintain a pattern of regularity in the spiritual life, and to make the performance of one's spiritual exercises a joy, not simply a routine or a burden, there must be regularity and balance in one's physical and emotional life. There must be also a careful and regular disposal of the twenty-four hours of the day. I have always been convinced that there is a basic connection between a good night's sleep and the spiritual life. For the priest, whose day begins with prayer and holy Mass in the morning, it is of the utmost importance that he retire for the night at a reasonable hour and regularly so.

It is easy to overlook or underestimate the importance of this observation. It is quite possible gradually to turn the night into day and the day into night. For some persons, interest in life and social activity begin after dark. The priest in active parish life may find that most of his parlor calls are in the evening. He may cultivate the habit of calling on friends and parishioners later at night. On his return, he may pick up a book and read into the small hours of the morning. If this develops into a routine, he faces the early rising in a mental fog. His prayers and Mass lack much in the way of concentration and spiritual satisfaction. He may feel it imperative to go back to bed in the morning, or the siesta after lunch may lengthen into an all-afternoon affair. He is, in the meantime, irritated by every demand upon his time, and it becomes increasingly difficult for anyone to approach him on business or even to find him available. Under these circumstances, the spiritual life reaches a low ebb; and one's usefulness as spiritual guide ends.

One must make a choice between regularity and irregularity in hours. There are times, of course, when one cannot get to bed on time; and circumstances may not make it possible, or even desirable, to maintain a clocklike routine without variation. Nevertheless, the priest whose primary objective is the proper discharge of his ministry and his personal sanctification will make it a point to arrange his program so that he gets sufficient sleep at the time when most law-abiding citizens sleep. He will endeavor to arise refreshed and fit to say Mass with recollection and dignity. And he will make it a point of principle to put in a good eight-hour day of labor in the vineyard, so that when night comes he will welcome repose.

It is all very well to talk about the love of God and the higher life; but the spiritual life and higher perfection must rest on the foundations of good common sense and the observance of sensible habits. In the words of Christ, "Not everyone that saith to me, Lord, Lord, shall enter into the kingdom of heaven; but he that doth the will of my Father who is in heaven, he shall enter into the kingdom of heaven."[7] Before the child can walk, he must creep. Before one can aspire to the mystic virtues, he must be solid in the moral virtues, and keep the Commandments. Before one can talk to God, he must be willing to examine his own conscience.

Here again, regularity and recollection in the essential things are far more important than brilliance, a multiplicity of devotions, or length of time on one's knees. It is far more important to say one's Mass with devotion, and to offer a short well-organized prayer afterward — adoration, thanksgiving, resolution, and petition — than to rush through Mass and spend a protracted time afterward trying to collect one's thoughts. It is far preferable to practice a fifteen-minute period of concentrated meditation than to drift aimlessly through one-half hour of spiritual woolgathering or to hope for an hour's meditation which never comes. A three-minute visit to the Blessed Sacrament after each meal may not seem like much; but if carried through as a daily practice, it becomes a treasure house of grace. One's morning and evening prayers, and even the little grace before and after meals, recited consciously, deliberately, and devoutly, lift the mind to God and open the floodgates of heaven. The Stations of the Cross, said throughout the year, on Fridays, are most helpful and fruitful for spiritual development. The daily Rosary, particularly if accompanied with meditation on the holy mysteries, is a formula which the saints have endorsed through the centuries. And the daily examination of conscience, particularly at the close of the day, is indispensable in keeping check on one's spiritual exercises.

4

For many priests, the most burdensome of all spiritual duties is the recitation of the Divine Office — the *opus Dei*. In many cases

---

[7] Mt. 7:21.

undoubtedly, its virtue arises principally from exercise of the virtue of obedience. There are several reasons for this, which we must recognize in all honesty. Despite impressions or pretenses to the contrary, many priests are not sufficiently adept in Latin to understand, without considerable difficulty, the text of the office. Even with fast reading, the Office normally requires forty minutes to one hour. To pause for translation, much more for thoughtful meditation, would prolong the task indefinitely. Generally insufficient time and attention are given in the seminary for study of the psalms or homilies; in later life, the busy priest finds it difficult, if not impossible, to make up for this deficiency.[8]

It has been suggested that the burden would be lightened if the Divine Office were shortened, particularly for priests in active ministry outside the canonical or monastic choirs. Permission to recite the Breviary in the vernacular has also been urged as an aid to its more intelligent and devotional discharge. Pending such adjustments, however, the priest can take steps to make the recitation of the Office something more than a sheer consumption of time and an act of obedience. For one thing, he can and ought to acquaint himself, on a planned basis outside of Breviary hours, with the psalter, the hymns, and the homilies of the Office. An excellent English translation of the entire Breviary is now available. Priests who have not previously studied the Breviary in this way will be amazed by its beauty and spiritual richness. The use of a commentary on the psalms and some research into the Old Testament and Old Testament history and geography will do much also to bring names and places into focus and make the pages of the Divine Office something vital and interesting instead of a mere reading exercise.[9]

---

[8] Cf. Letter of the Sacred Congregation of Seminaries and Universities, February 2, 1945, "On the Proper Training of Clerics to an Appreciation of the Divine Office," trans. by T. Lincoln Bouscaren, S.J. (St. Meinrad, Ind.: Grail Publications, 1955). Also Pius Parsch, *The Breviary Explained* (St. Louis: B. Herder Book Co., 1954).

[9] "For in truth," the Sacred Congregation reminds us, "the recitation of the Breviary is not and must not be a bare exercise of the intellect and memory, a vague reminder of past studies or a simple reading. It is and should be a prayer" (*op. cit.*, p. 12).

It is advisable also to schedule one's time for reading the Breviary, so as not to be caught with a large section unfulfilled at a late hour or in face of other obligations. This may not always be easy, particularly for the busy parish priest or on occasions and feast days when special demands are placed upon one's time. Nevertheless, it is embarrassing to find that one must rush through pages in anything but the spirit of dignity and devotion to beat the midnight hour. If this becomes a regular experience, it is obvious that other arrangements are indicated. In short, since the Divine Office is a daily obligation and consumes a not inconsiderable amount of time and attention, it should be performed well and profitably for one's own sanctification as well as a prayer for the Church.

Another matter that should be given serious attention in the spiritual development of the priest is that of so-called spiritual reading. Of course, all reading is in a sense "spiritual," whether for weal or for woe. The question here involved is that of literature, whether of an instructional or inspirational character, dealing directly with the moral virtues and motives that stimulate a greater love and service of God. Spiritual reading is a regular exercise in seminary training; it is expressly part of every spiritual retreat; and, as every priest knows, there is a most rich literature in this field, which may be called one of the legacies of the saints and of masters of the spiritual life to the treasury of the Church.

Unquestionably, every priest should have a program of spiritual reading. This should include, above all other material, a review of Holy Scripture, the inspired word of God, both Old and New Testaments. It should embrace also the best known writers of the outstanding classics, such as the *Confessions* and the *City of God* of St. Augustine, the *Imitation of Christ* for regular spiritual impulse, and other works of the Fathers of the Church and of the saints, which are now readily available. Moreover, the priest should maintain a working acquaintance with contemporary religious books and books on religious and moral guidance, both for his personal use and for direction of the souls under his care. There is comparatively little spiritual reading among the laity. The alert and well-informed priest can do much to direct the reading of the faithful into spiritually profitable channels.

In the field of spiritual literature, however, prudence and caution must be observed. Spiritual food, like food for the body, is of different richness and consistency; and what may be palatable and nourishing for one person may be a source of disturbance and confusion for another. Some of the writings of the mystics were never intended for general consumption, just as some of their practices and penances can hardly be recommended for general imitation. If Holy Scripture itself is subject to misunderstanding and distortion and frequently requires the authoritative voice of the Church, the same is even more true of various writings produced under great religious impulse of a highly personal character and directed to special circumstances. Spiritual reading which results in scrupulosity, religious disturbance and illusions, or discouragement should be strenuously avoided. Spiritual development should always be in *balance.*

The same is true in application of the principles of ascetic life to one's practice of penance and self-denial. What may be appropriate enough under religious rule and community life may be quite impractical, eccentric, and even dangerous when undertaken on personal initiative and without competent guidance. The regulations of the Church governing fast and abstinence are rigorous enough, but even these, as everyone knows, are subject to modification or dispensation if they cause serious inconvenience or endanger needful health and strength in any particular case. There is no spiritual merit in mechanical penance and self-denial as such. The merit arises from the motivation and must always be measured against the background of common sense. Everyone should learn to control himself, to bridle his appetites, and to forgo legitimate pleasures in the spirit of Christian realization and charity. But these practices should be part of a well-regulated life, not the spurt of sudden religious fervor or evidence of fanaticism.

There are times, of course, when one abandons one's normal occupations and social habits to devote one's entire energies to prayer and contemplation. The morning meditation, the annual retreat, periodic days of recollection, and special hours of adoration before the Blessed Sacrament call for full concentration on the Divine Presence, on one's personal accountability to God, upon the stark realities of death and judgment after death. At such times, the man of God cuts through the flesh and the world, and endeavors, so far as lies within his power, to come face to face with his Maker.

But the spiritual life and personal sanctification are never morose or brooding in character. A sense of the presence of God, a constant awareness and acceptance of the providence of God, and a truly abiding love of God — which are of the essence of sanctity — flourish best in the priest who is truly a man. Good cheer, a sense of humor, a willingness to serve and to share, a kindly spirit — these are more pertinent to saving one's soul than dark forebodings about the next life. Not theology, nor austerity, nor even long hours at prayer will help one to grow in grace, unless one has love in his heart for both God and man and is ready to express it.

"Priestly sanctity," writes Rev. John A. O'Brien, "is conceived in the womb of priestly zeal. It is born in the travail of daily duty. The greater the zeal and industry with which our priestly ministry is discharged, the greater is the fervor in the ministry of prayer and labor which rises as sweet incense before the Great White Throne. Labor done for Christ is but a form of prayer. *Laborare est orare* was the motto of the Benedictine monks, who spent long hours each day in tilling the fields. The kinship of labor to prayer was recognized even by a philosopher of the world, Thomas Carlyle, who pointed out so well the supreme importance of nobility of purpose in the worker. In his *Sartor Resartus* he expresses the selfsame truth voiced by St. Paul, when he exclaims: 'O man! It is not thyself but thy works as well that are infinitesimally small. It is only the spirit in which thou workest that is great!' "[10]

In his analysis of the instrumental means of perfection, Cardinal Manning declares that mortification and charity are the two condi-

---

[10] John A. O'Brien, *The Priesthood in a Changing World* (Paterson, N. J.: St. Anthony Guild Press, 1943), p. 30.

tions of perfection, and he adds that these "are called forth into
the fullest exercise by the demands of a priestly and pastoral life."[11]

As to the other means of perfection, he enumerates (1) the law
and obligation of chastity, (2) the life and spirit of poverty,
(3) obedience to the Church, (4) the habit of prayer and meditation, (5) the daily Mass and devotion to the Blessed Sacrament,
(6) the confessional, (7) preaching the word of God, (8) devout
recitation of the Divine Office, (9) the rule of life learned in the
seminary, and (10) "the law of liberty" referred to by St. Paul
and St. James, identified with our spiritual regeneration through
divine grace in the redemption of Christ.

"With such abundant means of confirming himself in the interior spiritual perfection in which he was ordained, and of at-
taining to the mind and life of his Master," the Cardinal concludes,
"no priest can fail of any degree of humility, charity, and sanctity,
except through his own fault. God has done for us more than we
could ask or think. And 'the gifts and the calling of God are without repentance' (Rom. 11:29) — that is, there is no change of mind
or purpose towards His priests, whom He has chosen to be His
representatives, and to be, like Himself, 'the light of the world'
and 'the salt of the earth.' "[12]

At the basis of priestly sanctification is undoubtedly the specific
mission of the priest, namely, to give Jesus Christ to the world. To
the extent that the priest identifies himself with the purposes of
Christ, endeavors to model his own character upon that of Christ,
and to effect a spiritual union with Christ, so that he becomes in
living reality "another Christ," he will keep his spiritual life ever
burning bright with increasing brilliance for all those to whom he
ministers.

"Never forget it," writes a master of the spiritual way for priests,
"we are instrumental causes in the hands of Jesus Christ for the
sanctification of the world. The instrumental cause must be closely
united to the agent who uses it: it can only produce its effect by

---

[11] Henry Edward Cardinal Manning, *The Eternal Priesthood* (Westminster,
Md.: The Newman Press), p. 60.
[12] *Ibid.*, pp. 60–62.

virtue of his activity. Let us accept our status as humble and docile instruments in the hands of God and never attribute to ourselves what the Lord accomplishes through us. The validity of our administration of the sacraments depends on our ordination and on the jurisdiction which we receive from the bishop, but the fruitfulness of our words in the confessional, in the pulpit, and in all our relations with the faithful depends principally on our union with Christ."[13]

---

[13] Abbot D. Columba Marmion, *Christ — the Ideal of the Priest* (St. Louis: B. Herder Book Co., 1952), p. 61.

"Who is a wise man and endowed with knowledge, among you? Let him show, by a good conversation, his work in the meekness of wisdom" (James 3:13).

CHAPTER III

THE CULTURAL LIFE OF THE PRIEST

I

ONE of the first challenges to the priest in parish work or administration is that of his own cultural life and development. A number of elements enter into this problem and may call for specific and even radical decisions. One is the question of time. How can the priest who is engaged in active work and subject to a thousand and one demands on every hand find sufficient time and peace of mind to give to his own cultural development, particularly in the line of systematic reading and study? Another is the matter of selectivity. With the wide range of interests connected with the priestly life and the broad appeals of attention, including those of the radio and the television, to say nothing of books, magazines, lectures, and various cultural events, how is one to choose judiciously so as to make progress along any particular line or lines? More practical still may be the question of energy. By the time one's regular duties have been taken care of, there may be little physical or mental reserve left for the development of the mind or for appreciation of the higher life.

Perhaps the most basic question is whether the priest should regard himself as an intellectual at all, or whether he will best discharge his mission by concentrating on works of piety, social charity, and organization. Much will depend upon one's conception of an intellectual. But if it is realized that the priest, like Christ, must teach by word as well as by example and that he is called upon to solve the moral problems of men by reason as well as by good example and simple exhortation, the importance of a developed and developing mind becomes clear. This responsibility rests upon all priests, regardless of whether they have the qualifications for great scholarship or an aptitude for deep appreciation.

"Piety in a priest, though indispensable," writes Cardinal Gibbons, "can never be an adequate substitute for learning. He may have zeal, but not the 'zeal according to knowledge' (Rom. 10:2) which the Apostle commends. Knowledge without piety may, indeed, make a churchman vain and arrogant; but piety without knowledge renders him an unprofitable servant. The absence of piety makes him harmful to himself, but the absence of knowledge makes him a stumbling-block to others."[1]

The fact that a man has gone into the priesthood is sufficient evidence that he recognizes the need for study, as this is a learned profession as well as vocation. For him to adopt a "low-brow" attitude once he is ordained and to go about as though he despised anything connected with education or higher cultural development is to betray the very nature of his calling. Not all priests have equal or even similar mental powers and tastes, even though they share the same ordination and priesthood. Some men pass their seminary courses through pluck and prayer rather than by the possession of a gilt-edge mind. But all must be prepared to sustain the prestige of their leadership, and all alike must make an effort to keep their interests fresh and their minds strong and alert in the service of God.

By the time a young man has reached the seminary, he should be sufficiently mature and developed to absorb knowledge in a reflective spirit, and he should have an ambition to improve his mental equipment and put it to work in the appreciation of truth and beauty. Whether he will do so or not may depend to a considerable extent upon the type of instruction and inspiration which

---

[1] James Cardinal Gibbons, *The Ambassador of Christ,* p. 171.

he receives during these formative years. If he gets the idea that the whole of Catholic truth is fully contained in his textbooks and that comprehension is exhausted by the effort of the memory in preparation for examinations, it is hardly probable that he will adopt an expansive view on his cultural life later on. Likewise, if in his course of training there is no opportunity for discussion, collateral reading, or wider approach through some kind of field work, or through literature and the arts, it is hardly to be expected that he will develop anything like dynamic appreciation or the ability to grow by himself.

These considerations are of the utmost importance in working out the educational processes of the seminarian and of the priest. Pope Pius XII, in his Exhortation on the Priestly Life, stresses the point that "particular attention must be paid to character formation in each boy by developing in him the sense of responsibility, the capacity to use his judgment concerning men and events, and the spirit of initiative. . . . Let directors have no fear," he adds, "in keeping them in contact with the events of the day which, apart from furnishing them with the necessary material for forming and expressing a good judgment, can form material for discussions to help them and accustom them to form judgments and reach balanced conclusions. . . . We urge that the literary and scientific education of priests be at least not inferior to that of laymen who take similar courses of study."[2]

2

Without this point of view and this mental alertness, a priest may deceive himself and endeavor to deceive others with the false assumption that he can solve all problems by a simple turn of his great mind. This eliminates the necessity of probing the facts. It gives rise to contempt, real or affected, for further knowledge or learning. Under the influence of this intellectual opiate, a man comes to regard any form of cultural activity as so much "prunes, pickles, and prisms." Schoolmen, scientists, and scholars are looked

---

[2] *Menti Nostrae*, nos. 84–87.

upon with a combination of suspicion, disdain, and fear. Reading becomes superfluous to the individual who already knows everything worth knowing. Lectures, forums, study clubs, and similar endeavors come under the dim view of waste of time promoted by queer and restless people who would do better to stay home and mind their own business.

Even more radical than this is the Manichaean idea that intellectual curiosity and development, beyond the most elemental phases, is mischievous, possibly a snare of the devil, and even dangerous for one's salvation. This notion has been dramatized, particularly in reference to occult knowledge and the immoral use of knowledge, through the literature of all peoples, as exemplified in the story of Faust. But it appears also to arouse the apprehension and alarm of various mystical and ascetical writers of the Church. The author of the *Imitation of Christ* warns repeatedly against the vanity and dangers of worldly knowledge and learning. Even the great St. Augustine finds peril to the soul in such pursuit. Many examples of similar thought could be adduced, which seem, at first glance, almost to consign this world to the devil and to reserve only the heavenly regions for Almighty God. I once heard a speaker of some consequence declare that every scientific advance brings only ultimate evil and that all exact knowledge is the work of Satan!

To a certain extent this negative view and these warnings — all of which contain an element of truth — stem from a conception of salvation and of the development of Christian personality. There are two aspects of the personality and teaching of Christ, one of a passive, mystical, and bucolic character, the other dynamic and expansive. It is possible to overemphasize the first at the expense of the second, and in this way to distort the full, true picture of the Christian message and philosophy of life.

Thus, one may concentrate on that aspect of Christ's character in which He refers to Himself as the Good Shepherd, with His followers as sheep. The parables of the lilies of the field, which "labor not, neither do they spin," and the birds of the air, "for they sow not, neither do they reap, neither have they a storehouse nor barn, and God feedeth them," might strengthen an attitude of passive dependence on divine providence.[3] "And which of you," Christ asks, "by taking thought can add to his stature one cubit? If then ye be not able to do so much as the least thing, why are you solicitous for the rest?"[4] This might appear to throw cold water on all intellectual endeavor.

The Master further warns us that, unless we become as little children, we shall not enter the Kingdom of Heaven.[5] "Learn of me, for I am meek and humble of heart," "my yoke is sweet and my burden light," "deny yourself," "seek ye first the Kingdom of Heaven and all things else shall be added unto you" — these are divine injunctions sounded over and over again to all who wish to know what to do to glorify God and save their souls. And in the prayers of the Church, there comes the upsurge of grief for us "poor banished children of Eve . . . in this valley of tears . . . this our exile." With exclusive focus of attention on this aspect of the Christian message, one might well take a desperate view of everything except death, the liberator and deliverer back to God.

While few have driven these expressions to such an extreme, it is probably true that many devout but misguided souls have dwarfed, not only their intellectual and cultural development, but also their basic spiritual growth because of their failure to grasp the full significance of Christ's teaching and example. As the result of a suspicious and dim view of human progress, science, and artistic excellence, mediocre standards have too often characterized the activities of the "children of light," and leadership has passed into the hands of the enemies of Christ. Strange, is it not, that the glory of expanding truth, which is a revelation of the mind of God, should be shunned as an obstacle to salvation, or that pre-eminence in the use of one's God-given intellect should be viewed as an occasion of sin?

Christ warned against conceit and that kind of pride which ignores one's dependence on God and responsibility to one's fellow man. Throughout Sacred Scripture as well as in the writing of the

[3] Lk. 12:24–27.
[4] Lk. 12:25, 26.
[5] Cf. Mt. 18:3.

saints referred to above, the searcher for human knowledge is cautioned that this must be related to eternal values, lest it be turned into an instrument of destruction. The force of divine providence and guidance is likewise stressed, but as an evidence to man of God's love and of His constant concern and assistance for all who love Him in return. But these lessons were never intended to blunt the instrumentality of the mind for truth and goodness and beauty in this life or to convey the impression that this world is other than the creation of God and an opportunity for men to live and advance in His reflected presence and glory.

3

One need go no farther than the parable of the talents to understand the doctrine of Christ on the use of one's faculties and energies. Those who use the talents that are given them may expect to hear the praise of the Lord: "Well done, good and faithful servant. Because thou hast been faithful over a few things, I will place thee over many things. Enter thou into the joy of the Lord." And those who retreat from the use of their talents, from fear of one thing or the other, will hear His rebuke: "And the unprofitable servant, cast ye out into the exterior darkness. There, shall be weeping and gnashing of teeth."[6]

There is abundant evidence in the Holy Scriptures not only that true religion is compatible with intelligence and the search for scientific truth, but indeed that the study of the physical universe reveals the nature of God Himself and knowledge of human affairs confirms and points up the ethical teachings of divine revelation. "The heavens show forth the glory of God," says the Psalmist, "and the firmament declareth the work of his hands. Day to day uttereth speech: and night to night showeth knowledge."[7] St. Paul sees in the phenomena of the physical world a reflection of the existence of God and of His attributes, and He upbraids the stupidity and intellectual perverseness of those who fail to recognize this fact. "For the invisible things of Him," he

[6] Mt. 25:14–30.
[7] Ps. 18:2, 3.

writes, "from the creation of the world are clearly seen, being understood by the things that are made. His eternal power also and divinity: so that they are inexcusable."[8]

In one of his most profound observations on the mentality of his times, St. Paul noted, "The Jews require signs; and the Greeks seek after wisdom. But we preach Christ crucified: unto the Jews indeed a stumbling-block, and unto the Gentiles foolishness; but unto them that are called, both Jews and Greeks, Christ, the power of God and the wisdom of God."[9] This dichotomy still exists in various forms, some obvious and others more subtle but just as real. Many religious persons are interested only in the testimony of miracles and regard the pursuit of knowledge as unrelated to salvation and even as a dangerous occupation allied with the work of the devil and leading to the loss of faith. Many irreligious persons regard the pursuit of truth as something which must be divorced from religion, and they refuse to consider even the possibility of supernatural manifestations or of a divine revelation. St. Paul points out that, for the true Christian, there is no such division. The increasing of one's knowledge, with the guiding wisdom of Christ and the prudent directions of the Church, is preeminently a process of salvation.

4

If there is validity in this reasoning, then the priest as the leader of men must be outstanding as a leader of dynamic thought and must himself exemplify growth in knowledge and culture. Christ is the perfect example of the learned man, the gentleman of refinement and power, and the tireless teacher. As a boy, he stood before the doctors in the Temple and confounded them with His wisdom. He addressed the scribes and pharisees fearlessly, for, in the words of St. Matthew, "He was teaching them as one having power."[10] As the bearer of Christ's truth to men, the priest must aspire to a share of this power, not with pretense, but with intellectual honesty,

---

[8] Rom. 1:20.
[9] 1 Cor. 1:22–24.
[10] Mt. 7:29.

as one who knows whereof he speaks and who can cope with the problems of the day.

"You are the light of the world," says the Master. "A city seated on a mountain cannot be hid. Neither do men light a candle and put it under a bushel, but upon a candlestick, that it may shine to all that are in the house. So let your light shine before men that they may see your good works and glorify your Father who is in heaven."[11] By "good works," we understand, not merely an act of faith, or even charitable deeds, but the pursuit of God's mind, wherever and however it may be revealed, and the tireless teaching of this truth. Spiritual growth must be identified with a deepening and broadening of one's perceptions and a profound reverence for the acquisition of learning, which is the virtue of intelligence. "I am the way, the truth, and the life."[12] "Going therefore, teach ye all nations."[13]

It is of the utmost importance that the priest, the Catholic educator, and indeed all Catholics become imbued with this dynamic conception of Christ's attitude toward life and learning, if Catholicism is to exercise a vital influence in civilized society or raise human standards anywhere. Otherwise, a deadly complacency sets in, leading to mediocrity and dry rot. It is quite possible for a Catholic educator to take a narrow and even anti-intellectual view of his faith and mission and to teach in a strictly routine manner. Such teaching depends entirely upon others to do the spadework, to carry the torch, to lead the way in expanding human knowledge. Where the element of competition enters into the picture, standards are maintained only by prodding from the outside. A dim and often resentful view of research, specialization, higher learning, and expression of opinion may come to characterize the sluggish disciple of Christ, who has his eye fastened on what he thinks is the easiest way into heaven. When, as a result of cultural insularity or unawareness, false prophets and strange doc-

---

[11] Mt. 5:14–17.
[12] Jn. 14:6.
[13] Mt. 28:19.

trines take hold, persecution follows and the Church finds itself in a position of having to start all over again.

History exemplifies these observations over and over. There are, of course, many elements which enter into situations where Catholic influence has waned and where the Church has lost its once strong position and been placed under severe disabilities. Greed for wealth and civil power, economic stress, social stratification, intellectual perverseness, and the plain immorality of men have been responsible, in different degrees, from within and from without, for attacks against the freedom of the Church and the functioning of its institutions. But in many cases, the problem has arisen as the result of a gradual deterioration of intellectual vitality among the clergy, with a corresponding alienation of cultured laity, and the transfer or usurpation of leadership by alien hands and minds.

The loss of the Catholic universities in practically all the traditionally Catholic countries of Europe and South America in the nineteenth century undoubtedly came on the wave of the free-thinking, rationalist, and atheist philosophies of the eighteenth century. But it is doubtful whether such a tremendous loss would have taken place, had there been a more alert and vigorous Christian mentality among the clergy and Catholic educators. What happened in many cases was a retreat of Catholic education into the seminaries, and a failure of competent Catholic minds to come to grips with the new scientific discoveries, methods, and theories that were shaking the faith of society. Instead of endeavoring to understand the problems that were disturbing the minds of men and of carrying them through a difficult period of intellectual ferment, the reaction was often one of hostility, withdrawal, or flight. One must take this into account, when studying the rise of liberalism, communism, and anticlericalism in the Catholic countries.

The Church is still suffering from this situation. Distinctly Catholic universities in most of these countries are new and small, practically all of the great old Catholic universities having been lost, secularized, and turned into cultural patterns far from Catholic thinking. In some of these countries, Catholic education is

forbidden by law. There is no mystery in this situation for ob-
servers who recognize the vital and critical importance of the
cultural and intellectual apostolate. If the Catholic Church — the
clergy and the laity — does not take the initiative and hold it in
expanding the frontiers of knowledge and of thirsting for truth,
other forces will.

"The Church," Pope Pius XII reminds us, "has no intention of
taking sides against any of the individual and practical forms by
which peoples and States are trying to solve the gigantic problems
affecting their domestic organization and international collabora-
tion, as long as these solutions respect the laws of God."[14] "The sole
desire of the Church," he reiterates, "is with the educational and
religious means she possesses, to transmit to all peoples without
exception the clear stream of their inheritance and the values of
the Christian life so that each nation, in the measure suited to its
particular needs, may use the doctrines and the ethical and religious principles of Christianity to establish a society worthy
of man."[15]

Commenting on these profound observations, Cardinal Suhard
notes, "But what she (the Church) cannot herself do, Christians
can do and must bring to pass; because, being also of this world,
they have an equal right with others to share in the search for
truth and to take part in all the debates and transformations of a
City to which they belong. The 'children of light' are only too
often less clever than the 'children of darkness'; and that fact, when
it was voiced by our divine Master, was not given as a precept.
That Christians have been behind-hand in ideas may be a fact,
but it is no virtue. We therefore tell you, Christian thinkers, that
your duty is not to follow but to lead. It is not enough for you to
be disciples; you must become masters."[16] Certainly these injunctions pertain pre-eminently to the priests of the Church who, by
their very position, are leaders in Catholic thought and expression.

---

[14] Pius XII, *Christmas Message*, 1942, in *Catholic Mind*, January, 1943, p. 46.
[15] Pius XII, *Christmas Message*, 1940, in *Catholic Mind*, January 8, 1941,
pp. 4, 5.
[16] Emmanuel Cardinal Suhard, *The Church Today* (Chicago: Fides Publishers, 1953), pp. 159, 160.

Similar observations might be made in all fields of cultural expression. A vast body of French literature of the eighteenth, nineteenth, and even twentieth centuries has found its way to the Index of forbidden books or been condemned in one way or another as unfit for Catholics. Much of the literature of modern Italy and Spain — including so-called classics — likewise reflects an anti-Catholic, anti-clerical bias. The same is true of the literature emanating from Central and South America. Yet all of these areas are known as traditionally Catholic. Many of these authors were the products of Catholic schools. What was wrong? Can it be that there is something inherently dangerous in thinking or in writing? This can hardly be so, if we recognize that the object of the mind and of communication is the truth. Yet, as somewhat humorously suggestive of a sector of theorizing on this subject, one of my students once informed me that he had no ambition to write, because "people who write books lose their faith."

The fact is, however, that there is no logical connection between writing books and losing one's faith. On the contrary, much of the world's great literature is a testament of faith. The Evangelists of the New Testament, as well as the Prophets of the Old Testament, were writers, thinkers, and preachers. The Fathers of the Church were writers; and their writings are one of the richest deposits of faith. The saints of the Church have been writers, poets, philosophers, scholars, and biographers, from St. Francis Assisi, St. Thomas Aquinas, St. Robert Bellarmine, and numerous others, down to St. Therese Martin, the Little Flower of our day, and Pope St. Pius X, who promoted good music and frequent Communion alike.

Loss of faith in brilliant minds has been due rather to a failure on the part of someone to guide and nurture them at a time when they needed religious strength and guidance. And, on the other hand, many a creative talent has been saved and brought into the greater service of truth by the sympathetic interest and generous encouragement and instruction of an intelligent and cultured priest. Christ brought Nicodemus into the fold by giving him instructions at night. St. Paul commanded the respect of the Athenians and

converted the cultured Greeks of his day by the force of his learning and understanding, as exemplified in his great Epistles, reinforced by the grace of God. Superior educational preparation,
coupled with virtue, has been the strength of Catholic missionaries
in all lands. And the level of the Catholic educational system,
directed by the Church, can be taken as the measure of directive
influence of the Church in the communities and countries of the
world today.

On the occasion of his visit to the Catholic University of America
as Cardinal Pacelli, on October 22, 1936, Pope Pius XII, declared
to the faculty and student body, "May yours be the grace of an
intimate realization of the greatness, the nobility, and the responsibility of those who, in the designs of God, are destined to be the
servants and custodians of learning. After the priesthood of the
altar, there is none greater than the priesthood of truth."[17]

5

To maintain cultural growth and attain intellectual maturity,
it is essential for the priest, as well as for anyone else, to begin
with and to continue in a spirit of humility and willingness to
learn. "If with so much solicitude," writes Pope Pius XII, "We
have, in the discharge of Our Apostolic office, recommended solid
intellectual training among the clergy, it is easy to understand
how much we have at heart the spiritual and moral training of
young clerics without which even outstanding knowledge can bring
incalculable harm on account of arrogant pride which easily enters
the heart."[18]

Without an abiding humility in one's desire to continue growing, the great advantages of priestly preparation and status may
degenerate in patterns of intellectual pretense and dishonesty. The
intellectually dishonest man pretends to have information which he
does not have. He passes judgment on matters that are beyond
his competence. He condemns persons and things without investigation. He treats reputations lightly, and dismisses as queer or be-

[17] Cf. Thomas McDermott, *Keeper of the Keys: A Life of Pope Pius XII*
(Milwaukee: The Bruce Publishing Co., 1946), p. 117.
[18] *Menti Nostrae*, par. 92.

neath contempt individuals, movements, and activities with which he has no, or superficial, acquaintance. He speaks dogmatically about books which he has never read. He gives advice on matters entirely outside his competence. He takes a strong stand and lets loose his oratory on subjects, when wisdom would counsel silence or, at least, honest study of the facts.

The humble man waits until he is prepared to speak. He is willing to listen and learn. He seeks out the truth and keeps himself posted on the development of facts. He endeavors to appreciate what wiser men have recognized as good and beautiful. He takes a sympathetic view of talent in others; and he opens his mind to profit by what others have to offer. He does not make the mistake of imagining that knowledge and information are intuitive. He is willing to work for the improvement of his mind, to read and study, to be deliberate and selective in his use of time, and to advance in his sense of values. The man who thinks that he knows it all or, worse still, who adopts an attitude of suspicion and hostility toward cultural expression and growth, cuts himself off from progress and blights the growth of others within his influence.

If humility is the first condition for the cultural growth of the priest, and a desire to learn is the second, we may well proceed to the third ingredient, which is the development of systematic progress. Without a systematic approach, one can expend a great deal of energy and time, without any satisfactory accumulation of knowledge or the achievement of any worthwhile objective. I once asked an eminent educator how he found time, amid numerous duties and activities, to write articles and books. "I cannot lay claim to any genius," he replied, "but I have endeavored to train myself to systematize my thinking, my reading, and my gathering of materials. With system, one acquires certain proficiencies. Knowledge takes shape into something tangible. One can become an authority, at least relatively such, on given subjects; and the dedication of one's time to observation and study renders it fruitful."

A great American educator once stated that fifteen minutes a day given to reading will make it possible for one to read the world's great classical literature. Deliberate selectivity, of course, is the secret. One can spend much more than fifteen minutes a day in reading and yet never read one classic. The priest who limits his reading to the daily newspaper and casual magazines may indeed acquire useful information; and, if he is a careful reader, he may derive much benefit from the practice. But, as a professional man with only a given amount of time at this disposal, he will not make much intellectual and cultural progress unless he selects his reading and directs his efforts in a continuous way to definite objectives.

This would suggest that every priest who can afford to do so should subscribe to at least one periodical which is edited specifically for priests. There are a number of such, including the *American Ecclesiastical Review,* the *Homiletic Review,* and the *Theological Quarterly,* in addition to more popular-style magazines like *The Priest* and various digests and reviews published in America and abroad. The lawyer, the doctor, the engineer, the musician, and the artist, worthy of the name and eager to keep abreast of his profession, makes it a point of principle to subscribe to one or more leading journals in his field. The priest should be marked by a no less professional attitude toward his calling and keep himself armed with the best in current thought and developments of specific interest to his sacerdotal life and work.

A similar principle of calculation and selectivity should govern one's acquisition of books and general reading habits. Reading may be regarded, and rightly so, as a form of recreation; and certainly, with this object in mind, there is nothing wrong in the habit of picking up a light novel from time to time or engaging in the pursuit of detective literature. I have known some great minds and administrators who devoured every book of mystery and crime they laid their hands on. Among others addicted to this passion, I am told, was G. K. Chesterton, whose Father Brown stories are an evidence of his mastery in this field of writing. But the serious priest cannot be satisfied to read merely for recreation or confine his reading to "pick-ups" and fringe literature of a casual character. He ought to acquaint himself with the significant books in contemporary literature, at least from the standpoint of positive critcism, and he should acquire and read, as a matter of plan, at least some of the best for his own professional development.

How can one tell what to read? The answer to this question will differ, of course, for different persons and for various interests. The man who is a specialist in a given field, such as history, will keep himself acquainted with recent literature by subscribing to a historical journal, such as the *Catholic Historical Review,* and following its comments and references to what is being written. More general readers will follow the indications and references in standard Catholic periodicals such as *The Catholic World, America, Commonweal, The Sign,* and *Best Sellers,* in addition to well-known sources in the general field like the *New York Times* Literary Supplement." Most Catholic publishers are more than eager to send their catalogues and other notices upon request.

Attention may be called also to various book clubs which offer some selectivity to their members, including a number of Catholic book-of-the-month" plans. It may be argued that the independent and mature reader does not have to depend upon any club to furnish him with what he should read. On the other hand, particularly for those whose time for reading is limited, as well as for those eager to encourage Catholic literature, there is much merit in the Catholic book club idea. Moreover, this provides a safe and constructive plan of Catholic reading, which the priest can recommend to the laity who are casting about for some guidance in Catholic literature. Information on Catholic book clubs is readily available from advertisements, bookstores, and publishers.

The alert and interested priest will find it to his advantage to avail himself of the facilities of the public library in his community. In addition to profiting by this agency which he as a taxpayer helps support, he can help to shape its policies and make suggestions as to titles which ought to be in its collections. It is a good thing for the priest to be seen in the public library, not only as an encouragement to the cultural development of his own people, but also as an indication to the entire community that the priest is a man of culture and that the Catholic Church stands for enlightenment and education on all levels.

In addition, the parish priest ought, from time to time, to use his pulpit to encourage good reading. Unfortunately, this is too seldom done. It is easier to issue sweeping condemnations of bad literature than to suggest books and articles that are worthy of attention. Yet, it is only on this positive basis that one can hope to achieve real good. Some years ago, I undertook to encourage weekly reading of a certain Catholic periodical in the "intellectual" class. The response was heart-warming. A weekly announcement of the diocesan newspaper, calling attention to a particular article, recommending a specific book, and occasionally devoting a sermon to the values of good reading, with some definite suggestions, can raise the standards and leadership of a Catholic community even beyond expectations.

The same general observations apply to the other fields of cultural appreciation. In the realm of the fine arts, every priest should have at least a basic understanding and an appreciation. The Church has always cultivated the arts as a reflection of divine beauty, an expression of creative prayer, and an aid to devotion. It is not to be expected that every priest be an artist; but every priest should cultivate an attitude of reverence for great art and share in its preservation and communication to others. Painting, sculpture, architecture, and the myriad forms of artistic expression should have a vital appeal to the man of culture; and every priest should humbly and devoutly put himself to the task of developing his own good taste.

Music likewise is worthy of serious consideration, whether one is talented in this line or not. The priest ought to know the difference between classical music and jazz. He should become acquainted with the history of music within the Church. And both for his own enjoyment and for the edification of the faithful, he ought to encourage the appreciation of the best. One who has received no musical education can, nevertheless, learn the basic facts by reading; and with the marvelous opportunities offered through radio, television, and records, as well as of firsthand performance in concerts, operas, and symphonies, in this age, a preciation of really fine music, on a selective basis, is available to everyone.

Patronage of the theater involves special considerations and local problems of a social character which touch upon prudence; and, in some places, special diocesan regulations govern theater attendance by the clergy. There can be no doubt that certain types of presentations, such as Shakespearean plays or grand opera, may be acceptable under most general circumstances. In the absence of positive regulations, the rule of Christian standards and consideration for community conventions will govern attendance at other productions, both of motion pictures and the legitimate stage. Whatever may be said about the social message of the drama, the simple fact is that most theater is for entertainment. The alert priest ought to know what is going on in his community, and he should be in a position to advise others as to what is acceptable and what is not in local theatrical and motion picture theaters; but this does not necessarily require that he attend everything in town. There are other ways of securing authentic information.

It is sometimes argued that the "cultural" priest becomes a dilettante, wasting his time on tidbits of art and curiosities of literature and trying unsuccessfully to impress his confreres with his superior knowledge. Such superficiality and posing is, of course, offensive. But this is not our conception of culture, even though there is certainly nothing wrong in even a superficial interest in worthy objects of knowledge. What we should keep in mind is, first of all, a sense of values and the realization that there is a difference between ignorance and knowledge, correct information and misinformation, crudity and finish, ugliness and beauty, effectiveness and ineffectiveness, propriety and impropriety, laudable ambition, initiative, and effort on the one hand, and crass inactivity, envy, and resentment on the other.

The cultured priest may be a man of deep, scholarly interests and production. But he may also be a man of genuine appreciation of the finer things of life, without being a genius. As such, he will reflect a Christlike spirit to all about him. His gracious understanding will be an inspiration to old and young alike. He will find himself at home among the rich and poor without distinction. He will never be a lonely man, because he carries within himself the wisdom of the ages and the power to discern beauty and goodness in all things and in all people. The priest of culture is essentially a gentleman, without ostentation or apology. And all who come in contact with his influence will be grateful for the spiritual experience of having touched at least the hem of Christ's garment.

> *"And in fine, be ye all of one mind, having compassion one of another, being lovers of the brotherhood, merciful, modest, humble"* (1 Peter 3:8).

CHAPTER IV

THE SOCIAL LIFE OF THE PRIEST

I

ONE of the most appealing and reassuring aspects of the personality of Christ was His social character. He loved to be with men and women on friendly human terms, and to share their joys and sorrows. The priest in active life need look no farther for justification and example in His attitude and dealings with people than in the pattern of practical life set by the Master.

"That Jesus did not close His heart to the joys of mankind," writes Karl Adam, "that He was not like the Baptist a man of the desert, clothed in a garment of camel's hair, whose meat was locusts and wild honey; that He went among people in everyday garb, a 'cloak without seam,' (John 19:23) adorned with hems (Matt. 14:35); that He took part quite naturally in their festivities and merrymakings so that his enemies taunted him with being a 'glutton and wine-drinker' (Matt. 11:19); that He did not hesitate to work His first miracle to please the guests at a marriage feast; that He would not have His disciples fast so long as the bridegroom was with them (Matt. 2:19); that He held one of His followers very dear and let him lean on His bosom (John 13:23); and lastly that the whole of this exhuberant vitality was set in a frame so full of charm and grace and loveliness, that in it alone we cannot fail to recognize a great, a supremely

57

great poet, who with a unique creative touch makes the whole of nature live for us — the fig-trees and the lilies, the mustard trees and the vineyard, the sparrow and the fox, the glad sunshine and the wild tempest; all this betrays such a generosity, openness of heart, breadth and responsiveness and tenderness and delicacy of spirit as had no counterpart in any heroic or strictly ascetical nature."[1]

No one can reasonably question that a well-balanced social life is legitimate for the priest, is fruitful and beneficial for all concerned, and is indeed an essential part of his ministry.

From the standpoint of mental as well as physical health, social recreation is important. While private calisthenics, the lonely walk, light reading, and sleep all have their value, it is a normal craving of human nature to enjoy some relaxation in the company of others. The average person who shuns the society of his fellows and communes only with himself is likely to develop eccentricities and a warped view of life which unfit him for leadership and develop mistrust in others. The priest is no exception to this. On the contrary, his celibate life and the more or less removed character of his social position can, unless he takes the necessary precautions, develop traits of a dictatorial and even cynical character and brand him as queer in the minds of the people whom he is called upon to guide and counsel.

A social mingling with people is required also for one to understand human nature and to have a real grasp of the problems which the laity must face in their daily lives. Study of psychology and a mastery of the principles of moral theology will give a priest the basic theories of behavior and the rules of conduct; but they will not, in themselves, reveal the practical dilemmas of men and women or provide those effective powers of the imagination so essential for a helpful spiritual adviser. One frequently wonders why clergy of intellectual brilliance sometime deliver sermons which are far "over the heads" of the congregation and lacking in practical application. The reason frequently is that

---

[1] *The Son of God* (New York: Sheed and Ward, 1934), pp. 131, 132.

their own social life is too circumscribed. They have never learned to make use of human experience and observation which comes from direct dealing with people, whether in the home, at work, or in the street.

The discharge of the pastoral duties of the priest requires him to get out among his people, to know them, and to be known by them. "I know mine, and mine know me," said Christ.[2] It is all very well to be available in the office or rectory parlor, on an official basis; and the considerate priest will make due provision for this. But good parochial administration cannot be handled simply from a desk, nor can the priestly ministry be fulfilled on a sheerly formal basis.

Too many people have a fear of their priests, for the reason that they know them only from a distance or engaged in a sacred rite; and they hesitate to express themselves on matters of critical spiritual concern, because of this fear. The priest who makes a real effort, as a human being, to give a friendly hand and a ready attention to men and women, at their clubs, in their homes, with their gatherings, their anniversaries, and their special projects, is in a position to do untold good. Many a difficult problem has been solved in an easy offhand way, which otherwise might have drifted on and led to disaster. Many a bigot has dropped his prejudices and antagonism because of the friendly, human gesture of a priest. Many a convert has been started on the road to the Church because of the chance to meet a kind and understanding priest.

On the other hand, there is no sadder comment than the expression, "Father So-and-so must be a good man, but no one ever gets a chance to meet him."

2

These general considerations are, of course, subject to further analysis and distinction. There is a difference between friendship and acquaintance. And there is a difference between friendship and association. As a man in the public eye, the parish priest

2 Jn. 10:14.

has a wide range of acquaintances. He is known by a great many people, some of whom claim close friendship with him, with faint or no recollection on his part. It is part of his business to be considerate and reasonably congenial with all; and he must keep in mind that he is recognized by persons who may be perfect strangers to him and in places where he might regard himself as unknown and anonymous.

His circle of personal friends will naturally be limited, from considerations of time, opportunity, interests, congeniality, and energy. A busy man has only a limited amount of time and energy which he can devote to strictly social and recreational engagements. One must choose between invitations, opportunities, and obligations of various kinds, to avoid waste of time and to conserve one's health.

A community of outlooks and interests will also determine the personal friends with whom a priest will feel most at ease, and he is certainly within his rights in cultivating such friendships within normal considerations of prudence. Christ was known to the entire country in which he moved. His personal acquaintances were legion. Yet, when He sought the shelter of a friendly roof, among friends with whom He felt perfectly at ease and whom He could trust unquestionably, He chose only a few, such as Martha and Mary and Lazarus. Even at the risk of criticism from busybodies and small pharisees, a priest has the right to make a similar choice and to make his own close friends, among clergy and laity alike.

Friendship on the basis of intimate and regular association, however, calls for more than ordinary circumspection on the part of the priest. For here he must take into consideration the special nature of his calling, the exigencies of his business and ministry, the safeguarding of his vocation and spiritual life, and the general regard of the people to whom he is required to give good example. Apart from the fulfillment of duties to his own family and the close bonds of affection which the family group normally implies, a priest cannot do better than to select his close associates, even on a social basis, from his fellow priests.

There are a number of reasons for this principle. While it may be argued, and with some justification, that priests are inclined to constitute a separate social caste, the fact remains that they have many things in common which serve to bring and keep them together. By special vocation, spiritual temperament and objectives, training, habits, and interests they naturally find a ready "calling card" with one another and an ease of mutual social approach which makes association practically taken for granted. Lawyers, doctors, and professional and business men of various categories are likewise drawn together, to such an extent that the man who shuns friendship or association with others in his calling or pursuit arouses wonderment and suspicion. The priest who takes no pleasure in the company of his fellow priests, who "disappears," so to speak, from his classmates and fellow clergy, and prefers to associate only with the laity or to remain by himself generally gives rise to the same unfavorable reactions.

There is, moreover, a high protective value in the association of priests with priests. Particularly for the priest living in the world, brushing up against all kinds of people, faced with all types of problems and dilemmas, and confronted with temptation of every kind, it is easy to become covered with the dust of worldliness and to be tarred with a material and secular outlook. A priest who stays close to his fellow priests cannot stray far from the spiritual path which has been cut out for him, without feeling the friendly hand of guidance or hearing the voice of warning. He may be deceived and misled by others and he may deceive himself for a while, but he will not succeed in deceiving his priestly associates. In this wholesome association, there is strength and encouragement and a sense of solidarity with Christ and the Church, which no one can deny.

"Next in warmth and strength to the fraternal charity displayed towards their housemates," writes Rev. Arthur Barry O'Neill, "is that which priests owe to the clerics of their neighborhood, the pastors and curates of adjacent parishes, fellow-members of their conference-circle, and the clergy of their diocese as a whole. The circumstance that one meets such brethren less frequently than is the case with the members of one's own household sometimes renders the observance of the rules governing brotherly love comparatively easy. Meeting a man only occasionally, and for a relatively brief period, is quite a different matter from living with him day after day and month after month, especially if his defects of character are (like our own, no doubt) neither few nor negligible. Even the most cross-grained, irritable, disputatious, or domineering cleric that ever merited the rebuke of Ecclesiasticus, 'Be not as a lion in thy house, terrifying them of thy household, and oppressing them that are under thee' (4:35), is generally on his good behavior when he is visited by brother priests, or when he in turn visits them. His normal self is for the nonce subdued, and he appears in the guise, or disguise, of an agreeable companion."[3]

In the company of one's fellow priests, there is a healthy antidote for loneliness which might otherwise find escape in dangerous tangents. In this association, a priest can relax without giving petty scandal. He can make himself "feel at home" without explanation or apology or fear of gossip. In public, on the golf course or in other legitimate sports, he need not attempt to dodge recognition or feel out of place if he is in the company of another priest. And in the rectory, if he wishes to have a game of cards or otherwise entertain, he can enjoy an evening of decent recreation among his priest friends without formality on the one hand or impropriety on the other.

In this association among the clergy, there are, of course, certain limitations. Social life which is restricted exclusively to priests can have a narrowing effect. The priest who never leaves his rectory becomes stale in his mental outlook and crabbed and superficial in his dealings with others. Mere association with priests is no guarantee of Christlike living. Priests can sit at the same table day after day and year after year, with no lay person about except the housekeeper, and lead the dullest of lives, in sullen or stupid silence, taking one another for granted

---

[3] Arthur Barry O'Neill, C.S.C., *Sacerdotal Safeguards* (Notre Dame, Ind.: University Press, 1918), p. 74.

and bringing no element of cheer or inspiration into their community existence. They may, although living under the same roof, dwell in worlds apart and never come to a friendly, human understanding and exchange.

A similar lack of interest and inspiration may characterize even those priestly associations which have the appearance of social conviviality. Possibly, because of the same training, the acceptance of basic truths, the same discipline and restrictions of activity, priests may come to regard each other as perpetual adolescents and to talk and act together on a plane of arrested development. No one can take fair exception to a keen or even playful sense of humor; but when it becomes a kind of defense mechanism employed constantly to thwart real human relationship and understanding, its validity is questionable. Some men never greet each other or carry on a conversation except on this basis. From the loud laughter, backslapping, and general evidence of good cheer, a superficial observer might gather that here fine friends are enjoying a choice anecdote or exchanging good fellowship. The actual fact may be that here are individuals sparring on a semi-hysterical basis, men who are really afraid of each other or fearful of revealing themselves, men who have never learned to deal with their equals in real, down-to-earth, honest social intercourse.

To effect a fruitful exchange of ideas and to make priest friendships productive of personal growth — not merely the passing of time — it is essential that men take each other seriously. It is important also that they learn to converse on matters of common concern, things that affect the Church and society, problems of parochial work, currents of thought involving faith and morals, contemporary literature, and Catholic Action. The fine mind and education of a priest may be hidden under the camouflage of being a "regular fellow" or the hesitancy to put some tone and value into a visit, an association, or a gathering which has started on a sheerly casual or social basis and apparently will carry along on a puerile level. It is not to be expected that priests, when together, must always be engaged in profound spiritual, philosophical, or pastoral discussion. Everyone is entitled to moments of sheer relaxation, fun, and even nonsense; but a constant program of conversational escapism and horseplay is most certainly an evidence of immaturity and irresponsibility.

Vigilance must also be kept regarding the level of one's language and sense of humor. Those who have read the *tischreden,* or "table talk," of Luther may be shocked at the coarseness of thought and expression that apparently characterized his circle. Nevertheless, it is amazingly easy for one's sense of humor to sink to low levels and for one to lose his sense of propriety in groups which specialize in risqué stories and double-meaning allusions. No one likes to be classed as a prude; but, on the other hand, even the priest must be on the alert against a turn of imagination and humor and the development of habits of speech and conversation that were never meant for the ambassadors of Christ.

Similarly in forms of recreation, the Catholic Church has never taken a puritanical stand on such matters as cards and other games of chance. There is no justification, however, for letting down the bars, to the point of scandalizing society or engaging in games beyond reasonable time and risk. Card playing which becomes a passion or runs into stakes that one can ill afford, or develops into all-night sessions with a corresponding dislocation of energy and daytime work, may call for pause and definite termination. It is easy to be drawn into such situations gradually and innocently, without realization that here is something neither worthy of nor consonant with good judgment and above all with priestly propriety.

Likewise with attendance at athletic events and participation in sports. The priest who enjoys a baseball game is a perfectly normal being. The interest and encouragement which the clergy show in clean sports are not only a healthy outlet for emotional and physical tensions, but also a source of respect and confidence from youth and all men who like to feel that their priests are red-blooded, human beings. In most communities, a priest can properly play golf with his fellow priests, roll up his sleeves at a picnic or with his friends, or enjoy hunting or fishing without having to dodge his parishioners or give elaborate explanations to justify himself. As a matter of fact, physical exercise, including the ancient and perhaps most adaptable of all, the art of walking, is something that every priest should make provision for if he possibly can. But no one can spend half his time on the golf course or in the sports field and take care of his business properly. The old adage "all work and no play makes Jack a dull boy" can be turned around with equal truth.

What is true of putting money on cards and other games of chance holds equally true in public sports. There is nothing wrong in itself about going to a horse race, for example — although diocesan regulations may have something to say on this subject. But the regular attendance of the clergy at such events and their display of green money in any abundance at the betting booths can easily leave a painful impression on the laity, particularly those who are conscious of the Sunday collection box and are sensitive as to where the money goes. One need not be too concerned about pharisaical criticism, particularly from those who would criticize under any circumstances. On the other hand, it is important to guard against giving scandal or giving false impressions; and it is even more important to guard against giving true impressions where such cannot be squared with priestly behavior and responsibilities. Priests, whether alone or together, in public are always a center of observation. They simply must keep this in mind and not nullify by their "off bounds" activity their Sunday sermon admonitions and general prestige and influence.

The friendships and associations of priests, in other words, should always be a source of mutual strength and helpfulness, not a stumbling block for one another or a cause for confusion among the laity. The story is frequently retold of the saint who gathered several members of his religious community about him for a walk through the town, alleging that he was going to preach a sermon. Upon his return from the walk, his companions asked him when and where the sermon would be delivered. "It has already been given," he replied, "while we were on our way."

3

In his relationship with the laity, there is only one rule for the priest, and that is to be a gentleman at all times. This means courtesy, consideration, and the urbanity of appearance and manners that one should expect from an educated person of responsibility. The fact that a man is a priest will never substitute or compensate for lack of etiquette, nor will it ever justify or excuse boorishness or slovenliness. The charity of Christ shines through kindness, perhaps more than through any other virtue, as Father Faber has pointed out so beautifully in his essays on this subject. A better-than-thou attitude in the priest, a position of cold detachment from the rest of the world, a technique of sarcasm, and a display of indifference to the amenities of social living, simply have the effect of alienating souls who look for example and inspiration in their spiritual shepherd.

The cultivation of the marks of a gentleman calls for attention to details, willingness to learn, and frequent examination of conscience. Because he lives the life of a bachelor, the priest generally lacks that vigilance and element of reminder provided by the women in a home. Consequently, he has to be more than ordinarily alert to his manners and appearance. He must be his own monitor. It is easy for a man living alone to slip into a kind of barnyard way of living. His speech may descend into a chain reaction of slang expressions. His table manners may be atrocious, revealing lack of instruction or complete indifference to civilized living. His clothes may be mute witness to many a season without benefit of a tailor and give testimony to many a slip twixt the fork or spoon and the lip. Even his cassock, noble garment of sacerdotal rank, may cry out from its assortment of spots and tatters and the burden of years against its wearer who places such little conscious valuation upon its appearance or is too lazy to give it the attention it rightfully deserves. Many a priest thinks that he can "get away" with this neglect; and it is true that the faithful are generally very patient and tolerant with the eccentricities and social deficiences of their priests. But there is no excuse for a situation which in itself is neither necessary nor really excusable.

The priest need not be a fashion plate; but he should be well groomed and properly dressed, within his means. His clothes should be clean and pressed, and his shoes shined. To the extent that he has hair, it should be combed. He should be clean-shaven, every day, by routine, preferably before Mass in the morning to greet his Lord properly. His shirt should be clean, and his other garments should be changed frequently. His hat should be kept brushed and in decent shape; it should be discarded when it has served a reasonable tenure. He should bathe regularly and as often as necessary to avoid giving offense. There is nothing extraordinary about these rules; nor do they impose a heavy burden. The priest who would command acceptance and respect must observe them.

Likewise in social manners. Because of their privileged position, the clergy are entitled to deference and first choice in many respects and circumstances. But this is no reason for insistence or for making a fuss if this is not always forthcoming. Nor does it include a general dispensation from those observances that distinguish the person of culture from the child of nature. If a man does not know how to use a napkin or how to proceed with table utensils, he should learn. If he has not been taught these matters in school and cannot obtain instruction from his friends, he might do well to purchase a book on the subject of good manners and social procedure and study it. If a priest is inclined to dismiss all this scornfully as superfluous or effeminate, he should also be conscious of the fact that he is selling his privileged position short and failing in practical demonstration of the truth that Christian charity toward one's fellow man is shown by correct etiquette in social matters in the same way as faith and love of God are shown by correct fulfillment of the Church's liturgy.

These principles are just as valid in a rural community as in the big city and among sophisticated society. True gentlefolk and people of refined instincts are found in the countryside and in the cottage as well as on the boulevards and in palaces. On all levels, the priest who is aware of his responsibilities as well as of his privileges will show himself a gracious person and a leader who can point the way to Christian living by his personal bearing and example, quite as much as by exhortation.

4

A favorite adage for religious is that while they are in the world, they are not of it; which is to say, so far as the priest is concerned, that he should be a human being, with a human understanding of, and sympathy with, his fellow men, but never a playboy. Even when enjoying the casual company of the laity, whether in social recreation or in sports, he should never forget or allow others to forget his sacred calling. I recall a certain pastor who loved to go on hunting expeditions with his parishioners. Even when in rubber boots and up to his hips in water behind a duck blind, he always wore his clerical collar and a derby hat. Perhaps this show of clerical dignity was somewhat exaggerated and unappropriate under the circumstances; but his companions realized that they were never to take unfair advantage of his comradeship. The priest who thinks he can go along on the same basis as all of his lay friends, punctuating his conversation with profanity and being a regular fellow without any distinction or reservations, will soon find himself in a compromising position. And those who lead him on to see how far he will go are usually the first to turn against him, talk behind his back, and capitalize on his indiscretions.

In the United States, priests enjoy a singular range of social freedom, which is evidence of their general maturity and is highly to be prized. With local and regional exceptions, depending upon conditions, they may attend the theater, enjoy motion pictures, participate in general gatherings and clubs, drive their own cars, and travel with ease without having to give an elaborate explanation either to ecclesiastical authorities or to the world in general for every movement. But the continuance of this liberty, which has been purchased by their general good sense and prudence, depends upon individual and group circumspection. There are many places and occasions which are acceptable for the laity but not proper for the clergy. There are night clubs, dances, forms of entertainment and recreation quite innocent in themselves, which a prudent priest will regard with great caution or stay away from altogether. The fact that he is invited is no reason why he must accept; and if he finds himself more or less forced by circumstances to be present, he will always find ways and means of quickly bowing out at a convenient moment and an early hour.

There are times when groups and clubs welcome the visit of a priest and are honored by his presence. But the priest who appears without reason or warning in gatherings of the laity or lounges in clubs and hotels, more or less as a permanent fixture, is definitely out of place. Bars and taverns and known gambling establishments are generally not the proper place for priests to frequent; nor are priests wanted in these places.

There are times, as on a holiday or vacation, engaged in a game of golf or cards or visiting casually with close friends, when a priest may wish to relax in a loose shirt without the clerical habiliments and to remain anonymous for the time being. Certainly there can be no objection to this. But it is always a mistake for a priest to imagine that without the clerical collar he is in complete disguise and can therefore engage in activities and forms of recreation out of harmony with his calling. Even the assumption of disguise is of doubtful validity. There is something about the face, the bearing, and general appearance of the Catholic priest that identifies him through any mufti. Any protracted conversation puts him under suspicion with others, although they may not be able completely to solve the mystery. Out of character, he can proceed only to a limited extent in reference to his knowledge and acquaintances and then must trail off into vague or evasive remarks. Moreover, no matter how far from home, he is almost certain to run into someone who knows him; and for everyone who gives him a nod, there are several who see him without evidencing their recognition.

For these reasons, no matter how satisfactory the motives for casual costume or disguise or how innocent the holiday diversion, one cannot safely discard caution, without risking misinterpretation and running into trouble. If circumstances justify the use of a sport shirt and slacks on a vacation or holiday, no one can reasonably be scandalized, provided the priest appears in appropriate clerical garb at the proper times and does not attempt to pass himself off on people as something other than he really is. The immature, if belated, desire which might seize a clergyman, to "see how the rest of the world lives," by dropping out of character and assuming a lay role, holds special dangers and can lead to tragedy.

The attitudes and practical policy which the priest takes relative to membership in, and co-operation with, lay organizations and fraternities, ranging all the way from interfaith and civic groups to Catholic societies such as the Knights of Columbus and the Catholic Order of Foresters and to general groups like the Elks, Lions, Rotarians, Kiwanians, and so forth, will depend in the first place upon the attitude of the Church and the indications of the bishops. Even when dealing with lay groups on a social, not necessarily official, basis, it is always the part of prudence and good consideration to secure the approval or at least the *nihil obstat* of the Chancery. There are times when the individual may find this distasteful, with his own ideas of propriety in disagreement with the diocesan authority. Nonetheless the priest must remember that he is part of an organization, and he will make it his business to conform to the voice of authority.

When permitted or directed to join in the activities of such groups of laymen, the priest will usually find his position most secure and his presence most effective by maintaining a certain reserve and concentrating his attention on the stated objectives of the order. In this way, if any good is to be accomplished, he can make his contribution with little waste of time and keep himself free from the petty politics frequently involved. Through contacts of this kind a priest can perform a real service for the Church, by breaking down prejudices and giving men of all faiths a better and more personal appreciation of what we stand for in a constructive way. Often the opportunity is opened for lapsed or weak Catholics to find their way back through the extended hand of friendship. But an argumentative approach to business and professional men, on the one hand, or a backslapping, back-room technique, on the other, is offensive and detrimental to any real influence and leadership so far as the clergy are concerned. For the prudent priest, friendship and dignity will always go hand in hand.

5

In his social dealings with women, the same general principles of consideration and common sense are applicable. There are some priests who seem to think that the only women above suspicion are the Blessed Virgin Mary and their own mothers. All others are somehow regarded as necessary evils, difficult to understand and not to be trusted. It should be noted, however, that a number of women, including at least one repentant sinner, Mary Magdalene, figure in the life of Christ; and when all the Apostles had fled, faithful and courageous women remained at the foot of the cross. They were the first to return to the tomb on Easter Sunday, and it was to them that the risen Christ first appeared, with a message to reassemble His scattered flock. Religious orders of women are one of the strongest arms of the Church, in teaching and charitable work; and every priest in parish life soon learns that, without the ready and generous co-operation of the laywomen in the community, he can do little indeed.

The fact is that God created women as well as men; and in every respect they are human beings, with the same sensibilities, reactions, aspirations, and strength and weakness in moral and physical stamina as the masculine sex. The mature and effective priest must take a realistic view of their existence and place in life and society. A picayunish attitude, finding fault with little details of dress, accusing women of constant gossip, or regarding them as of inferior intelligence and only secondary rights, is unfair and un-Christian.

If danger lurks in association with women, the danger is within the man himself. Because a man has taken the vow of celibacy is no proof that he is exempt from sentiments of a romantic character or from sexual appetites. Nor is the fact that the seminarian has behaved very well in the seminary full guarantee of maturity and discretion once he is released into the freedom and personal responsibility of the priesthood. To be prepared for the contingencies of life in the world, it is important to have some advance understanding of how human nature operates in the social contacts of men and women, and to be prepared against the natural weakness of the flesh.

In many ways, the life of a priest is a lonely one. At the same time, his unique position of social responsibility and trust brings him into close touch with women as well as men. Under given circumstances, familiarity easily generates the spark of affection; and without the steady control of intelligence, the human instincts become operative as an independent unit, to create dissatisfaction and yearning. These signals appear in the life of every normal layman, whether single or married. They appear also in the life of every normal priest. Wisdom shows itself in the recognition of these signals and the exercise of self-control with appropriate action to avert possible dangerous developments.

Defections, thank God, are comparatively few, but even these could be averted, in men of good will, by the application of perhaps a little more sophisticated understanding of self and some psychological foresight. The old adage "pride goeth before a fall" is certainly pertinent in this field of human relations, particularly for those who think they know considerably more than they really do, and whose native innocence is matched only by their stupidity or stubbornness. It should be noted, at the same time, that persons of strong affections and even of sexual attraction are by no means necessarily bad. On the contrary, many of the greatest saints, like Magdalene, St. Paul, and St. Augustine, had to put up a valiant struggle against their passions; and possibly they derived much of their spiritual energy and generous enthusiasm from a sublimation of their animal instincts and emotions.

As a general rule, temptation will present itself to a priest, not in the crude form of sexual desire, although this is a possibility for all men of flesh and blood. Rather it will develop from a feeling of loneliness, a desire for company and companionship, and for attractive opportunities to fill the void with apparently innocent social contacts. The important thing for the priest to remember is that, in human inclinations and appetites, he is no different from the rest of mankind. Consequently, he cannot impose either upon himself or others more than a layman could under similar circumstances, without endangering his peace of mind and his celibacy.

If a man finds his steps turning regularly and frequently toward the same address where there are women, he may well ask himself why. It may be on legitimate business. It may be legitimate social recreation. It may be that he is making a nuisance of himself with people who are too polite to remind him that he has worn out his welcome. It may be that, consciously or unconsciously, he is pursuing an affection that will do neither him nor anyone else any good. His visits may be the subject of unfavorable conversation within the family group which he is apparently patronizing; and they may be the cause of wonderment and even scandal in the neighborhood. Perhaps no one can answer these questions better than himself. Under certain circumstances, he may have to ignore petty and unjustified criticism and gossip. But, on the other hand, he may be obliged, if he is honest, to give an unfavorable answer to the question and take decisive steps to break off an unnecessary and dangerous connection. One step backward in time may save nine.

6

For some men, the most insidious danger to their moral fiber and spiritual usefulness comes from drink. Here again, the principles of Christian humanism, so to speak, are involved. St. Paul reminds us that "a little wine" is good for the stomach.[4] Christ took wine and was accused by His enemies of being a wine bibber. His first public miracle was the conversion of water into wine at the marriage feast of Cana; and following the custom of the Jews at the Passover, He used wine at the Last Supper to be transformed into His body and blood in the holy sacrament of the Eucharist. From time immemorial wine, or some derivative of the vine or of grain, was served to signalize the toast to friendship and give honor to a worthy cause. But like every other gift of God, including friendship

---

[4] 1 Tim. 5:23.

itself, wine and alcoholic drink of all varieties must be used with discretion.

Some persons can take drink for enjoyment and sociability, without any difficulties. Others find it a problem to manage their drinks. And for others, drink is a poison, a false friend, a character assassin.

How can one tell? By experience and observation. And how can one meet the problem? By determination and the help of good friends. For all priests, there is at least the rule of temperance. For the priest who, by physical or psychological allergy, cannot drink without going to excess, there is only one rule — total abstinence. It is of the utmost importance that one should come to a definite understanding with himself on this matter and make his stand perfectly clear to his friends. Too much is at stake to fool or temporize with this matter.

I am told of a splendid young layman whose father died of alcoholism. Dismayed by this example, he took the pledge of total abstinence until the age of twenty-one. Then he took his first drink. He died two years later (of alcoholic poisoning and delirium tremens), after running through a bad marriage and resorting to dope. This may be an extreme case, but it points to the fact that drink is capable of effecting a complete moral and physical disintegration in short order.

The danger signal appears in the form of small but frequent samplings, beginning with an "eye-opener" in the morning and a cocktail or two before lunch. This may be followed by a couple of "bracers" in the afternoon, an appetizer before dinner, and a powerful nightcap before retiring. The effect of this kind of drinking is to keep a person in a state of mental fuzziness or false exaltation. Under this regime, many a man of talent and promise has dreamed and frittered away his life, never accomplishing anything, and wondering why.

Some people never acquire a chronic habit, but when they drink they take on a new personality, becoming silly or argumentative after a few cups, and yielding easily to each new round of libations. For some, the problem arises in social drinking. With others i develops into the more vicious habit of solitary drinking. For the priest who lives alone, or who suffers from loneliness, or pities himself as disillusioned or disappointed, there is special danger. Anyone can rationalize the need for one more drink; and everyone, no matter how fine in character or lofty in aspiration, must be on his guard. In this, as in most other respects involving the weakness of human nature, a priest is no different from the rest of men. But for him, the risk of scandal and moral deterioration is usually greater. Everyone can make a mistake. The smart man is he who recognizes his limitations and special vulnerability and takes the necessary steps to reduce and eliminate the danger of a repetition.

7

Perhaps in a discussion of the social life of the priest, it is misleading to stress the dangers and the pitfalls. Certainly they do not appear in actuality as so many hurdles which a man must jump in order to attain a well-regulated and happy life or an effective ministry. The highway of life for the average priest is a joyous one. If he meets the world with a smile, he will find a welcome on every hand. His career does not require a dehumanized personality or a policy of distrust. Like St. Paul, he should be "all things to all men." Social problems and dangers are only incidental. In keeping a steady vision ahead, the priest will learn to mingle easily with men and women, to share their joys and sorrows, to learn of their problems and point the way to their solution, as a friend, a guide, and a leader. In the service of the Master, he will truly, following the counsel of St. Peter, be a lover of the brotherhood — "merciful, modest, humble."

The best way of appraising positively the value and propriety of the social life of the priest is to relate it to the over-all purpose of his vocation. In other words, it must never become an end in itself but should serve as a means in furthering his apostolate. With this as a measuring rod, one can easily determine whether one's social life and recreation serve a constructive purpose or leave a serious question in one's conscience. At that same time, one can judge whether these activities are reasonably limited in time and scope or whether they are consuming such an amount of time and attention as to constitute a real waste.

In commenting on the value of a priest's time, Cardinal Manning writes, "Happy the priest who knows its value, and unwise the priest who wastes it."[5] Social activities and recreation are no waste of time if they are planned with a calculated effect, whether it be to meet one's parishioners or the people with whom one must deal, to encourage Christian social living by one's personal appearance and example, or simply to refresh one's physical and mental powers. There are times, indeed, when the priest must attend social events even against his personal desires and inclinations, but for the good of the parish and of Catholic Action. There are times when a man must slow down for his health's sake. But when social life or recreation becomes a preoccupation or an escape from idleness or boredom and the priest becomes a social butterfly, the time is at hand for a fundamental reappraisal of life purposes.

In most parishes, schools, and institutions, provision is made for the priests to take a holiday of one day a week. This is good practice, and every priest is within his rights in insisting on this consideration. A definite time should be set aside every day when a man can have at least an hour he can call his own, to relax or to take care of personal business. Every priest should plan an annual holiday and make it truly worthwhile. It is good to get a change of scenery, to relieve the tensions that build up in the course of a year, and to freshen one's outlook with new ideas and experiences. Travel is educational and, if carefully planned within one's time and means, will deepen and enrich the spiritual and cultural reserves of the priest for the benefit of those whom he serves. The priest who budgets his time for recreation as well as for work need never accuse himself of idleness or a wasted life.

"Most men," writes Cardinal Manning, "give one-third of every day to sleep, with its circumstances of rising and lying down: about three hours are due to Mass and office: who can say how much to

---

[5] Henry Cardinal Manning, *The Eternal Priesthood*, p. 132.

private prayers and spiritual reading, to study, to the confessional, to the care of souls? and of all this who can fix the measure? To the world and to society some priests give little; many give too much. If then, we live to seventy years, we shall have spent more than three-and-twenty in sleep: about seven years in Mass and offices — that makes up about thirty out of seventy years. How are the other forty years bestowed? It would be well for us if in every place we heard the words, *Quid hic agis, Elia?* and in every hour of our day, 'Did you not know that I must be about My Father's business?' "[6]

---

[6] *Ibid.*

> *"But if a man know not how to rule his own house, how shall he take care of the church of God?"* (1 Tim. 3:5.)

CHAPTER V

THE PRIEST'S HOUSE

I

SOME years ago, while visiting one of our neighboring republics, I attended a course of lectures given on various aspects of that country, some of them none too friendly to the Catholic Church. One of the speakers, describing his travels into the interior, related his visit to a local priest's house. He was surprised to find that the pastor possessed a radio and considerable taste in the general adornment of the place. The visitor was afforded the facilities of an elemental bath, given a decent meal, and put to bed under what he described as a luxurious cover that would have done credit to the nobility of Europe. It is quite possible that the lecturer had no intention of dishonoring the gracious hospitality he had received in this remote spot; but certainly the reactions of his audience were of confused wonderment.

A buzz of comments went around the room. Why should a priest have a radio, when most of his parishioners had none? How could he afford good food in so poor a place? And the bath, and that bedspread! I was somewhat annoyed by the recital and the audience reactions, until I began to reflect that practically everything a priest does or has is a source of wonderment. Even in the most staid communities, the rectory is a kind of public monument. Every visitor is noted, and an atmosphere of interest and remote mystery intrigues the place. Sometimes the comment is favorable, and sometimes it is mixed with various emotions.

78

In any case, the priest's house is a public property, intended not merely to house a private individual, but also to render a community service, identified with the mission of the Church. As such, it is a place of the utmost importance. It reflects the personality of the man who has been sent to interpret Christ to the community, as well as of the parish which he serves. It is intended to provide office or reception space, where members of the parish and others may come for spiritual guidance. It is intended to be accessible to all who are in need of the sacraments, particularly in an emergency. It is presumed to furnish office, library, workshop, and living quarters for the priest, where he may conduct the business of the parish, keep the official records under his charge, prepare his sermons, and live in decent comfort. This means that the priest's house should be well ordered and equipped for the transaction of its proper business.

At the same time, the priest in charge should recognize the official character of his residence and render the public service for which it has been provided. He should be available within reasonable hours. Callers should be received with a courtesy and dignity befitting the nature of their business; and they should be given the satisfaction to which they are entitled in a businesslike but kindly and Christian way. Telephone calls should be handled promptly and in proper form; and appointments should be made and kept in a responsible and punctual fashion.

Among the principal means of coping with the "all-purpose" character of the rectory is that of physical layout and arrangement. It would appear wise, wherever practicable, to have a clear-cut distinction between the office space and visiting parlors, on the one hand, and the living quarters and strictly domestic sections, such as the dining room, on the other. The offices which serve for the reception of persons with some business in mind, whether commercial or spiritual, should be ready of access from the outside and, if possible, cut off from a view of the other sections of the house. They should be fitted up neatly and simply for their purpose and should provide a reasonable amount of privacy.

It may be advisable to have the record books, such as for the entry of Masses, baptisms, marriages, and other references for which there is frequent call, placed in one special room, under proper custody, so as to be available without the necessity of making a search for them and without breaking in on the privacy of callers who may be engaged in conference. The room or rooms used for the counting of collections and the recording of the financial affairs of the parish should likewise be kept distinct, if possible, from the offices used for callers. The installation of sufficient telephone and buzzer service may also be regarded as good economy since they eliminate the embarrassment that arises from priests' and housekeepers' or others' shouting through the corridors or up and down the stairways.

A decidedly unfavorable and often ridiculous impression is created where these arrangements are neglected. The visitor is ushered practically into the center of the house, possibly in full view of the dining room with the priest or priests seated at the table. Then there is a quick scurry to close the doors or to pull the curtains. On occasion, the visitor is announced by the housekeeper who cries out to inquire whether Father So-and-so is upstairs. Further shouts from the second floor may reveal that he is or is not at home. Additional inquiries may require a lengthy and sometimes fruitless search for the record books. Meanwhile, the visitor is initiated into the entire organization or lack of organization in the domestic establishment. No good purpose is served by such procedure.

Dignity and convenience should be the keynotes also of such social or religious functions as are appropriate to the priest's house. It hardly seems fair to thrust mixed marriages, for example, into a small office with nothing more than a desk and chair. Ultraseverity not only is humiliating to the Catholic party but may serve to accentuate such antagonism as lurks in the breasts of non-Catholics. If the parish can afford it, the rectory should have a decently furnished parlor where such a function can be performed without any offense and in keeping with the dignity of the event.[1]

---

[1] In many dioceses provision is now being given to perform mixed marriages within the church proper.

In addition, it is entirely reasonable that a priest should have at his disposal such a room where he may entertain guests of both sexes, without criticism, and make provision for such parochial occasions as confirmations or receptions, when gracious hospitality requires the facilities of something more than a business office. Such a room might also be used as a common room for the clergy to assemble for conversation or recreational purposes after meals or on other occasions. It seems proper that such provision should be made where there is more than one priest in the rectory.

The constant assembly of the curates in the pastor's quarters or their segregation elsewhere can become a nuisance or give rise to undesirable social discriminations among the priests of the house. The priests, including the assistants, have a right to consider the rectory as their home as well as the parochial headquarters and should be encouraged to build their happiest hours around it instead of being obliged to go elsewhere for recreation and relaxation.

So far as the domestic aspect of the rectory is concerned, considerable thought should be given to the dining room, its service, and the decorum of the table. It is easy for men, living alone or together, to drift into an extremely casual and even uncouth attitude toward their meals, to bolt their food in a way that bodes no good for their digestive apparatus and in a silence that gives no indication of a community of interests or of mental alertness and exchange. Sometimes the food itself is served in a fashion that is anything but appetizing and on dirty tablecloths that bespeak no appreciation for the old adage that "cleanliness is next to godliness."

In the matter of meals as well as of the furnishings and general appearance of the priest's house, the display of luxury, particularly to the general public, is always to be avoided. No good is ever accomplished by conveyance of the impression of high living or of a scale of personal comfort and convenience in contrast with that of the parishioners whose contributions are the support of the priest. The size of the rectory, the quality of its appointments, and the standard of living of the parish priest will naturally differ in various localities. In some places, the priest may want for nothing; in other places, he may be called upon to make great sacrifices in the material order. But in all events, he is entitled to and should strive for an establishment which is clean, decently furnished, and a symbol of the culture and spiritual leadership which he represents. Less than this, where this minimum is possible, reflects small credit upon either the community or himself.

Particular stress may be placed upon the virtues of cleanliness and orderliness. These are luxuries which can cause reasonable scandal to no one. Nevertheless, some men allow the worst possible disorder in their rooms. Books and magazines are strewn on the floor. The desk is piled high with books, letters, both answered and unanswered, catalogues, bric-a-brac, and even clothing in indiscriminate mixture. Over all this, a liberal layer of dust throws its protecting mantle. The clothes closets become a catchall for items which will come in "handy" at some future date which never arrives. This condition may extend itself throughout the entire house, so that the first impression of a visitor is that of a dusty atmosphere, with wonderment that a man of education and culture should permit his place of business and residence to become so unkempt.

Where the priest is actually aware of this condition, there may be a ready tendency to blame the housekeeper; and it is true that desirable domestic help is not always easy to secure. On the other hand, the difficulty may go back to the lack of habits of cleanliness, neatness, and order on the part of the head of the house himself; or it may be the result of his failure to insist upon the desired standards and to point out to the housekeeper, in some detail if necessary, just what is desired.

Needless to say, the decoration of the rectory should always give evidence of its sacred character. Good taste in the selection of furnishings is always in order; but above all, due provision should be made for appropriate symbols and reminders of Catholic faith. "The exclusion of foolish and unseemly pictures," as Cardinal Manning has observed, "needs no comment. The presence everywhere of the crucifix and sacred pictures is most wholesome as a mental discipline for ourselves, and as a silent witness to the world. A priest's house cannot be like the house of a layman without our seeming at least to be ashamed of our Master."[2]

2

Any discussion of the physical arrangement of the rectory may well be more theoretical than practical, for the simple reason that in most cases the house is already an accomplished fact. The priest has only to accept and move into it, for weal or for woe. Some rectories give evidence of careful planning. Others show obvious signs of additions and subtractions, with "step-ups" and "step-downs" and dark corners and places where it is difficult to make any decision. Still others were never intended to be rectories. Everything is so bunched together that it is almost impossible to consider the segregation of various elements or the privacy that is necessary for serious work.

Segregation and privacy, however, are necessary, at least in an elementary form. The kitchen and the maid's quarters should be kept separate and distinct from those of the clergy; and the clergy's quarters should be separated from that section of the house which is designated as the office or reception parlor. Otherwise, confusion and embarrassment are bound to result, with a consequent loss of proper dignity and efficiency and the rise of misunderstanding and bad feeling.

Within the limitations of the house, each one of the priests, if there are more than one, should be entitled to return to the sanctity of his own quarters and close the door behind him. Some men are inclined to regard the exercise of this privilege as a form of snobbishness; and there are some restless souls who never feel at home except in someone else's room. But it is impossible to do serious meditation, reading, writing, or planning of various kinds, unless one has occasional peace and quiet and some control over his schedule of privacy. Every business executive knows this; and every priest who seriously endeavors to prepare his sermons and to organize his work will insist upon it for himself. In a well-ordered house, there should be plenty of time for common discussion, at

---

[2] Henry Edward Cardinal Manning, *The Eternal Priesthood*, p. 240.

meals or later, without constant interruptions during the day for matters of no significance. And where some formalities are observed in this matter, it is probable that men will have more of interest to discuss at the proper time.

This may suggest also, wherever possible, that each priest should have ample quarters, not only in which to sleep, but also in which to study. It is perfectly understandable that in some rectories, because of the inadequacy of the house or because of expanding requirements, this may not be possible. In such cases, a reasonable man will adapt himself gladly until more appropriate provisions can be made. It seems unfair, however, that the pastor should have a large suite at his disposal, whereas the assistants have only one small bedroom and are obliged to stack their books in the clothes closet or put them under the bed. Moreover, while it is only proper that the individual priest should pay for such special items of equipment as he wishes to regard as personal property, there is no reason why he should be obliged to furnish at his own expense such essential pieces of equipment as bed, desk, chair, and bookcase, which the parish should pay for and own as part of the rectory property.

It is in the considerate observance of these amenities that the priest's house not only serves its public function, but also maintains something of the happiness and comfort of a home, which every priest has a right to expect. Notwithstanding their sacred calling, their special education, and their ability to counsel others in the arts of social living, priests remain men, with the same propensities to irritation as their lay brethren. To live together under the same roof for a period of time, even with our own families, requires considerable patience and adaptability. The problem is not lessened by the fact that the persons involved in the rectory may be of different ages and temperaments and in nowise related except by priestly vocation and appointment of the bishop.

3

Unfortunately, the best aspects of the rectory are not always shown to the public. In some instances, the worst possible impression is given to people who wish to contact the pastor or one of the priests; and the rectory acquires such a reputation for haphazard methods and even discourtesy that people of self-respect are not going to risk the embarrassment that a visit may involve. There have been cases in which the pastor has refused to install a telephone in the house, when he could easily do so, or has refused to list his number in the telephone directory, lest he be disturbed with undesirable or inconvenient calls. In other cases, telephone calls are answered in so curt or casual a fashion, by the housekeeper or the priest himself, and information of any sort is so difficult to wring from a stupid or unwilling servant, that it is hard to believe one is calling an educated man who styles himself a priest of God and the leader of his people.

A somewhat similar curious experience occasionally transpires in connection with admission to the rectory. After long or repeated ringing of the doorbell, the housekeeper finally appears, in a nondescript dress or wrapper, and cautiously opens the door part way, as though unwelcome and dangerous characters were abroad.

"Is Father So-and-so in?" asks the visitor.

"No," comes the answer in positive tones.

"When will he return?"

"He didn't say," replies the doorkeeper. And with that termination of the interview, the door is abruptly closed. Or, if the caller is admitted to the interior, it is with the definite impression that this constitutes a serious exception to the rule.

Sometimes, whether over the telephone or at the door and in the parlor, the information takes a much more voluble form. The caller is advised that "Father is shaving now" or "Father is sleeping and cannot be disturbed." If time and circumstances permit, the stranger may be treated to a good deal of information about the life and likes of the various clergy in the house and other matters which are pertinent neither to the business at hand nor to the individual who is thus entertained.

If a priest were to receive this type of reception from his doctor, lawyer, banker, or any one of the people with whom he does business on a serious basis, he would undoubtedly have some strong comments to make and might well change his connections. On the other hand, people are hesitant to offer suggestions to the priest although they may have plenty to say on the subject among themselves. A man cannot be held responsible for every *faux-pas* of the people working under him, but he should give definite instruction on correct and courteous procedure and occasionally check into the situation. Where the behavior of the domestic and office help is simply a reflection of the mind of the priest himself, then, of course, there is nothing for the faithful to do except to pray that Father So-and-so may mellow in the course of time or somehow be shocked into the realization that his manners need mending.

4

On the subject of female help in the rectory, Canon Law has made definite regulations and offers some indications for the observance of fundamental proprieties and the avoidance of anything that might cause scandal.[3] Beyond that, the individual pastor has the responsibility of securing domestic and secretarial assistance that will measure up to certain standards of efficiency and good judgment. Because of the special requirements involved, it is not always easy to obtain and retain persons of the type that one would desire; and fortunate indeed is the man who can count on the loyalty, stability, and efficiency of his workers in this field.

The difficulty with some priests is that they do not know how to manage or treat their help. They are either too strict or too lenient, and often fail to comprehend the problems of the particular position they wish filled. There are very few people who respond automatically to commands in the manner of a machine. They have their good and bad days. They appreciate a word of thanks, a little consideration, an occasional gift. They recognize weakness as well as strength; and in adjusting to a situation, they often take advantage of weakness in their superior. They become irritated and upset by inconsistency and lack of decision in the head of the house; and if unfairly treated, even in their own minds, they may cause a great deal of mean talk in revenge.

---

[3] Canons 133, 2176.

There is very little that gets done properly without supervision. If a pastor wishes the domestic help to be properly attired, and they should be so attired, he should make his wishes clear and specific, and correct the situation if there is a tendency to lower the standards. If he wishes the telephone answered properly and parlor calls treated with Christian courtesy and restraint, he should outline exactly what the procedure shall be. If he wishes the meals served on time, properly, and up to a certain standard, it is his responsibility to make this clear and to point out in some detail just what he has in mind. It will not do to complain to the curates, one's clerical friends, or the neighbors about the shortcomings of the housekeeper. If the soup is served cold, she is the one to be reminded of it. The same is true relative to the cleanliness of the house. If the rectory is unkempt, the furniture covered with dust, lint accumulating on the carpets, dirty linens on the table, and bathrooms in unsanitary condition, the fault is due quite as much to the negligence or timidity of the priest who heads the establishment as it is to the lazy, evasive, or possibly overworked housekeepers.

An unfortunate situation sometimes develops where the housekeeper, who may be a perfectly virtuous and splendid woman, becomes a combination of mother confessor, first assistant, and general policy maker for the pastor. This can easily happen when the latter begins to complain to her of his secret sorrows — his disappointment in the curates, his problems with the trustees, his differences with the bishop, the shortcomings of his fellow priests, and the eccentricities of his parishioners. If the housekeeper becomes a kind of buffer between the pastor and his assistant priests and her judgment takes precedence over theirs, an unhappy situation arises which is difficult to correct, except by removal of one or the other. These little household feuds have a way of being carried out into the parish, sometimes by the indiscretion of the pastor, sometimes by that of the curates, who derive a dubious comfort by unburdening their domestic problems to persons who cannot be expected to keep a confidence.

When the impression gets abroad that, not the pastor, but the housekeeper, or the janitor, or the secretary, or some layman — no matter how stainless their reputation — is the real head of the parish and in charge of its functions, the time has come for a reckoning and a decisive adjustment. The Catholic Church cannot function that way.

An equally unsatisfactory condition may develop where the laity, no matter what their business, are allowed to run through the house as they would in a club or a hotel. That part of the rectory which is devoted to living quarters should be regarded as private. An appropriate section of the house should be provided for conducting the business affairs of the parish and for entertainment, particularly where the company is mixed. While a priest should have a reasonable amount of freedom in the entertainment of his friends and in the negotiation of business in his own quarters, he should exercise his rights and privileges with prudence and with regard for the privacy and the rights of others.

In general, the pastor who allows the complete freedom of his house to the vestrymen on Sunday morning is making a mistake. There should be a particular office or space for the depositing and counting of the collections. Cordiality and appreciation for services are always appropriate. But financial matters and related affairs should be kept on a disciplined and business basis. Any other procedure can easily lead to abuses and misunderstanding. In the same way, the assistant pastor should remember that the second floor of the house is no place for the children of the school or the baseball team or the Holy Name Society. The school hall and parish center or, at most, the parlor or reception room of the rectory are the proper places for such activities.

The same principles may be enunciated concerning the families and relatives of the clergy. A discreet hospitality is always desirable; but this does not mean that the parish house is to be regarded simply as the personal possession of the pastor. If, for good reasons, a member of the family or a relative is introduced as domestic, or secretary, or in some other business capacity, the conditions of employment and residence should be made perfectly clear. A mother or sister who is engaged as housekeeper, for example, unless endowed with a great capacity for tending strictly to business, can easily develop a possessive complex that makes life disagreeable for the rest of the household and gives origin to mis understanding and resentment, both inside and outside the domestic fold. Whether justified or not, priests do not normally relish the idea of having some lay person established as a regular boarder at the table. There is no objection to the occasional introduction of a guest; but more than this may rightly be protested as an imposition upon the privacy and professional character of the priest's life and his house.

5

One of the principal problems which a priest in parochial life has to face is that of organizing his time into a definite program and routine. This is particularly true in a large and busy parish, where there are constant and conflicting demands. Frequent office or "parlor" calls by transients and others, whose importance and urgency is often in reverse proportion to the time consumed; sick calls, day and night; funerals, wakes, and weddings; meetings of the parochial societies; classes and supervision in the school; in structions to converts; organization of bazaars and other affairs calculated to make ends meet; and an incessantly ringing telephone – these are the familiar components of rectory life in many places. On the other hand, in all frankness, it must be admitted that some men have difficulty in ordering their time in some tangible pattern, even where there is comparatively little to do or where compara tively little is done.

In all cases, the basic problem consists in determining what is of first importance, what amounts only to a series of details or duplications, and what may be simply a waste of time. Some men have the precious faculty of recognizing essentials and of organizing their energies and the energies of others around these central con trols. Others are less happy in their acumen and either allow themselves to be bogged down in an accumulation of demands or never rise to a point where they can distinguish between mountain tops, so to speak, and small hills or valleys. Thus a busy priest may in reality be simply a drudge, doubling back on his own trail; and the priest who thinks there is little to be done in his field may be missing the whole point of his ministry, with tremendous opportunities crying for action all around him.

Thus it frequently happens that with a full church at the several Masses on Sunday, the man of God delivers a poorly prepared sermon; and then spends the rest of the week delivering fine "fervorinos" at small special devotions or to little circles of pious souls who reappear as the same faithful members of a half-dozen parochial organizations. A busy pastor may find himself at the mercy of salesmen or small gossips or insignificant parlor calls and imaginary social obligations, and never get beyond the front door to take a census of the parish or learn the people and problems of his parish. Or between counting the collection, organizing bakery sales, answering needless telephone calls, doing an amateur job on the plumbing, and God knows all what, his life may be consumed by an endless chain of details without heading in any particular direction or accomplishing anything of spiritual worth.

Sometimes the difficulty arises from the unwillingness of a man to delegate tasks to others. There are some pastors, for example, who insist upon taking all office calls themselves. They will not allow their curates even to record a Mass intention, but treat them like children and then complain that the men of the younger generation are worthless drones. In matters of parish business, organizations, and general contacts, they are likewise of a mind that no one but themselves is capable of doing things, and they resent such initiative or popularity as their assistants may achieve.

A similar situation may develop in a rectory where there is more than one priest, if there is no clear-cut schedule or division of duties. One man then resents what the other is doing, as invading his own territory; and when an important matter is not tended to, all can blame one another for the neglect. A sulky reaction sets in; duties are attended in an unwilling manner, and a disorderly, haphazard manner of running the house is the result. At times, no one is at home to take care of calls. At other times, the personnel are getting in each other's way, and the place becomes known familiarly a a "madhouse." All may be present in the house, and yet not a single priest available to tend to business.

The precise remedy for these difficulties will differ according to the circumstances. The first step is a serious, professional attitude and determination relative to the purpose of the priesthood. No business can prosper unless properly regulated. This means regular hours and a full working day. It means a desire to be of service, to be available and courteous to all who are prospective customers — in this case, the faithful who are committed to the care of the priest. If people approach the priest in fear and trembling and are given the impression that every service is a distinct favor and condescension, they will soon find ways of solving their problems elsewhere.

In some cases, definite office hours may have to be established; but such a schedule should be made clear to the parishioners, so that they do not come to the rectory in the expectation of seeing a priest, only to be told that he is "out" or "cannot be seen." A definite time should be allotted to parish and civic societies and projects. Definite time should be given to inspection or teaching in the school, and definite time should be kept for privacy and study.

A definite assignment of time for rest and recreation is desirable but within reasonable limitations. Some men never begin to find themselves until ten o'clock at night. Then they sit up until all hours of the night reading or discussing the problems of the world. They pull themselves from bed the following morning only with the greatest difficulty and retire again after Mass or spend the afternoon in a "siesta."

One of the advantages of a rectory is that the priest has his living quarters and office under the same roof, so that time is not consumed in traveling from one place to the other as most businessmen must do. But this has its disadvantages also, unless something of a clean-cut distinction is made between the business of the rectory and the home life of the priest. The businessman, who has his office separated from his home, must tend to business while he is at his place of work. When he returns home at the end of the day, he does so with a certain sense of relaxation and comfort. With the priest, remaining under the same roof all day long, a kind of staleness may set in, a feeling that people are interfering with his domestic privacy during the day and an urge to go abroad at night. Another problem of schedule arises from the fact that many people have time to see the priest only in the evenings, when their own working day is over. Nevertheless, there are ways and means of solving these problems, which will suggest themselves to the thoughtful and orderly priest.

In the last analysis, men can suffer various forms of physical privations and discomforts without complaint or unhappiness; but if their human relationships fail in the application of Christian justice and charity, not all the modern conveniences at their disposal will bring them contentment or real efficiency. One of the keenest disappointments that can come in the life of a priest is to find, after all his striving for high ideals, that his home life is drab, disorderly, and disagreeable. Such a man, having preached the beauties of a Christian home and counseled others on the means to attain it, finds that he has become a castaway himself. A realistic outlook on the problems of the priestly life, as well as on those of human nature, and careful, considerate planning will avoid the pangs of disillusionment and make the rectory a source of strength and joy in the divine ministry.

"To come at length to the everyday actualities of sacerdotal life," writes Father Arthur Barry O'Neill, "the law of fraternal charity calls for genuinely cordial relations between a pastor and his curates. Of all the residences in the parish, the rectory, while necessarily lacking both the figures and the affections primarily associated with the idea of the Christian family — father, mother, children, with their concomitant conditions of conjugal, parental, and filial love — should none the less be the one house in which more than in any other habitually abide the peace, concord, mutual consideration, and bearing-one-another's-burden spirit that characterize and bless the true Christian home. The ideal pastor stands to his curate in the relation of father or big brother according as the disparity of their respective years is great or small; and he sincerely desirous that the younger man shall look upon him, not as an exacting and unsympathetic taskmaster, but as a kind-hearted and considerate senior partner in the business of ministering to the spiritual needs of the people. . . . While mindful of his duty properly to train his assistant in the various works of the ministry, he relies for the success of that training more on the example he sets than on the orders he gives; and even when reproof becomes imperative, administers it calmly, charitably, and in private, not passionately, harshly, and before others."[4]

This atmosphere of cordiality and attitude of co-operation within the rectory and among those dwelling in it are the result of determined effort. The fact that men are priests does not in itself create an ideal situation. They must put themselves to the task of being gentlemen, of exercising a mutual courtesy and consideration, and of observing all those amenities that make a domestic establishment and home life attractive.

The graciousness of Christ that should characterize the priest in his relationships with the people ought to be manifest first in his own home. He cannot take it for granted that things will take care of themselves. Whether he leads a drab existence or an inspiring one, whether he implements Christian charity with the little remembrances that should mark the milestones of life or lets the years roll by without thought of these things, whether he goes down to his grave with the grateful tears of those whom he has taught and befriended as one truly deserving the title of "Father" or with a sigh of relief that another mean man has passed on to eternity, will depend in large part upon his attention to the small details and provisions that change his house into a home.

The words of St. Paul offer sage warning and positive advice for the priest who believes that order and progress are basic to his apostolate: "If a man know not how to rule his own house, how shall he take care of the church of God?"

---

[4] Arthur Barry O'Neill, *Sacerdotal Safeguards*, pp. 71, 72.

"But godliness with contentment is great gain. For we brought nothing into this world: and certainly we can carry nothing out. But having food and wherewith to be covered, with these we are content. For they that will become rich fall into temptation and into the snare of the devil and into many unprofitable and hurtful desires, which drown men into destruction and perdition" (1 Tim. 6:6–9).

CHAPTER VI

THE PRIEST AND FINANCE

I

THE problem of money is an important one in the life of every priest who is required to administer a parish, school, or plant of any kind. The fact that the Church is a visible body, an organization of men and women in this world, immediately ties into material considerations. The assembly of people to worship God indicates the need of a place to assemble which is at least decent and protected from the weather. The instruction of the youth in any systematic form of Christian education points to the need of a schoolhouse. The care of the sick, the orphaned, and the aged in fulfillment of the injunction of Christian charity involves hospitals, asylums, and homes, with facilities and means of keeping body and soul together. These considerations are elemental, and only the hypocrite will attempt to divorce them from the worship of God "in spirit and in truth."

As the custodian of a spiritual flock with human, material needs, the priest himself must live; and it is only proper that he should derive his sustenance from those whom he serves. St. Paul, who found himself obliged to make tents in order to eke out a living, nevertheless pointed out that the laborer for the Lord is worthy of his hire and should look to his ministry as providing for his necessities. Whether the priest is a member of a religious order with the vows of poverty or of the diocesan clergy under obligation to support himself with his personal means makes little difference. Someone must assume the responsibility of providing for his livelihood.

For the diocesan or secular priest, particularly if placed in charge of a parish or institution, the question of finance is a real one of pressing importance. His is a twofold problem, that of making provision for the organization which he has been appointed to administer and of insuring a decent livelihood for himself so that he can carry on his work properly. Both divisions of the problem call for serious consideration and for the establishment of attitudes and procedures that are consonant with his spiritual mission and, at the same time, prudent and ethical from a business standpoint.

In dealing with the whole question of finance, two extremes should be avoided. One is based on the idea — whether from detachment or irresponsibility — that money and money matters, or related material considerations, are beneath the dignity or outside the proper scope of the clergy. The other extreme is an engrossment or obsession with finance and material expansion, as though this were the object of the ministry or a priest's first concern, "supposing," as St. Paul says, "gain to be godliness."[1]

Detachment from all monetary considerations may arise from various suppositions and take a variety of forms, so far as the diocesan priest is concerned. An airy or cavalier attitude may spring from the fact that a man has never learned the value of a dollar. The seminarian who has never had to work at a gainful occupation or to save for himself or his family, but whose living has been

---

[1] I Tim. 6:5.

provided for him through the labor and sacrifices of others, may come to the priesthood with a disdain for anything but pocket money and with a total lack of understanding of the processes by which money is gained, saved, and accounted for. Some people are congenital "dead beats" — irrespective of whether their calling is sacred or profane — with little or no attention to the meaning of expense accounts or contractual obligations. Their attitude toward debts is like that of the college boys toward the tailor in *Charley's Aunt,* a combination of comedy and contempt for the creditor, whose claim has no more validity than his ability to catch up with and collect from his elusive debtors.

A more lofty and spiritual view may be entertained by others. This may stem from the thought that if "the desire of money is the root of all evils," the priest of God should have as little to do with it as possible. The conclusion often drawn from this premise is that ignorance of money matters is a badge of sanctity. Another false derivative is that the truly spiritual priest should not be called upon to give his precious time to such mundane concerns or to dirty his hands with filthy lucre.

It would indeed be wonderful if priests engaged in the active ministry, as well as those sheltered in the contemplative life of the monastery, were spared the necessity of having to take up collections, pay bills, put up buildings, provide for their maintenance, invest funds, and support themselves. But such, generally speaking, is not the case. As a matter of fact, the business of parochial and personal finance enters so constantly into the life of the average diocesan priest, that a large part of his salvation depends upon his proper concern for and right administration of funds, both Church and personal. For this reason, ignorance of or contempt for business methods and financial responsibility on the part of the priest in the active ministry should not be confused with virtue or high spirituality. On the contrary, every priest should have a healthy respect for money, its value, its exchange and investment, and know at least the difference between a debit and a credit. Every seminary course in pastoral theology would do well to include at least the elements of bookkeeping and the imparting of such com mercial information as to give the priest the essentials of business procedure.[2]

As a result of ignorance, inattention, naïve gullibility, or mental attitudes of superiority and contempt, with the easy dismissal of temporal matters to take care of themselves or turning them over to God as His burden, many a Church venture has come to naught or been shipwrecked, to the loss of many whose trust of funds in a worthy cause was misplaced. Many a splendid project has been starved or crippled, instead of going ahead with health and success, for the same reasons.

The other extreme, against which the priest must be equally on his guard, is an obsession for money and temporalities, whether this takes the form of extreme preoccupation with the raising of funds for the Church or an overzealous concern with one's private fortune. It is from such confusion of the primary objectives of the pastoral ministry or deviation of personal interests and energies that St. Paul sees the origin of "conflicts of men corrupted in mind and who are destitute of the truth, supposing gain to be godliness."[3]

It has often been alleged that the greatest abuses in the Church have been those which have arisen as the result of wealth, either of the clergy or of the Church as a body. Historians hostile to Catholicism have worked on this theme to derive the principal causes of the Protestant Reformation, and there is no end of attempts to show that the Church can attribute its woes to its riches. Thus the Church in Mexico has been denounced for the endowments which it held from the early days of the Spanish colony until their dispersal in the Masonic Reform of the mid-nineteenth century. In the words of Oliver Goldsmith,

> "Ill fares the land, to hastening ills a prey,
> Where wealth accumulates, and men decay."[4]

I, for one, have never subscribed to this as a sure principle of cause and effect. For one thing, wealth is not an absolute, but is

---

[2] Cf. Dumas Leon McCleary, *Parish Accounting* (Washington, D. C.: The Catholic University of America Press, 1948); W. J. Doheny, C.S.C., *Practical Problems in Church Finance* (Milwaukee: The Bruce Publishing Co., 1941).

[3] 1 Tim. 6:5.

[4] *The Deserted Village.*

relative from age to age, country to country, man to man. The man or the institution that has little in one parish, country, or era may be called wealthy compared to one that has nothing. The man or the organization with plenty can put material treasure to good use as well as to ill; and poverty is no guarantee of virtue. The Church has been persecuted when it has been at its best quite as much as when at its worst. The great cathedrals and works of religious art are proof of the great inspiration of faith and devotion in times of prosperity and not necessarily evidences of the decadence that follows on an era of prosperity. The great educational and philanthropic works of the Church would never have been possible without adequate resources to finance and maintain them. Likewise with individual clergy. Without referring to any needless, massive accumulation of money and material goods, the priest who lives amid abundance is in no greater danger of the loss of his soul than he who must put up with wretchedness and squalor, never knowing where his next penny is coming from.

On the other hand, it cannot be doubted that there are corrosive elements in the acquisition and possession of money and the symbols of wealth. "If wealth could contribute to the peace and happiness, as well as to the real glory of the priesthood and the salvation of souls," Cardinal Gibbons has observed, "Christ would certainly have chosen for Himself and have recommended to His Apostles, a life of affluence and luxury."[5] A priest who is not deeply rooted in spiritual ideals and endowed with the power of honest soul-searching in his activities may spend his life, not in raising the standards of his flock and bringing them closer to God, but in sheerly material expansion. His whole ambition may be that of collecting more funds to put up more buildings; to invest funds simply to have a rich reserve for the parish; or to campaign for money, for the sheer love of demonstrating his ability along these lines or because he knows of no other tangible way to exercise his ministry.

Under certain circumstances, a priest may find the way open for him to amass a fortune and become a rich man in his own right.

[5] *The Ambassador of Christ*, p. 119.

The danger in this course is reminiscent of the slogan of a well-known confection — "the more you have, the more you want." There is a curious psychological effect in making gains and winnings in gambling, which is a kind of giddiness, where neither brains nor brakes appear to function. The desire for gain is much like this and accumulates speed and momentum as it proceeds. A variety of motives can be drawn upon conveniently to rationalize and justify this interest or hobby, up to the point of obsession. The adage that the laborer is worthy of his hire, with this impulse, can lead to a dissatisfaction or reluctance to do anything that does not immediately result in a stipend. Perhaps the motive is to buy more books, or to take a trip, or to buy a car, or to provide for one's old age, or to meet the needs and demands of one's family and poor relations. All these motives are good in themselves, up to a certain point; but when they serve merely to feed an insatiable appetite for more and more gain, or to turn a man's attention from his spiritual growth to the manipulation of savings and investments, his priestly character becomes atrophied and his ministry becomes sterile.

"The experience of nineteen centuries," as Cardinal Gibbons has noted, "has amply proved that the Christian ministers who have set their heart on the accumulation of money, to the neglect of higher and holier interests, have never been happy, nor has their honor been augmented in public estimates by their temporal possessions. They have forsaken the Fountain of living waters, and have digged to themselves cisterns, broken cisterns, which can hold no water.' "[6]

Too much is as bad as too little. The man of God particularly must keep in mind that money is only a means to an end, not an end itself. The value and the good of money lies in its adaptation to a worthy cause. Its abuse lies in its waste in frivolous and needless activities or in pandering to a selfish and miserly egotism. These observations are applicable to all men. The priest who wishes to follow in the footsteps of Christ cannot afford to ignore them.

---

[6] Ibid.; Jer. 2:13.

"Give me neither beggary nor riches," prayed the Wise Man. "Give me only the necessaries of life."[7]

2

Prudence in the handling of money, as well as in its acquisition, is basic for every priest. The young levite, fresh from the seminary, is perhaps the most gullible of men, ready to be plucked by every salesman who wishes to start him out in life properly. Some men jump this hurdle with comparative ease or survive the first onslaught with only minor losses. Others remain easy prey all their days. Encyclopedias and other library sets which no self-respecting clergyman can do without come high on the list. Insurance policies of all kinds, safe investments with a high yield of interest recommended by friendly agents, and all kinds of gadgets for house and transportation are urged upon him. And if he is easily touched by "trouble" stories, he may be sure of a wide range of appeals, from those delivered in person by gentlemen of the road, to mail campaigns for worthy causes at home and abroad.

To a certain extent, there is no substitute for experience. Bitter experience in this regard, however, can be minimized and perhaps eliminated altogether if a man is willing to solicit and accept advice from older and wiser men. And there are certain basic principles and considerations which should be of assistance to every priest in the matter of finance, whether personal or parochial.

The first principle is that money, in any form, carries a corresponding responsibility. The priest who has money to his credit should consider carefully whether this entails any obligations. If these obligations are in the nature of a contract or trust or promise, then this money should be classified as a liability, and he may not spend it without reference to the purpose for which he received it. The acceptance of Mass stipends, for example, sets up a liability. The Masses must be said, and the priest has no clear title to the stipends until he has fulfilled this obligation. He should set aside this amount or have it available for another to assume the obligation in case anything should happen to him to prevent his

---

[7] Prov. 30:8.

personal fulfillment. Money collected or received for a designated purpose from individuals or the parish, with the priest acting as agent or trustee, may not be diverted into other purposes or spent otherwise than in accordance with the designation, even with the hope of replacing it sometime in the future.

If the money in question assumes the nature of a debt, then the debt should be paid in full as soon as possible. Some men are notoriously lax in settling such obligations. They buy on credit, without knowing how or when they will pay. When bills are rendered, they put them aside or postpone settlement month after month. If they take exception to the amount, they let the matter slide along without informing the creditor of their claim. If they receive a bill with a notation "past due," they become incensed, write insulting letters, and make the creditor wait just that much longer. These attitudes and procedures are inexcusable, especially in a priest, who preaches the doctrine of justice and should know at least the elements of business routine. The priest who contracts debts should do so only with the reasonable assurance of making payment within the time specified; and he should comply with his obligations like a gentleman.

The second basic principle is that the priest should never mix or confuse his personal finances with those of the parish or institution for which he is responsible. Bank accounts should be completely distinct, and properly named, so that, if anything should happen to him at any time, there could not be the slightest question of which is his personally and which is that of the parish, society, institution, or trust fund. The same is true of investments. The priest has no right to purchase and hold in his own name securities or property with money which belongs to the parish. Nor has he any right to pocket as a commission for himself the yield or profits involved, with any such argument as that the gain is due to his enterprise and genius. Moreover, while he may take a certain amount of risk with his own personal funds, under certain circumstances and within reason, he is never entitled to gamble with parish funds or to put them into speculative investments, particularly those involving real danger of attrition or loss, no matter how attractive the market or fancy the yield. Disregard of or compromise with this principle cannot be justified; no amount of covering up losses will excuse or heal a situation which is intrinsically wrong.

With respect to the matter of personal finances, it is assumed that the priest will exercise the same prudence as a layman in comparable circumstances. The income of the clergy differs from diocese to diocese and indeed from parish to parish within the same diocese. This should be clearly understood and accepted as a matter of fact by all aspirants to the priesthood, whose calling is the service of God and not necessarily the accumulation of money. With this understanding and within the means at his disposal, the prudent priest will endeavor to make provision for the contingencies of sickness, old age, special emergencies, the demands of charity, and the eventuality of death. Spending up to the hilt does not make good sense.

Everyone should take out enough life insurance to provide for his decent burial, without pulling upon the resources of others. There are numerous plans for health and accident insurance at reasonable rates for the clergy, so that a priest in average circumstances need not go to a hospital as a complete charity patient or remain at home without any means of obtaining medicine and care. Likewise, annuity insurance may be recommended as a conservative plan for saving and a sensible means of building up a source of at least supplemental income for one's later years or possibly a small estate to leave for a worthy cause.

Every priest should make a will and not wait until his old age to do so. No one knows when death will come, or in what form. It is well to have one's disposition of earthly goods in proper shape at all times, and, if advisable because of changing circumstances, to change the will so that it represents one's true intentions. There is nothing more revolting than the squabble of relatives over the estate of a dead man who has left no will or who has left his will and his estate in such doubtful condition as to invite trouble and scandal. This is particularly true if there are any considerable assets involved. The processing through courts, the publicity, and legal expenses involved are all highly undesirable. It is well to seek good legal counsel well in advance and to plan one's affairs quietly and fairly, so as to arouse the least possible attention and opposition.

A priest may well have family obligations which he must duly consider, and he cannot be rightly criticized if he makes appropriate provision in his estate for those to whom he is bound by blood ties or obligations for faithful service rendered. At the same time, it would be tragic if he should fail to make a suitable apportionment for works of charity, religion, and education. Normally, most of his income is derived from the offerings of the faithful, in one form or the other, because of his religious service. He cannot rightly ignore this fact and fail to return in generous measure the remainder or surplus after his death to the propagation of the faith for which it was originally received. This matter should be given careful thought, so that legacies and bequests are not delivered haphazard but represent a sound investment in Catholic Action which will survive the deceased.

If careful disposition of one's surviving estate is important for a priest, it is even more important that he handle his current assets with a mind to Christian giving. Nearly every priest is at one time or the other the victim of panhandlers and confidence men of some description. The rectory is a marked spot for tramps and hardship cases ranging from outright fraud to troubles truly deserving assistance. Often the needs within one's own family call for special attention and sometimes with an appeal that may strain the priest's limited resources. In addition, a wide variety of pleas for funds come through the mails, so that the total of all of these items of casual or repeated charity may represent a substantial sum.

Nevertheless, it is not sufficient that a priest with financial means his disposal content himself with giving on the basis of casual charity or appeal. He ought to devote some positive thought and planning to contributions or donations to Catholic and general civic, cultural, and charitable causes of a more stabilized and permanent character. And through his careful examination of the merit of various projects, he should be in a position to give sound advice to others who are in a financial position to be of assistance to

Catholic and community causes of genuine value. It is truly amazing the amount of money that is given to ephemeral schemes of little worth or to spot-cash charities, on the basis of a personal appeal, when a broader comprehension and public-spiritedness could produce far greater results. The priest who plans his giving, within his means, will probably give much more in harmony with the spirit of Christ and will watch his personal expenditures more carefully as the custodian of a Christian trust.

3

If the priest who is responsible for his own livelihood in the pursuit of his vocational labors must exercise prudence and common business sense in personal financial matters, he is called upon to employ the same principles to an even greater degree for those of the parish or institution over which he is placed in charge. Personally, he has to keep in mind that he did not go into the priesthood to make money, but that with what he possesses he must deal in a thoroughly ethical manner. Likewise, in his priestly work, he must remember that, however great the needs, he cannot allow the accumulation of funds to become the preoccupation of his life. And, on the other hand, whether the contributions of the faithful be great or small, he is responsible for their exact accounting and proper administration.

A certain amount of spiritual perspective and human realization is necessary to keep this balance. And it is particularly necessary that the young priest be properly oriented during his formative years. It may be observed that the attitude of a priest toward a practical philosophy of life is often developed more decisively during the first year of his apostolate than during the six or more years of his seminary training. Many a young levite reacts with disillusionment and even cynicism upon his first contact with the material aspects of the ministry. In the seminary, he gave his time almost exclusively to prayer and study, centered around philosophy, theology, and meditation. Practically all of his financial and material needs were taken care of. Upon arrival in parish work, almost his first duty is to announce the Sunday or special collections and count the money. Soon he is called upon to conduct bazaars and parties, solicit funds, and plunge into the whole business of parochial or institutional finance. With such a program of activity, philosophy and theology soon appear very remote and alien indeed, and even meditation may come with difficulty. "My God," he may find himself praying, "was it for this that I was ordained?"

It is important to keep in mind that, as the individual human being is composed of a body and soul, with material as well as spiritual needs, the Church as a visible body or society of human beings likewise has material as well as spiritual needs if it is to continue to exist and flourish. The attention of the faithful must be called to the importance of their contributions, and the priest in charge must give his serious and continued attention to these temporalities, right down to the details of counting and accounting for the collections. The financial problems of the Church differ greatly from place to place; but many a priest on the mission finds that only by the greatest attention, ingenuity, and frugality with good management can he keep a roof over his head and the parish organization solvent. Every priest in parochial work or other administration may as well reconcile himself to these facts from the outset and be prepared to integrate the corresponding responsibilities into the work of his divine ministry.

There is the other danger, already noted — that of excessive preoccupation with money matters and the temporalities of the Church, to the point where these practically edge out the spiritual life of the priest and of the parish or Church institution. For some priests, the problem may present itself in the form of a temptation or fascination for dealing with business matters or money-raising, to the point of obsession and spiritual vacuum. For others, it may take the form of a constant and almost desperate worry lest the organization fall apart for lack of adequate funds. In either case, the effect upon his personal spiritual life, as well as upon that of the parish, school, organization, or institution under his care, may be disastrous.

With such mentality and attitudes, the entire activity and objectives of the priest may become dislocated, from that of saving souls to raising money. The measure of success or failure of parochial organizations becomes their ability to provide revenue. All planning and programs are centered around a booming financial report as their primary purpose. Ideas, friendships, time, projects are all viewed under the cold calculating criterion of what they will produce in terms of dollars and cents. The pulpit becomes a sounding board for money, with all announcements somehow tuned in to this theme, and the sermon backed into a position of subordinate importance. Collections are multiplied, from the preliminary "seat money" at the entrance of the church, to the offertory basket, with another collection after the Communion of the Mass, and possibly the selling of raffle tickets in front of the church after services.

There is nothing more distressing for the faithful than the impression that the Church is just another money-raising organization and that the Sunday Mass and sermon, instead of offering an opportunity of grace and spiritual inspiration for the week, will be simply a repetitious plea of the pastor for bigger collections. Where such appeals take the form of scolding, nagging, insulting, and denouncing the parishioners for their stinginess, the effect may be to drive people out of the Church and to turn others away from it. Certainly such wearisome procedure contributes nothing to the spiritual life of the parish, but may do incalculable harm.

The priest who is called upon to ask for money or donations of any kind for the Church, including his own support, will do well to give the most careful thought to his methods. It is probably true that people will think twice about giving a dime to the Church on Sunday, although they experienced no pain in spending freely on drinks or various forms of entertainment and luxuries the week before. But there are different ways of reminding them of their obligations to God. A reasonable explanation of the need and of an apportionate assessment or distribution of the costs will normally produce more generous results than peevish or demanding tactics. An expression of appreciation and thanks for co-operation and generosity is usually more fruitful than complaint and upbraiding about smallness and delinquency. And the record of good service and spiritual activity and leadership of the clergy is undoubtedly far more persuasive of cheerful giving than a good half hour of bitter reminders from the pulpit every Sunday.

The problems of special finance and extra collections differ from place to place, and there is no simple method of solution that can be prescribed. In parishes where there is a more or less steady and permanent congregation, the envelope system seems to offer a constructive plan, with its separate compartments for the regular Sunday offering and for special projects. There are several advantages in this system. It offers the individual or family a definite and tangible form of donation. It provides the pastor with a means of recognizing the contributors to the parish. And it avoids the annoyance of reaching into the pocket several times during Mass for a contribution to various collection boxes on their rounds.

Careful thought should be given also to the necessity of special campaigns for funds and to the methods proposed. It may be that under given circumstances strenuous efforts must be put forth to pull a parish out of debt or to keep it afloat. It must also be recognized that the social aspects of events sponsored to raise money for the Church have a legitimate and useful place in Catholic community life. Nevertheless, a certain circumspection and prudence are advisable, particularly where the events share the character of gambling and make their appeal to the public on this basis. Carnivals, bazaars, various forms of bingo, slot machines, and games of chance are certainly not wrong in themselves; but where they border on the illegal, or partake of the nature of a commercial "racket," or induce people to spend beyond their means, or produce attitudes and habits of gambling in the youth, it may be seriously questioned whether the net results are a benefit or a detriment for the Church and public morality.

Sometimes, the constant appeal for money and the feverish activity of money-raising events is an evidence of the spiritual poverty or superficiality of the priest. It may be that he has run out of spiritual thoughts and counsel and has reached a point where the only thing he can talk about is money. This is a sad and perhaps even brutal thought; but it is not beyond the realm of possibility. In other cases, it may be an evidence of the fact that the priest has never discovered any systematic way of solving his financial problems. If such is the case, he should take counsel.

A great deal of this confusion and expenditure of time and energy could be avoided by a careful study of the problem, with the assistance of a trained accountant and good business advice. This may indicate the need of a survey, which will take into account the expenses of operating the plant with reasonable needs and expectancy. Such a survey will segregate the value of the plant and make provision for its depreciation. It will also differentiate between projects for expansion and current operating expenses. With these facts in hand, it is possible to draw up an annual operating budget based upon realities of needs and expectancies, and possibly make some provision for surplus, upon which plans for future replacements or expansion can be formulated. With such a program in hand, the pastor or administrator can go to his parish or directors or general public and make an intelligent appeal with something more than the blue sky as his limit. Generally speaking, people will appreciate a position of this kind; and their response may eliminate the need for interminable appeals and money-raising activities.

Such a procedure should, of course, be carried through logically. In other words, having installed a system, the priest should follow it through by an accurate set of accounting books, with a periodic audit by a competent accountant or bookkeeper. These books should be thoroughly accurate and be kept current at all times. The trustees of a parish or Church institution should not be asked to sign any report without an appropriate and certified test; and no self-respecting trustee will do so. A last-minute slapping together of figures and request for approval without even the privilege of examination is certainly poor business and of at least questionable ethics.

With respect to the undertaking and financing of special projects, such as churches, schools, convents, and rectories, the first rule in all cases is for the priest to consult his bishop and to follow his directives. Without the specific approval of the Ordinary, all such projects are headed in the wrong direction from the start. One may disagree with the decision and possibly suffer a major disappointment. The responsibility for mistakes, however, lies with the higher authority, which must also bear the burden of mistaken judgment on the part of enthusiasts who failed to solicit advice or to secure proper authorization to proceed.

More than one sad story could be written around the pious zeal of good men who have proceeded to build without funds and to borrow without adequate security. There is something touching and sometimes humorous in the innocence of priests and religious who blindly rush into plans for expansion without ever asking where the money is coming from, beyond a trust that Divine Providence will work one miracle after another to pay their bills and keep them out of jail. But at the same time, a darker story could also be told of houses built on sand, defaulted bond issues, and obligations incurred with little thought of the sacrifices imposed upon later administrations.

Enterprises involving financial outlay should never be undertaken without careful thought, a keen sense of responsibility, sound advice, and adequate provision. Liabilities should not be incurred without reasonable assurance that they will be discharged. Loan issues should not be floated without security that will provide for payment of the interest and amortization of the capital within the stipulated term. In all cases of financial negotiation, the advice of prudent and conservative businessmen and financiers should be sought. Easy money offered by financial adventurers, wildcat schemes, and highly personalized advances should be avoided like poison. The fact that a holy cause is involved does not exempt it from fraud or the machinations of plausible but corrupt confidence men. The price of solvency, like that of freedom, is eternal vigilance.

Properly handled, duly subordinated and directed to a spiritual mission, the finances of the Church are an instrument of good. Clumsily, stupidly, and loosely manipulated, they engross the attention of the priest which should be given to spiritual matters; they stifle spiritual development, end in unethical tangles, and result in loss and general disgust.

4

One of the dangers to be avoided by the priest in charge of a definite territory is that of small-mindedness, which may take the form of a narrow provincialism or parochialism. Some men become extremely resentful of anything that seems to take money out of their parish or jurisdiction. Societies or organizations with an extraparochial or national character are viewed with a jaundiced eye as though they had no right to exist. Causes beyond their territorial limits, even those of a diocesan character, appear to them as a threat to their own integrity, a leech upon local support, an enemy of parochial finance. This attitude not only reflects a lack of consideration for the mystical body in its larger aspects, but actually hurts the generosity of the people to their local parish or cause.

People who are encouraged to give to diocesan charities and education, to contribute to the missions and to the Peter's pence, to support worth-while extraparochial and interparochial projects are not going to cut one cent from their own parish or pastor. On the contrary, their awareness of needs beyond their own boundaries makes them better Catholics and stimulates their appreciation of the place of their own parish or local cause in the over-all organization of the Church. The priest who can look above and beyond his own immediate horizon is Catholic in the true sense of the word. If he can learn to live and let live, to share of his bounty and that of his people, no matter how great or small it may be, he has learned the first and greatest lesson of Christian finance — that of giving with a heart and "godliness with contentment."

In commenting upon the spirit of charity and detachment that should characterize the priestly ministry, Abbot Marmion writes, "As for the great number of priests who live modestly, even austerely, their merit is great before God. Bethlehem, Nazareth, and Calvary furnish eloquent lessons in this regard and teach us that such priests are approximating more and more closely to the divine model."

To maintain this spirit, it is obvious that the priest must be grounded in the highest supernatural motivation, a full reliance in Divine Providence. The same writer refers to this as "a complete abandonment of oneself to God by the confident and loving acceptance of all His hidden designs in our regard, the surrender of oneself to the divine good pleasure, not merely as regards the pains of the moment, but for all the uncertainties of the future."

This does not mean an abandonment of common sense, of normal prudence, or of a reasonable appreciation and concern for the things of this world. The priest must live in God's world of three dimensions and apply the teachings of Christ to the daily affairs of men. But it does signify the importance of an abiding supernatural trust in God and a constant recognition that all human experience, all material gain and loss, must be related to His greater wisdom and goodness.

"For who is there," asks Abbot Marmion, "who can know for certain what is to his best advantage in the supernatural sphere? Do we always appreciate the value of failure, of trials, of suffering, to purify us, to enlighten us, to unite us to God? He alone can see the soul with a clearness which is incomparable; He alone knows how to heal it, to liberate it, to strengthen it, and to help it on its journey. By holy abandonment man accepts his daily life with its annoyances, its difficulties and its misfortune, *Dominus est,* and also his future as Providence has arranged it; he embraces with the most complete confidence the unknown which awaits him, including the time and the circumstances of his death. By this, he glorifies God in His power, in His wisdom, and in His love, by this also, he draws closer the bonds which unite him to the heavenly Father. You understand, therefore, that in the spiritual life holy abandonment is the climax; and without it, charity could not elevate us to the point of a complete and absolute gift of ourselves.

"We should like to repeat with the psalmist: 'The Lord ruleth me and I shall want nothing . . . for though I should walk in the midst of the shadow of death, I will fear no evil, for Thou are with me' (Ps. 22:1, 4)."[8]

The priest who endeavors to cultivate this spirit, whether in the midst of plenty or in the depths of want, will truly be one of the poor of spirit, to whom Christ has promised that "theirs is the kingdom of heaven."[9]

---

[8] *Christ — the Ideal of the Priest,* p. 150.
[9] Mt. 5:3.

"The word of God is living and effectual and more piercing than any two edged sword and reaching unto the division of the soul and the spirit, of the joints also and the marrow: and is a discerner of the thoughts and intents of the heart" (Hebr. 4:12).

CHAPTER VII

PREPARING AND DELIVERING THE SERMON

I

THERE are few activities in the active ministry of the priest so important as the delivery of the sermon. Whether it be a Sunday instruction or a homily on a special occasion, in a small chapel or in a great cathedral, the sermon represents the most effective opportunity of the priest to reach the mind and hearts of the people. Through the vehicle of the sermon, he finds the basic fulfillment of Christ's injunction to the Apostles: "Go ye into the whole world and preach the Gospel to every creature."[1] To a large extent, it is through the medium of the sermon that the priest becomes known to the people. Through it, he brings Christ and interprets the message of Christ to a world hungry for the truth. And, largely dependent upon his proficiency in expounding the word of God, the priest creates an attitude of acceptance and respect in the community for the Church he represents.

It is of the utmost importance that every priest who is called

---

[1] Mk. 16:15.

upon to do pastoral work should have a full appreciation of the power of preaching and that he should bend every effort to become an effective preacher. To realize the power of the spoken word and to exploit the potentialities of the pulpit for the dissemination of Christian doctrine, he cannot maintain a detached or diffident attitude. Much less can he allow himself to be dominated by nervousness or motives of false modesty and self-consciousness when facing a congregation or audience. In entering the priesthood, he has assumed a definite responsibility. Preaching stands foremost among his pastoral duties. It is up to him to face this task positively and seriously and to use this marvelous opportunity to the fullest for the salvation of souls.

It is probably true that temperament has something to do in the formation of a good preacher. The extrovert and creative type of individual is undoubtedly more adapted by nature for ready and easy expression and more likely to avail himself, without urging, of the opportunity to speak. It is also true that some men are more gifted than others, in personal presence, voice, and command of language. Some are outstanding in power of imagination and ability to organize their material; others have to struggle with themselves as well as with their audience to maintain interest and project their message. Nevertheless, these differences are only incidental to the task in hand.

Preaching is not in the nature of a contest, where the best preacher wins. Each man is heard by the faithful on the merits of his doctrine and the honesty and sincerity of his effort. Every priest, with determination, diligent effort, and training, can become an effective preacher and has a positive obligation of becoming such.

The place to start training for public speaking is the seminary, if one has not had previous opportunity and practice. In every seminary course there should be time and systematic attention under competent direction, for the preparation and delivery of sermons and other types of public address. It is not enough to be a good student, whether of philosophy or theology or of any other subject, to acquire an automatic proficiency in teaching or preaching. Some of the most brilliant men I have known have been terri fied by the mere thought of facing an audience. Some of the best known authors have shown themselves dismal failures when suddenly thrust upon the lecture platform. Some very holy and learned priests, from lack of what is now called "know-how," present a singularly flat and uninspiring message even when reading the Holy Gospel. To bring forth one's knowledge and convictions from the reservoirs of the mind, and to present a lesson or an exhortation in acceptable and appealing form, requires both training and practice. But with the recognition of this need and with persistent effort under direction, there are few men who cannot develop into truly effective speakers.

A good sermon has three ingredients — substance, form, and delivery. By substance, we understand the thought, the matter, the meat, or message of the discourse. By the form, we indicate organization or logical presentation of the matter under consideration. Delivery signifies the manner in which the speaker makes contact with his congregation or audience, the arts he employs to secure and hold their attention, the impact he makes upon them, by voice, stance, and gesture. All three ingredients must be given careful consideration if the time consumed by the sermon is to be fruitful and effective.

With respect to the substance of a sermon, it is obvious that a man cannot put into a discourse something which he does not himself possess. A thoughtful sermon requires thought. A practical sermon requires a background of knowledge of human nature and affairs. A powerful sermon requires a sense of conviction developed from keen realization and appreciation of truth and pertinent fact. In other words, the sermon requires remote as well as immediate preparation, just the same as any other kind of presentation which is developed from knowledge and skill. A pianist cannot hope for concert success simply by practicing a few hours the day before his appearance; his art calls for years of professional interest, study, and work. A dramatic artist, or an aspirant to the stage, needs far more than ambition and the ability to memorize a few lines; these must be reinforced with the power to comprehend character and situation and long hours of understudy and rehearsal. The lecturer cannot expect to win a reputation for himself and carve out a platform career, simply by reading up on his material an hour or two before his appearance. An audience may have to accept a thin and hastily-put-together performance once; but it will not demand a return of the imposition.

These examples may seem to labor the obvious. It is extremely important, however, particularly for the priest who must deliver sermons regularly, to recognize the fact that one cannot habitually live in a mental vacuum and suddenly come up with a sermon that is worth delivering or listening to. The false idea that the seminary training so impregnates a man with the truths of philosophy and theology that he can solve any problem at the drop of a hat, speak on any subject with little or no preparation, and preach a worthwhile sermon simply from his native resources, deceives no one except the individual who attempts to act upon it. One must continue to grow mentally and culturally, if he is not to go to seed quickly. One must learn that facts are constantly changing and must be restudied. The world moves on. Attitudes change. New problems arise. New challenges, new adversaries, new opportunities knock at the door. The notion that a bundle of basic truths and a revamping of one's seminary sermons is all that is necessary through the years may be fatal so far as one's ministry in the pulpit is concerned.

It is one thing to be orthodox in doctrine. It is another to clothe that doctrine in attractive form, to stimulate the imagination of one's listeners, to bring applications of the truth right down to everyday life, to convince, and to persuade. This calls for a long-range program of preparation, of reading, and of daily observation. The alert priest will keep up on his reading, keep abreast of what is being written and what is being read. This includes both secular and religious books, even a judicious reading of novels to catch the trend of events and to feel the pulse of the times and of people. He will keep an eye on the current magazines and select those articles which bear upon the problems of the day. It is not necessary to agree or to be pleased with everything one reads; the important thing is to keep aware of

what is going on and what people are thinking or what they
are exposed to.

The priest's library should reflect, at least for himself, a vital
interest in human affairs. More than that he should make it a
point to clip pertinent articles for further reference and to keep
a file cabinet of articles and clippings to which he can refer
for facts and ideas. He ought to keep a notebook or pad on his
desk, where he can jot down points or ideas as they come to
him, for appropriate filing and reference. In this way, one's
reading becomes selective and analytical, not merely a pastime;
and one's knowledge becomes cumulative and organized, not simply
casual process.

With this procedure, one can develop a treasury of material for
various occasions. Poems, aphorisms, anecdotes, and even humorous
stories that are worth remembering and retelling as part of the
speaker's stock in trade may also be filed in this manner. One's
library, as well as one's daily reading and experience, thus becomes a working bank which increases its assets with every de-
posit and pays ready and rich dividends upon demand.

Among the primary materials with which the effective preacher
should be thoroughly conversant, Holy Scripture, of course, stands
in first place. Every priest should know his Bible history well and
make it a point to review regularly all of the New Testament.
Not only the Gospels, but the Epistles as well, should be at his
ready command. As one grows in wisdom and experience, it is
remarkable how much more one finds in the Inspired Word. In-
cidents in the life of Christ and the details of His teaching grow
in significance upon restudy. The Epistles of St. Paul are a
mine of spiritual treasure; and a fresh, deepening perception of
the Christian philosophy of life comes with every new reading of
the writings of the other Apostles. Direct quotation from both
the Old and the New Testaments notably strengthens the authority
any sermon.

2

There are times when the priest is called upon to deliver a

sermon without previous notice; in such cases, he must draw
from previous discourses or put together his thoughts as best he
can. Under these circumstances, one is grateful for the back
ground of preparation at his disposal. As a general rule, however
it is folly to depend upon immediate inspiration or what is called
the *dabitur vobis*. From the standpoint of the faithful, people are
willing to overlook defects in delivery and even to accept inferior
content, so long as the preacher gives evidence of having sin
cerely endeavored to prepare his sermon. An impromptu dis
course, put together while one is vesting for Mass, betrays scant
respect for either one's obligation or for the needs and expectance
of the congregation. This kind of spiritual food, offered to the
faithful as a regular fare, results in general disgust and a weaken
ing or even loss of faith.

If we consider the weekly sermon, delivered at the Sunday
Mass, it is not too much to expect that one should start prepara
tion early in the week. This means that the preacher should
determine upon his subject and begin thinking about it, so that
his thought has time to mature and develop with a sense of
personal conviction. As ideas occur, they should be jotted down
One should search for illustrations to bring the points into focus
and to stimulate a human interest. The topics should be organized
into a sequence that is both logical and dramatic. Then the out
line should be drawn up, so that one knows exactly where the
sermon starts, what points are covered, where the climax is
reached, and when it is time to stop. The time to get good ideas
and to put them in their proper place is during the preparation
of the sermon, not after one has begun to speak.

Authorities differ on the question of whether a sermon should
be written out and memorized or delivered from an organized
outline. Of course, a great deal will depend upon the prefer
ence and the talents of the individual. In theory, at least, a ser
mon can be brought to the greatest literary polish if it is written
out. The preacher who has a good memory and the ability to
deliver a memorized sermon with all the force and freshness
that went into his original conception is indeed in an ideal posi

tion. There are occasions when a read sermon is appropriate and acceptable; and the preacher is willing to forego the embellishments of natural eloquence and directness of appeal, in the interests of delicacy and exactness. But as the effectiveness of a sermon is largely in the personal contact of the preacher with his congregation, many preachers are willing to sacrifice possible literary excellence in the interest of holding their attention by concentration upon thought rather than upon expression.

As a practical matter, whether one writes out his sermon in full or develops it in outline form, most priests find their most effective sermons those in which they are not bound to the words and lines of a manuscript. If one has carefully decided upon the two or three points to be discussed under the general topic and has determined just how he will develop each one in turn, he can be reasonably confident of himself and proceed upon the momentum of his thought. If he wishes, he can further clinch each of these points in his own mind with a practical example or graphic illustration or story; and the congregation will find it easy to follow his thought and to recall his points later, with this assistance. To make sure of his termination, he may memorize a concluding paragraph with a "punch" paragraph or one. Even the most elaborate written and memorized sermon should follow this prescription. Literary skill and all the artifices of eloquence cannot compensate for wandering logic and disorganized, disjointed, and half-developed presentation of ideas.

This leads to the question of how long a sermon should be. The answer again depends largely upon the nature of the occasion. When the sermon is the principal feature of the religious event, such as a Lenten series, a dedication, or a jubilee, a longer discourse may be expected than for a Sunday Mass, with only a limited period at one's disposal. The fervor of a special occasion or the exuberance of one's thought may tempt the preacher to extend his sermon; but, in general, it may be said that one half hour should be the limit. Beyond that time, one tests the patience of his congregation and runs the risk of undoing his good work. The average Sunday sermon should not exceed fifteen minutes;

and where a rigid schedule must be observed, it may be advisable to cut the time even more briskly. Even a five-minute sermon, carefully prepared, can present an effective message.

As a matter of fact, a short sermon requires more careful advance preparation than the wandering homily which consumes the time and effort of both the preacher and the congregation to bring the thought into focus. To achieve brevity, it is important to remember that one or two points conceived sharply are far more telling than a half-dozen points which only serve to confuse the issue. In the preparation of the sermon, one should aim at precision and cut all irrelevancy and side remarks. The good preacher will use short sentences and make certain that every statement is cast in the form of a true sentence with a subject and predicate. Parenthetical remarks, afterthoughts, and dangling participles retard the movement of logic and needlessly prolong the process of explanation. It is far better to run the risk of forgetting some brilliant flash of thought than to clog one's rhetoric with parentheses.

To assist in achieving brevity and conciseness, the preacher should also resolve that every sermon which he delivers will be worthy of his best efforts. With concentration on a short message it is easier to achieve this objective and to maintain a consistently high standard of excellence. The notion that because a sermon is long, it must therefore reflect great preparation and profound thought may deceive some persons; but it usually results in a restless and bored congregation.

3

Much might be written on the subject of sermon delivery. This question is complicated by the fact that the basic attitudes and temperaments of individual priests in the pulpit differ widely. With some men, the problem begins on the elementary level of psychological or physical handicaps. With others, the difficulty may be one of correct pronunciation and even of sentence structure. Voice power and placement, modulation, gestures, and mannerisms enter into the picture. But whatever one's speci problem or problems may be, there is no reason why every priest with normal powers of articulation cannot develop into an effective and even eloquent preacher. By the same token, the good preacher can improve himself and expand his powers for the greater good of souls.

It is, of course, fundamental to recognize the fact that preaching, like any other form of public speaking is an art. While some persons have more native ability than others in this field, most of us need training and all of us can benefit by instruction and experience, both to avoid pitfalls and to develop our confidence and ability in a positive way. Effective public speaking is now generally recognized as a most valuable asset for businessmen and, in fact, for all men and women who aspire to any measure of leadership and advance. After achieving a position of eminence through various circumstances, many personages have suddenly realized that they labor under the woeful handicap of ineffective public speech; whereupon they hasten to remedy the defect by taking lessons in speech delivery. Particularly since the entry of radio and television into the field of public communication, the possession or the lack of ability to deliver a speech effectively has become a critical determinant of both careers and vital policies.

More than one pastor, to my knowledge, has insisted that the curates appointed to his care directly from the seminary shall supplement their seminary training with a course in public speaking under professional direction. The results are invariably beneficial. For several years, The Catholic University of America has conducted a special Preachers Institute during its summer session to give priests an opportunity to improve their preparation and delivery of sermons; other Catholic institutes are pursuing the same objective in various centers. More and more priests are recognizing the value of courses in public speaking and are taking advantage of the opportunity by following classes or securing special coaching under competent instruction.

The theory behind this action is simple but sound: The pulpit is not the place to practice one's sermons, any more than the concert stage is the place for a musician to rehearse his scales. If one has definite defects or shortcomings as a preacher, these can best be ironed out behind the scenes; and this is a process that may well be continued long after one has acquired sufficient skill to appear before the public.

These observations are not intended to discourage the diffident, timorous, or self-conscious individual. On the contrary, they point to the fact that, just as no preacher is so perfect that he is incapable of improvement, so no one is so hopeless a preacher that he cannot achieve genuine proficiency, with determination, practice, and persistence. Nervousness can be overcome with patience and encouragement. Embarrassment and a sense of failure on any particular occasion should never be regarded as more than incidental to final success. Defects of speech, such as stammering and stuttering can be overcome by coaching. Faulty pronunciation can be improved, if one is willing to accept correction and to practice deliberately the habit of correct diction. The ability to discourse in complete sentences is a skill that comes with self-discipline and study.

In addition to improvement under instruction, one can now take advantage of various recording devices, to play back one's sermon or speech. In this way, mistakes and defects, which one might never otherwise detect, come to one's attention for improvement. If one is not too proud or sensitive to accept criticism, a fellow priest or even someone in the congregation may be willing to stand by and offer friendly, positive suggestions. This kind of assistance is valuable for the trained and experienced preacher as well as for the tyro and the man working under a handicap. Without realizing it, anyone may develop strange mannerisms of speech or gesture that detract from pleasing delivery.

I have in mind the case of a certain priest who regarded his sermons as models of perfection and insisted that the class in shorthand in the parochial school should take down and transcribe one of his presentations. The more proficient members of the class succeeded in capturing his sermon exactly and gave him a transcription in which every third or fourth word was followed by a prolonged "a-a ah." Without realizing it, one can fall into the habit of following every statement with a parenthetical question such as "Do you see?" or "Do you understand?" These eccentricities develop in the best of speakers, unless a friendly critic is permitted to call attention to their existence.

Similarly in stance and gestures. Some preachers develop the habit of rocking on their feet throughout the sermon, or standing on their toes and bobbing up and down whenever they wish to emphasize a point. Others pound vigorously on the arm of the pulpit, like a judge trying to restore order in the courtroom. Some pick away at their ears or scratch their heads, as a nervous mannerism somehow connected with the extraction of a thought. Some preachers gesture with a windmill motion or resort to a kind of jerking of the elbow as their standard method of reinforcing an idea. All of these eccentricities can be brought under control by an occasional checkup with someone who is willing to tell the truth and not have to suffer the loss of one's friendship.

The same is true in the matter of voice placement. A large part of the effectiveness of delivery consists in distinct enunciation and in the projection of the voice, so that it can be heard and understood by the entire congregation. There is nothing more distressing than to have to strain one's ears to hear a speaker, particularly if, even with this effort, most of his discourse is muffled or unintelligible. If the church or hall is large or the acoustics are poor, special effort may be required to speak slowly and to enunciate clearly. It may be necessary on occasion to use a microphone and amplifying system. One should not hesitate to use this device whenever advisable; and it is recommended that every preacher accustom himself to the microphone and learn to use it effectively.

I recall the incident of a well-known lecturer who was confronted with a large audience but became very temperamental when it was suggested that he use the loud-speaker available on the platform. In addition to a soft voice, he labored under the handicap of a foreign accent. To prove that the microphone was unnecessary, he stepped to the front of the platform and asked in his loudest natural tones, "Can you hear me?" Practically the entire rear section of the audience shouted back, "No!"

"See," he replied triumphantly, "you can!"

As a matter of fact, they did hear him, but they understood very little of what he said during the course of the excellent lecture which he delivered for the next hour; and most of them went home feeling that their time and money had been wasted. Every preacher and speaker should keep in mind the fact that the only reason for his appearance before an audience is to deliver a message. If he cannot be heard or understood, he is wasting his own time as well as that of the disgusted people whose expectancy has been frustrated. This applies not only to part of the sermon. Every bit of it should be intelligible. Some men start their sentences in a good tone and then drop their voices at the end of every sentence or trail off in a series of whispers and mumbles. At one moment they are shouting, and at the next they are communing with themselves. This is positively frustrating to a congregation; and every preacher should be on his guard against it.

Audibility, however, is not the only objective of a considerate and effective preacher. To retain the attention and interest of the congregation, a change of pace and variety of tone and delivery are required. Students of the psychology of attention and of hypnosis recognize two general types of mental reaction to external suggestion and stimuli. One is that of stimulation and the other is that of drowsiness. Stimulation, and aroused fascination are the result of movement, variety, and uncertainty. Drowsiness is induced by uniformity of action, monotone, and repetition of the same pattern. Application of these principles to the art of preaching is obvious. Monotone or a uniform pattern of inflection induces sleep in the congregation. To maintain interest, to stimulate thought, and to persuade one's audience to follow a proposed course of action, the preacher must inject verve and variety of tone and approach into his own voice and inflection.

One of the most familiar forms of pulpit hypnosis inducing drowsiness and sleep is that which is known as the "preacher's tone." This may be described as a kind of sanctimonious inflection, with a slightly mournful note, and a suggestion of fatalism in the voice. Musicians may recognize it as a kind of recitative invariably terminating in a minor note. Whether this tone serves as a natural accompaniment to a certain cast of thought or whether it is copied unconsciously by preachers as a sort of classic pulpit tradition is difficult to say; but it is at once so facile and so deadly as to demand an eternal vigilance against it.

A similar hypnotic effect is produced by pitching the voice at a certain level and holding it with little change from sentence to sentence. Much the same effect is produced, after a short time, whether the voice is pitched low, so as to result in a kind of purring effect, or it is placed on a high note and shouts consistently through the sermon. Related to these effects is what may be called an "intellectual" monotone, very much like that of reading a learned or scientific paper. The contents of a sermon must indeed be superlative to hold the interest of a congregation in a sermon with these kinds of delivery.

Between these forms and the theatrical or melodramatic types of presentation, which easily become offensive and suggestive of insincerity, there is certainly a middle ground. The effective preacher ought to pause from time to time to ask himself whether he is really convinced of what he is saying and really feels the impact of his own message. It is true that the sermon is not simply a kind of one-sided conversation or monologue. It must maintain a certain formality and dignity. But it should also have flesh and blood and be clothed with those human qualities of realization that establish a genuine contact and relationship between the preacher and his congregation. At the end of a sermon, the congregation should feel refreshed, exalted, and inspired, determined to be better men and women as a result of the lesson and experience. They will derive these benefits if they come away with the impression that they have been in contact with an exemplar of truth, who understands and has compassion for the various problems and emotions of his fellow men. They will not react in this way if they feel that they have been listening to a machine.

4

To a considerable extent, as already indicated, the effectiveness of a sermon depends upon mechanical factors in both preparation and delivery. No one can afford to overlook or minimize their importance. But from a long-range point of view, the priest's career and success as a preacher depends essentially upon his attitude toward life and his own sense of values. These factors will largely determine the importance he attaches to preaching, his choice of subjects, his handling of subject matter, and his pulpit approach to his people.

One basic test is the comparative amount of time which the priest devotes Sunday after Sunday to announcements and to the sermon. It is quite understandable that, from time to time, extra time and special emphasis must be given to announcements of parish events and societies and to diocesan announcements and pastoral letters. But if, Sunday after Sunday, these announcements crowd the sermon into a position of insignificance or wipe it out altogether, there is something radically wrong. Many routine announcements can and should be printed in a leaflet or parish bulletin for distribution at the church door. Many of the announcements pertain only to limited groups; others can be presented most effectively in written form, such as the Mass intentions for the week. First concern should be given to the bulk of the congregation. They come to receive a spiritual message, not to hear a long list of announcements, most of which are none of their concern.

Another test is the amount of time given to appeals for financial support compared with that given to the sermon. Certainly, there can be no legitimate criticism of a request for the funds needed to support the Church and its wonderful works of charity and education. Such support is one of the basic works of religion. From time to time, special pressure may have to be exerted, where the need is great and the response inadequate. But when, Sunday after Sunday, the main theme is a cry for money, with the sermon as an afterthought for which little time is left, something is wrong. It has been frequently stated, and I think with much truth, that where genuine service is given, the parishioners respond generously to the material needs of their parish without much prodding. A good sermon fits into the category of genuine service; and while most people must be reminded from time to time of their duty to contribute to the support of the Church, they are likely to be far better disposed to the task if they are spiritually conditioned to a fulfillment of all their religious duties.

Still another test which may involve the preacher in a personal examination of conscience is the general mood and spirit which he breathes from the pulpit. It is true that one must not compromise with the devil. Evil must be denounced, and wrongdoers must be called to an accounting for their evil deeds. But when the pulpit becomes simply a sounding board of denunciations and jeremiads, it loses much, if not most, of its power for good. Christ did not hesitate to denounce sin, and he even used invective against hypocrites and scandal-givers. But the vast bulk of His preaching and His teaching was positive, friendly, and inspiring to higher perfection. "Learn of me, for I am meek and humble of heart."[2] "Blessed are they that hunger and thirst after justice."[3] "Feed my lambs, feed my sheep."[4]

The preacher who habitually scolds, denounces, and complains to his flock and resorts to bitterness and sarcasm is defeating his own purpose. He communicates his own sourness to others and thus creates an attitude of resentment and resistance. Most people respond to a friendly pat on the back and make a more earnest endeavor to please God and man if they recognize some note of appreciation. Particular caution must be observed in the pulpit in praising or in blaming particular individuals, even by hint or suggestion. Imprudent praise, even though deserved, can easily give rise to envy and even justifiable criticism that others equally worthy were not mentioned. Blame, even if deserved, when publicly administered from the sacred precincts of the pulpit, may mortally wound sensibilities and drive persons from the Church.

---

[2] Mt. 11:29.
[3] Mt. 5:6.
[4] Jn. 21:16, 17.

An interesting and significant test which the conscientious preacher should apply to himself from time to time is his attitude toward the intelligence and cultural level of his congregation. It is possible to pitch the level of one's sermon too high, or at least to give the impression that one is talking "over the heads" of the people. On the other hand, one's approach may be on such an elementary and condescending level as to insult the congregation. It is always advisable to study one's congregation in advance and to direct one's discourse in such terms as will be easily grasped by anyone of average intelligence in the group.

A great deal that passes for "intellectual" is simply the confusion that results from the use of technical terms with which others are unacquainted. The word *troglodyte* may produce only a raising of the eyebrows: but when we say *cave man,* everyone knows what we mean. The same is true of theological and philosophical terms. The effective preacher will do well to translate these for himself first, to make sure that he understands them, and then deliver his message in language that the layman can understand.

The classical story is often retold of the two women who met on the doorsteps of the church, one coming out from Sunday Mass, the other going in.

"How was the sermon this morning?" asked the one entering the church.

"Simply wonderful," replied the other.

"Well, tell me," continued the first, "what was it about?"

"I don't know," said the second. "He didn't say."

It is equally bad, and possibly worse, to "talk down" to the congregation as if they were morons or unable to understand anything above the level of a child. The fact that the Sunday congregation is a "captive" audience may lead the preacher unconsciously to adopt the attitude that anything will satisfy their requirements and then to set the requirements on a very low level. To correct any false assumptions in this regard, it is always well to remember that education and intelligence are not synonymous. Persons of only elementary education and even those in primitive communities have the same brain capacity and the same powers of comprehension as those of more developed educational opportunities; it is a profound mistake to underestimate their intelligence and their needs, and to feed them spiritual crumbs, fragments, and stones. Where the level of culture and formal education is low, it is one of the obligations of the pastor and preacher to raise that level by a measured program of teaching and action.

In many instances, an analysis will reveal the fact that the congregation includes persons whose education is equivalent to that of the preacher and whose reading and experience may be considerably wider than his. While this thought should not terrify the preacher, it should assist him in maintaining a worthy and dignified presentation of his subject that will command the respect of all concerned. It is generally a mistake to think of the congregation as children and to use such expressions as "the penny catechism teaches us," or to hint, by manner or expression, that the congregation is incapable of grasping more than the most elemental conceptions.

It has been observed by many experienced preachers that Christian doctrine, even in its most sublime mysteries, is within the grasp of those whose formal training is limited as well as of the educated provided it is presented clearly and directly, in language comprehensible to the layman. With regard to the moral problems of people, one may say that they approximate the same for persons of high and low degree. Human nature is the same in all of us. Hence, the preacher is generally safe in formulating his sermon, clearly and simply, always drawing a practical lesson or conclusion, with the assurance that the entire congregation will be grateful for the respect paid to their intelligence and all alike will profit by the spiritual message.

5

A question frequently asked by preachers is, "What shall I talk about next Sunday?" Sometimes the question is answered by the existence of a set of instructional outlines established by diocesan orders. Particular seasons, such as Lent, the month of the Holy

Rosary, and November with its devotion to all the saints and the holy souls in purgatory will suggest appropriate subjects. Certain outstanding feasts such as Christmas, Easter, Trinity Sunday, and the feast of Pentecost call for a special message, which can be prepared well in advance. The Epistle and Gospel of every Sunday are rich with subjects of both inspirational character and practical application; all that is necessary is to study them well in advance, as already suggested, and to concentrate during the week on the development of one particular theme.

For truly effective preaching, however, it is important that one be in touch with the problems of the day and with the particular moral issues and dilemmas of this generation. One should never forget that man is destined for life beyond the grave; but the fact is that the people in the pews are still on earth and have to face the world as it is. The principles preached from the pulpit should be as lofty as heaven itself; but unless they are brought down to earth and applied to the life of the home, the farm, the factory, the office, the child, the youth, the man and woman, private and public life, and the community itself, they will appear remote and impractical in face of the pressing realities of human existence. This means that the priest should know what is going on around him and make it a point to talk with people and to study his own city and parish.

People are looking for practical guidance, and they are willing to take it from the priest who knows what he is talking about, even when it hurts. They are eager for the preacher to break through the curtain of pious generalities and to teach the truth about honesty, justice, fair dealing, the rights and duties of employers and employees, as well as about purity, prayer, and spiritual motivation. But they insist that the priest know his subject well and maintain a balanced view of life. They are ready to hear about the art and the beauty of the Church from one who has taken the pains to study it himself. They are looking for guidance on good reading, not merely denunciation of bad books. They would like to know the facts of Catholic activity — the missions of the Church, its work in education, in science, in hospitalization, in charities, and in social work. They would like more practical guidance in human relations, to give their individual lives a better sense of direction, their social and business contacts a more Christian and co-operative impulse, their married and family lives a more happy and positive adjustment.

The alert priest who continues to grow himself in the comprehension of life and of the people in it, as well as in his love for God and for his pastoral mission, will never be at a loss for vital and important sermon topics. He will never allow himself to become obsessed with one or two banal subjects or imagine that he is delivering a powerful message when he is simply contributing to the scruples of more tender souls and preaching damnation to people who are searching for the bread of life. He will not rest content with brushing up and delivering over and over again, year after year, the few gems that he produced during his seminary days or on special inspiration thereafter. With his own growth in maturity, experience, and wisdom, he will recognize in the pulpit a constant challenge and opportunity to guide and guard and strengthen souls. In the words of Christ, "Every scribe instructed in the kingdom of heaven is like to a man that is a householder, who bringeth forth out of his treasure new things and old."[5]

Needless to say, the elemental strength and ultimate success of the sermon depend upon something far more basic than the learning and expertness of the preacher. The fundamental purpose of the sermon is not merely to enlighten minds but also to move men's wills to accept the grace of God. This power itself comes only from God's grace. In the words of St. Paul, "I have planted, Apollo watered: but God gave the increase. Therefore, neither he that planteth is anything, nor he that watereth: but God that giveth the increase."[6] The priest who would be an effective preacher, not merely an orator or lecturer, must therefore be himself first a man of God and reflect his own faith and virtue in his sacred eloquence. His preaching will, by the same token, make rich use of the words of Holy Scripture.

---

[5] Mt. 13:52.
[6] 1 Cor. 3:6, 7.

A vigorous and discerning faith, writes R. Garrigou-Lagrange, O.P., "is absolutely essential for apostolic preaching. Without it, one's preaching may well be academic, but it will certainly not be apostolic. Without it, the priest is a mere orator, not a Christian preacher."[7] The same writer adds, "There are three forms of the apostolate — prayer, daily sacrifice for the conversion of sinners, preaching. Without the first two, the third will never be fruitful."[8] At the same time, he retells the story of a successful preacher whose constant associate was a lay Brother, who prayed without ceasing while the priest delivered his sermons. While many souls were won to God as a result of these sermons, it was revealed to the priest that the source of his success was the sincere and humble prayer of his companion.

There can be no doubt that the Catholic priest is in true character as a preacher only to the extent that he identifies himself with the personality and the purpose of Christ. While addressing his congregation "as one having power, and not as the scribes and Pharisees,"[9] he will remember that his Master and prototype was always able to say, "Take up my yoke upon you and learn of me, because I am meek and humble of heart."[10] While unafraid to preach the straight doctrine of Christ and to castigate sin, he will never forget the charity of Christ the Good Shepherd toward sinners or His words, "He that is without sin among you, let him first cast a stone."[11]

Preaching is not an end in itself but only a means toward an end, namely the conversion of sinners, the increase of virtue, and the salvation of souls. The priest who is intent on making his sermons effective will do well to remember the injunction of Christ to His Apostles, who wondered why they were unable to cast out a devil: "This kind is not cast out but by prayer and fasting."[1]

---

[7] *The Priest in Union with Christ,* trans. by Rev. G. W. Shelton (Westminster, Md.: The Newman Press, 1954), p. 126.

[8] *Ibid.,* p. 130.

[9] Mt. 7:29.

[10] Mt. 11:29.

[11] Jn. 8:7.

[12] Mt. 17:20.

Faith, personal penance, and preparation through prayer must therefore be added as the supernatural ingredients of successful preaching, underlying the natural ingredients of the effort. Indeed, the Catholic priest will always approach the preparation and the delivery of his sermons in the spirit of prayer. And in this very important phase of his ministry, he will always keep in mind the principle of the union of work and prayer: "We pray as if everything depended on God; but we work as if everything depended upon ourselves."

> *"For every high priest taken from among men is ordained for men in the things that appertain to God, that he may offer up gifts and sacrifices for sins"* (Hebr. 5:1).

CHAPTER VIII

THE PRIEST AND THE LITURGY

I

THE priesthood, as we understand it in the Catholic Church, is essentially a participation in the ministry and power of Christ, to teach the divinely revealed word of God, to administer the sacraments, and to lead in public religious exercise and worship. All three of these functions the Catholic priest performs, not on his own initiative or even as a venerable elder designated by the community, but as the called and anointed representative of God, duly ordained by a bishop as a successor of the Apostles, and authorized by the Church to exercise his spiritual powers in accordance with given mandates.

All three of these functions are essential to the life and activity of the Church. All three are inextricably joined together and in some respects are identical. Nevertheless, the most distinctive evidence of religion in any community, and of the organization of the Church in particular, is the existence of worship in common. Whatever his other activities may be — education, administration, organization, writing, guidance, or contemplation — the Catholic priest is, by the very nature of his calling, ordained to lead in prayer and serve in offering sacrifice at the altar of God. Even the priest in a religious order devoted to silence and meditation shares in the public ministry of the Church. His daily recitation of the

Divine Office is for the spiritual intentions of the Church; and his daily Mass, even in the most remote chapel, is essentially a public service.

The Catholic Church has always been aware of its primary obligation to provide for public and community worship. This it has done consistently against the distorted interpretation of Christ's words "But the hour cometh and now is, when the true adorers shall adore the Father in spirit and in truth. For the Father also seeketh such to adore him. God is a spirit: and they that adore him must adore him in spirit and in truth."[1] The context of this passage clearly indicates that Christ intended that all men everywhere should come to the knowledge of true religion and that His doctrine and worship were not to be confined to the Jews. It was never His idea that true worship was to be exclusively personal, private, and secret. He taught "For where there are two or three gathered together in my name, there I am in the midst of them."[2]

There are, of course, many cogent arguments from natural reason why public, community worship corresponds to human nature and is a duty in the natural order of things. From supernatural revelation, we have the commandment "Remember that thou keep holy the Sabbath day."[3] As this principle was developed in the Mosaic Law, it came to represent an elaborate ritual of worship which brought the Jews together in the Temple and in their synagogues and indeed organized their entire nation into a community of prayer. In the New Testament, fulfilling the prophecies of the Old, the Catholic Church has regarded the institution of the Holy Eucharist as establishing the distinctive sacrifice and service of the Christian religion. In the injunction of Christ, "Do this for a commemoration of me," following the sacramental conversion of bread and wine into His body and blood, the Church recognizes a positive obligation which it has enshrined in the Holy Mass.[4]

---

[1] Jn. 4:23, 24.
[2] Mt. 18:20.
[3] Exod. 20:8.
[4] Lk. 20:19.

The Catholic priest, as foreshadowed in the type of Melchisedech, is ordained with this same power conveyed by Christ to His Apostles at the Last Supper; and it is primary among his priestly duties to offer the Holy Sacrifice of the Mass for the faithful with all the dignity and devotion which his Christlike character demands.[5] And just as St. Paul was called upon to instruct and reprove the faithful, so it is his commission to see that the faithful understand this divine service and conduct themselves in accordance with a full realization and appreciation of its supernatural character and importance.[6]

One of the first things that a priest should resolve for himself is the recitation of the prayers of the Mass completely, correctly and distinctly, in accordance with the rubrics and approved directives. As Latin is a foreign language and many of the prayers are recited from memory, there is a natural tendency for one to slur words, to abbreviate expressions, and even to change case endings unconsciously. This tendency is accelerated by the speedy recitation of prayers, so that, unless one is on his guard, the end result may be far from devotional or even intelligible. One should always keep in mind that, although the faithful may not be able to understand the Latin or notice the unfortunate habits of diction into which the priest has fallen, God does. And it is to God that the prayers are offered. From time to time, the celebrant of Mass should ask himself what his reaction would be to prayers or petitions offered to himself in the manner of his own address to Almighty God.

Primary among the reasons for an unsatisfactory recital of the Mass is the desire or habit of unnecessary speed. It is true that exaggerated devotion and a dragging of the time of the Mass by a slow, scrupulous mouthing of the words are quite unwarranted. The Mass proceeds by a steady, forward pace, with the words and ceremonies exactly set forth. In the course of time, most priests memorize the principal parts of the Mass, so that there is no reason for delay or hesitation. There is no provision in the Mass

[5] Gen. 14:18; Hebr. 5:10; 7:17.
[6] 1 Cor. 11:16-29.

for extended pause. Nevertheless, when the recitation of the Mass becomes so rapid that not even the experienced of the faithful are able to follow along intelligently with their missals in English, it is time to stop and take stock of what the speed is all about.

Moral theologians lay down a certain minimum of time within which Mass can be worthily celebrated. Some priests may pride themselves on the fact that they are able to come close to this minimum, and some of the congregation may share in the satisfaction of complying with their obligation of Sunday Mass in the shortest possible time. But when one skates on such thin ice, dealing with the Holy Sacrifice as one would with a foot race or with a distasteful function which one must endure, the whole meaning of the Mass has become grossly distorted. If the Mass is worth saying at all, it is worth saying well, with at least the same recollection, intelligence, and devotion as one would pay in a secular ceremony where something of importance is at stake.

Similar observations may be made regarding one's general conduct and performance of the rubrics of the Mass. In the course of time, it is almost inevitable that one fall into certain errors or eccentricities which call for a review or checking of the directives for the Mass. There are definite rubrics for the tone of voice to be used for the words of consecration and for the Canon of the Mass. There is a certain decorum for the elevation of the host and of the chalice. The extension and height of the arms and position of the hands during the Mass may call for correction. There is such a thing as, not only correct, but also beautiful recitation of the Mass. On the other hand, one's stance, gestures, and tone of voice may become, not only incorrect, but positively distracting and disedifying. This matter is of sufficient importance for every priest to consult his references, from time to time, as a matter of principle and to invite the suggestions of his confreres.

These problems may become particularly acute in the more elaborate functions of solemn Mass. If one is not called upon frequently to participate as an officer in such functions and a trained master of ceremonies is not at hand to issue ready directives, the situation can easily become embarrassing, despite one's best intentions. It is advisable for every priest in active life to make a periodic review of the *ceremoniale* and to study one of the recognized authorities, such as Fortesque or Martinucci, for the correct movements of the celebrant, the deacon, the subdeacon, and the other officers of solemn Mass. Some priests have a special interest in the liturgy and a particular talent and ease for the sacred ceremonies; others have an allergy and even dread of appearing on these occasions. But with determination, some study and observation, with sufficient advance rehearsal, everyone can acquire sufficient competence to meet the challenge and even develop an enthusiasm and love for this beautiful ritual.

What is applicable to the priests themselves is of importance also in the training and conduct of the altar boys. The theory governing the servers of Mass is that they represent the congregation in answering the dialogue prayers of the priest and assist with the Offertory and such other functions as may be necessary to warn the congregation or minister to the needs of the celebrant. In this capacity, they perform a most important and sacred role. They occupy a privileged position; and their prayers and actions become an integral part of the Mass. There should be no guesswork in their procedure or frivolity in their behavior. They should know their responses perfectly and conform to the rubrics as exactly as the celebrant.

To achieve these objectives, of course, there is no substitute for competent training. The altar boys should be taught their Latin carefully and be told what it means. If the task of learning is not too difficult for the boys, then the task of teaching should not be too difficult for the priest. If one has school Sisters, they can begin the work and even teach the boys the complete routine and etiquette of serving. But it is the priest himself who must ultimately assume responsibility, to rehearse the altar boys and to make certain that they measure up to requirements and necessary standards.

There is no good excuse for the mumbling and pretense of Latin response that one sometimes hears from poorly trained and supervised altar boys. Such conduct, as well as clumsy bungling on the altar steps, or irreverent behavior in the sanctuary, is a dire eflection on the priest himself who has neglected or failed one of is primary duties. The same observation is true when the servers re provided with torn or dirty cassocks and surplices, when they ppear regularly late for services, or arrive in an unkempt condi- ion unfit to appear on the altar. The priest who is getting these esults should ask himself whether he is really interested in his york or is giving his altar boys a reasonable consideration. If the ltar boys are simply taken for granted, with no evidence of ppreciation and encouragement, or — worse still — if their only eward is public reprimand and humiliation from the priest, not nuch can be expected in the way of co-operation.

Altar boys are people. If they are given considerate treatment nd taught in a kindly manner and given an occasional reward or eat, they will regard their position as one of distinction and will spond to the privilege. A thoughtful priest can work wonders for oys of this impressionable age. Many wonderful vocations have eveloped among altar boys. And many laymen recall with pride nd gratitude the incomparable training and experience they quired as acolytes.

2

An integral component of the sacred liturgy to which the Church is given a high position of honor and which calls for the careful onsideration of every priest is sacred music. Comparatively few iests ever pause to regard themselves as musicians. Yet, they are gularly called upon to render the sacred chant in public, and as loists, so to speak, in Holy Mass, Benediction, choir recital of the oly Office, and in numerous other liturgical functions throughout e year. Moreover, they are held responsible, in parochial life, r the organization of a parish choir and for the correct and autiful rendition of music at liturgical functions.

Compliance with this obligation and the presentation of litur- cal music, in accordance with the mind of the Church, do not cessarily require native music talent or advanced musical train- g. What is essential, however, is, first, a recognition of the im- rtance of music in Catholic worship and of one's priestly responsibility in this matter, and, second, a determination to do everything humanly possible to bring and maintain the liturgical chant and sacred music to a position of the highest excellence as an expression and adornment of divine worship. Not everyone is gifted with native musical ability; but everyone with rudimentary perceptions, elementary training, and some study can achieve basic musical skill and an advanced appreciation of music.

Every seminary should provide facilities for group study of liturgical music, including both Gregorian Chant and the various forms of polyphony and sacred compositions, according to the directives of St. Pius X and the other popes who have issued letters on this subject.[7] Moreover, the seminary should provide opportunity for each individual to develop a musical ear and learn how to sing the chant correctly and with dignity; and no one should be exempted from this requirement.

Some men seem to have absolutely no ear for music. They are unable to distinguish one note from another, and their attempt at singing result in no more than a droning monotone. This condition can be corrected under competent instruction and with determination on the part of the individual to learn. The seminarian or priest with this handicap may never become a great or melodious singer; but if he can distinguish between notes, learn to read at least Gregorian notation, and place his voice correctly, he has achieved the minimum requirements for an adequate rendition of a High Mass or any other sung function.

At the same time, it is important to recognize that, with the acceptance of basic values and a determination to learn, everyone of normal powers can achieve a genuine and satisfying appreciation of musical composition and performance. Comparatively few people who enjoy music on the radio, television, or concert platform are musicians themselves. Many persons who thought that they could never appreciate and enjoy fine music have learned to do so through the encouragement and assistance of a friend. In the

---

[7] Cf. *Motu proprio* of Pope Pius X, November 22, 1903; Apostolic Constitution of Pope Pius XI, December 20, 1928; Encyclical Letter of Pope Pius XII on Sacred Music, December 25, 1955.

ase of the priest, particularly of the parish priest, there is no question but that this is an imperative, at least so far as liturgical music is concerned. The directives of the Church are clear. The sacred nature of the liturgy requires that its musical accompaniment be worthy of the occasion. The congregation who participate in the sacred function are entitled to the best consideration. And the priest who takes pride in maintaining the dignity of his church and of Catholic worship under his direction will see to it that the music for which he is responsible is always correct and inspiring.

The task of organizing and supervising a choir is not always easy. Musical talent may be lacking in the community; and where it exists, there is sometimes the problem of temperament to be coped with. Musical taste varies considerably, and where the norms of ecclesiastical music have not been understood or observed, there may be difficulty in adjusting standards and securing conformity. This is the human side of the problem, for which tact, diplomacy, and patience may be even more important than musical competence in the busy pastor.

The key to the solution of these problems is usually to be found in securing a qualified and co-operative choir director. To secure such a person may well entail expenditure or an adequate honorarium and a willingness to provide and maintain a satisfactory organ, a good musical library, and facilities for practice and performance. One cannot be stingy and demanding at the same time - expecting the choir to pay for its own music, requiring performance on short notice, highly critical of a volunteer group that holds together from sheer, desperate devotion to the Church — and hope to get the best results.

Every choir needs encouragement and praise; and nothing can take the place of the understanding, personal interest, and co-operation of the pastor or priest in charge of parochial music. An occasional visit during rehearsal and a tangible expression of appreciation are the least that should be expected of the pastor. But more than this, the priest in charge should take pains to explain to the members of the choir the meaning of the Latin texts of the music they are endeavoring to render. The choir should be made to feel that it is truly an integral, active part of the divine service, whether it is within the sanctuary rail or in the choir loft at the rear of the church. Unless this is done, the entire significance of sacred music may be lost, the singing becoming simply a profane exhibition of musical talent, rivalry, or vanity; and abuses may creep in which make the choir loft a place of anything but edification.

A great deal has been written about the comparative merits of the Gregorian Chant and of polyphonic music for liturgical service; and even more might be said as to the artistic value and appropriateness of modern compositions for the Mass. Whatever one's personal preferences may be, the fact is that Gregorian Chant has been designated by the popes as the classical and basic norm of liturgical music. This does not mean that part music or compositions for mixed voices, even of an elaborate nature, are regarded with disfavor. But it does mean that the authentic Catholic choir should have a genuine appreciation of Gregorian Chant as embodying the authentic spirit and feeling of liturgical music and be able to render Gregorian Chant with competence and devotion. With this background of appreciation and training, the choir is always in a better position to evaluate music as it fits in with the spirit of the Church and to distinguish between true and false Catholic music, between what is appropriate and what is simply florid exhibition, quite out of harmony with Catholic belief and sacred worship.

Of course, the first one who should have this basic understanding and appreciation is the priest. It should constitute part of his seminary training; but if this has left any gaps in his preparation he still has the obligation of bringing himself into a position where he can give some constructive and positive indications to the choir. In some cases, it is possible to anticipate opposition from the choir particularly if its background of training has left much to be desired. Brusque demands, sudden changes, and attempts to inaugurate reforms that are really beyond the capacity of the group are not advisable. Friendly interest, tactful suggestions, and gradual approach to the problem, however, will serve to correct abuses, win the confidence of the choir, and stimulate its ambition

o conform to the best standards of selection and performance. The
results are almost certain to repay sustained effort.

3

One of the most essential things always to keep in mind about
the sacred liturgy is that it is public worship. While the priest con-
ducts the service, he does so on behalf of the people. The more
the congregation is brought into active participation, the more the
service becomes a truly community prayer, not simply a formality
or cold ritual. Everything possible should be done to impress this
realization upon the faithful, so that their presence becomes an
intelligent and devotional union with the priest as he offers their
spiritual aspirations to Almighty God upon the altar or leads them
in public prayer.

This is pre-eminently important in the Holy Sacrifice of the
Mass. Catholics should be carefully instructed in the meaning of
the Mass. Its sacrificial character should be constantly stressed, as
exemplified both at the Last Supper and on Calvary. The Offertory
should be explained as a participation of all the congregation in
providing the celebrant of the Mass with the material for the Holy
Sacrifice and in presenting a union of prayer. The Consecration
and the Elevation should be understood as the moment of transub-
stantiation, when the bread and wine are turned into the Body
and Blood of Christ. The Communion should be represented as a
completion of the Sacrifice, when as many of the faithful as possible join with the priest in receiving the Sacred Species to complete
the sacred action of the Mass.

To insure this reverential attention and devout participation, the
utmost care should be given to the details of what, for a better term,
we may describe as the etiquette of the Mass. The Mass should
start promptly, as scheduled; and the congregation should be assembled and ready for the emergence of the priest from the
sacristy. They should be taught to rise as soon as he appears and to
remain standing until he begins the prayers at the foot of the
altar. They should know when to kneel, stand, and be seated. And
they should understand that they are not to leave their seats, as a

matter of Christian courtesy, until the final prayers have been completed, and the celebrant has returned to the sacristy.

Of course, this calls for co-operation on the part of both the priest and the people. It may be necessary, from time to time, for the priest to remind his congregation of what is right and proper. He will do this most effectively by explaining the spiritual significance of this precious time and of the importance of making the most of it to gain all of its spiritual benefits. Simply denouncing people for coming late, demanding that they come forward to fill the front pews, or glaring at those who leave before the service is ended, causes needless embarrassment and resentment. The celebrant may well ask himself whether his own erratic observance of time may not be a source of general confusion, as to the starting of Mass. His perfunctory, rushed, or indistinct recitation of the prayers at the end of the Mass may give the impression to many that it is of little importance whether one leaves the church early or lingers to the end.

The conduct of the Mass should be so ordered that it is possible for all to concentrate on the sequence of the prayers and to follow the celebrant as he proceeds from the *Confiteor,* at the foot of the altar, to the prayers, the Epistle and Gospel, the Offertory, the Canon, and the Communion. This becomes impossible if one priest reads announcements or attempts to preach the sermon while the celebrant is carrying on with the Mass. There may be special occasions when a great number of Communions requires the distribution of Communion while the Mass proceeds; but this should certainly be only tolerated under extraordinary circumstances. The correct time to give Holy Communion is at the Communion of the Mass, when the available priests can co-operate in its distribution in order to save time. Similarly, special circumstances may warrant giving Communion before and after Mass; but this can easily become an abuse, leading to an irregular scheduling of Mass and a general distortion of the liturgy and significance both of the Mass and of the sacrament of Holy Eucharist.

During weekdays, there can be no valid objection, as a rule

against the celebration of several Masses simultaneously, for the convenience of visiting clergy. But on Sundays and holydays of obligation, this practice in the parish church is inexcusable. An orderly congregation should not be confused by several Masses going on at the same time. Possibly in the great shrines there may be extenuating circumstances for this condition; but in the average church, where the regular congregation must be served as a body and on a given schedule, it is advisable to have a private or secluded chapel where a visiting priest may be accommodated without disrupting the regular service.

Much has been written and discussed on the subject of the best way for the faithful to assist at Mass. There is no standard or required procedure beyond that of physical attendance, with reverence and such devotion as the individual is able to summon. It is the usual practice at children's Masses for prayers to be said in common with hymns interspersed. Sometimes children are taught to sing a community Mass, such as the *Missa de Angelis*. Adults are generally allowed to follow their own private devotions, whether at Low or High Mass, saying the rosary, following a prayer book, meditating, or just drifting, as the case may be. No "best" way to hear Mass has been laid down by the Church. In the humble opinion of this writer, however, the use of the missal, following the Mass as it is said by the celebrant, may be highly recommended to the faithful.

Various missals are now available in the vernacular, and with a minimum of instruction, their use is within the grasp of anyone of average intelligence. As a start, the leaflet missal may be recommended. As one masters this, he will almost invariably wish to proceed to the complete missal. The logic of using the missal is obvious in the fact that these are the prayers prescribed by the Church for the Mass and actually said by the celebrant. Other prayers and devotions, however excellent, simply are not the Mass. The person who follows the Mass with the missal, not only is united with the mind of the Church as the celebrant proceeds with the Holy Sacrifice, but has the further benefit of the Epistle and

Gospel of the day, as well as of the special prayers and commemorations of the saints. The intelligent and consistent use of the missal ties the individual right into the liturgical life of the Church.

Promotion of the use of the missal by the laity deserves encouragement by the clergy. To achieve the desired results, it may be advisable to conduct classes in the use of the missal and to give such further instruction in the history and significance of the Mass and its rubrics as is feasible. Moreover, to make the use of the missal practical, the celebrant must guard against inordinate speed in saying the Mass. The argument that the Latin of the Mass is recited much more quickly than its English translation is quite invalid and deceives no one.

In pursuance of the principle that the laity should participate as fully as possible in the liturgy, and particularly in union with the celebrant of the Mass, it may be suggested that more consideration be given to having the congregation join in reciting aloud certain prayers of the Mass. This does not mean that the responses of the altar boy are to be displaced or that there is to be any disturbance in the regular celebration of the Mass. But, under the direction of a precentor, certain prayers can be said together by the congregation at the same time as they are recited by the priest at the altar. Thus, the *Confiteor*, the *Gloria*, the *Sanctus*, the *Pater Noster*, and the *Agnus Dei* may be selected as community prayers. Recitation in English is undoubtedly easier and perhaps of more significance to the average congregation. This, however, may be subject to directives from the Chancery Office, as in some dioceses definite regulations are established for the use of Latin and the vernacular in public prayers at the Mass and other liturgical functions. If children can join successfully in this recitation, there is no reason why adults cannot do the same. This method supplements the private use of the missal and has proved to be practical and spiritually rewarding wherever it has been given a serious trial.

The same thought may be applied to community singing of High Mass. With a little practice, under competent direction, almost any congregation can master one of the Gregorian Chant Masses and sing the responses as well. One of the most impressive

Masses I have ever heard was sung by an Indian congregation in a remote Mexican village. Everyone took part; and at the end of the Mass I had the impression of a general spiritual exhilaration from the exercise.

These considerations should govern the general conduct of all liturgical and devotional services. In other words, while the priest alone has the power to offer the Sacrifice of the Mass and, as the duly ordained minister, leads in other religious services, he should always keep in mind the fact that he is co-ordinating the prayers and devotion of the faithful. His own recitation of prayers should never descend into a matter of routine and speed, but should always be thoughtful and deliberate so as to command attention and inspire religious sentiment. To the extent permissible and appropriate, he should endeavor to secure the active participation of the congregation in these exercises; and he should see to it that they are properly instructed in the meaning of the services and of the prayers that are being offered. This applies to all services, not only those which are conducted in the vernacular such as novenas, the rosary, litanies, and the Way of the Cross, but also those which are conducted in Latin, such as Benediction of the Most Blessed Sacrament. In the administration of the sacraments likewise, such as Baptism, means should be taken to insure that the participants realize what is taking place and understand the meaning of the words and of the ceremonies.

Question often arises as to the special devotions which are to be provided, particularly in parochial life. The answer to this will be governed both by the prescriptions of the Church and the desires of the faithful. The considerate priest will always be eager to offer to his people such special and seasonal devotions as they desire and are willing to attend. At the same time, he will avoid the needless multiplication of devotions, the introduction of novelties or melodramatic display, and anything that smacks of opportunism and commercial motivation. Eccentric devotions and whatever borders on or encourages superstition must be strenuously avoided.

The soundest general procedure is that of following the liturgical year as it has been drawn up by the Church, with emphasis upon the liturgical seasons and approved feasts. This calls for advance planning and a determination to use the liturgical prescriptions and ceremonies to the fullest extent practicable. The novenas in preparation for Christmas, the Immaculate Conception of the Blessed Virgin Mary, and Pentecost should always be observed with the utmost devotion and solemnity. The Lenten season, culminating in the beautiful ceremonies of Holy Week and Easter, should be observed with the time-honored and officially approved rituals. The patronal feast of one's parish church ought to be marked with special observance. The more actively the ecclesiastical calendar and the daily commemoration of the saints enter into the consciousness of the faithful, the more their Catholic faith is nourished and the more vital a force their religion becomes in their daily lives.

4

In the faithful and dignified observance of the liturgy, one should never lose sight of the importance of correct liturgical equipment and furnishings. In every Catholic church, whether large or small, rich or poor, the basic requirements for the Sacrifice of the Mass are the same. Definite regulations are laid down for the placement of the altars, erection of the Stations of the Cross, and the propriety of sacred images and general adornments.

Within these limitations, a great deal of latitude is allowed for local and individual taste; and, of course, the budget of the church or parish will have a bearing upon the quality and extent of the decorations. Whether the church be simple or grand, however, there should be no compromise on the subject of cleanliness and decency. Even in the poorest of chapels there is no excuse for a rickety altar, dirty linen, or an unkempt sanctuary. The altar is the sacred table for the celebration of the Last Supper, the consecration of bread and wine into the Body and Blood of Christ. It should be worthy of its sublime function and be presentable at all times. The linens should be immaculate. The holy precincts within the altar rail need not be covered with expensive carpets; but they should be in good repair and representative of a high regard for the sacred liturgy that they serve.

Likewise with the sacred vessels and vestments. Chalices and ciboria should be regularly cleaned and replated as necessary. If worn vestments cannot be replaced, they can at least be kept mended and presentable. There is no reason for extravagance in these matters; but there is less excuse for penuriousness or neglect. There is nothing more disedifying or more indicative of a decaying faith than a shoddy treatment of the instruments and symbols of holy Mass.

Where dirt and disorder are apparent within the sacred precincts, the fault may be charitably ascribed to poor training or low standards of those responsible for the premises. It is true that men are not always as observant of these details as women, or as demanding of high standards as they should be. The priest who is bewildered by such considerations can and should engage a competent sacristan to take care of the altar. It is nearly always possible to organize an Altar and Rosary Society of women who will deem it a privilege to care for the sanctuary, the linen, vestments, and candles, and to arrange for flowers and whatever is needful for the decency of the house of God. As a matter of fact, everything about the altar and throughout the church should sparkle with cleanliness and good maintenance.

Regular attention should be paid to the holy-water fonts and the baptistry. If not from a sense of reverence for holy things, then, at least, from a sense of responsibility for the health of the community, these appurtenances should be frequently inspected and kept in a sanitary condition. The old saying that cleanliness is next to godliness is nowhere more valid than in the church. The priest who takes pride in himself and in his ministry will be vigilant on both scores.

There is a mistaken notion in some quarters that attention to these details is an evidence of vanity and that somehow a devotion to cleanliness and good taste is indicative of worldliness and a materialistic spirit. It is, of course, possible to concentrate on the external appearances of things to the exclusion of inner significance. The priest who is truly interested in serving his people need not worry about such allegations. Whatever he can do to provide for the comfort and convenience of his congregation, to beautify the church, and to make the liturgy attractive, he may well regard as in fulfillment of his sacred ministry, in accordance with the mind and precepts of Holy Mother Church, and as bringing down the blessing of God.

"It appears odd," writes Father Sadlowski, "that any law should be necessary regarding the care and preservation of the sacred furnishings. That such furnishings should be kept neat, clean, and in good repair follows from their very nature as something sacred Hence it can be said that the care and preservation of them is a corollary of the divine law, namely, that respect and reverence are due to sacred things.

"Nonetheless, it is clear that the Church has found it necessary in a way has been forced, to issue legislation on the matter because of the negligence of individuals, which negligence at times was apparently quite widespread. . . . The present law, as contained in the Code, is a concise restatement of the former pronouncement on the care and preservation of the sacred furnishings. It states that sacred furnishings, particularly those which are consecrated or blessed in accordance with liturgical laws, and which are used for public worship, are to be carefully preserved in the sacristy of the church, or in some other place which is safe and becoming and they are not to be used for profane purposes.[8]

"Although the Code itself does not go into detail regarding the neatness, the cleanliness, and the condition of the sacred furnishings, these matters can be deduced particularly from the law as found in the liturgical books. Of utmost consideration is the statement of canon 1150, that the things which are consecrated or blessed with a constitutive blessing be treated with reverence (reverenter tractentur). This reverence most certainly postulates that the sacred furnishings, at least those which have such

---

[8] Canon 1296, 1.

consecration or blessing, should be kept neat, clean, and in good repair."[9]

This leads to further consideration of good taste and artistic expression in church architecture and furnishings and in all the symbolism and appurtenances relating to the sacred liturgy. "Christian art," as the distinguished liturgist Stapper observes, "can be of great service to liturgy. The reason is that liturgy aims to present in as vivid a manner as possible, through the medium of symbolical expression, the most sublime ideas of Christianity, namely, the work of redemption and the efficacy of the sacraments in producing grace. When art recognizes the service it may render and seeks to contribute, in union with Christ, to the glorification of God and the sanctification of man, it becomes ecclesiastical or liturgical art."

"True liturgical art," he adds, "must always seek the manner of expression which is both in keeping with the times and in accord with the unchangeable ideas of Christian worship. The artist must point out the way to Christ and through Christ to God. In doing this, he must strive after an expression of his art which is clear and harmonious and intelligible to his contemporaries, and which gives evidence not only of religious feeling, but also of maturity of character and moderation."[10]

These observations are of particular importance to the priest who is planning a church or is responsible for the selection, installation, and care of sacred images and ornaments within the church. While it is always easiest and, in some ways, safest to copy pictures and statues of the great masters whose works have merited the approval of the centuries, the priest will do well to avail himself of the original talent of contemporary and local artists and craftsmen. The expression of a fresh, living comprehension of the faith in artistic form is itself an important contribution to divine worship.

In accordance with these principles, the pastor or church ad-

[9] Erwin L. Sadlowski, *The Sacred Furnishings of Churches* (Washington, D. C.: The Catholic University of America Press, 1951), pp. 27, 28.
[10] Richard Stapper, *Catholic Liturgics,* translated and adapted by David Baier Paterson, N. J.: St. Anthony Guild Press), pp. 43, 44.

ministrator should be careful and selective in accepting pictures or images for devotional use or display. Anything which might contribute to superstition must be strictly prohibited. But one must be on his guard also against cluttering up the church with statues and other representations which create an atmosphere of false sentimentality or give the impression of a museum rather than a place of prayer.

Good taste and prudence should, moreover, keep one on guard against the introduction of strange figures and novelties which contribute more to confusion and wonder than to devotion. Canon Law makes it clear that any unusual pictures or statues must be submitted for the special approval of the Ordinary, to determine whether they are in accord with the approved usage of the Church.[11]

Special expert care is required also in the repair of outstanding works of ecclesiastical art.[12] Clumsy restoring has sometimes ruined precious things which can never be replaced.

It may be pertinent also to call attention to the importance of securing adequate protection for church properties and furnishings and of providing ample coverage for their replacement in case of loss. "In church administration," Msgr. George D. Mulcahy observes, "the obligation to safeguard property held for the faithful and dedicated to the works of religion assumes a sacred character. While insurance as such is not mentioned in the general law of the Church, it is certainly one of the administrative duties of the pastor to see to it that the physical possessions of the Church are safeguarded from loss by fire and other fortuitous causes. Most synodal statutes require adequate insurance protection, and the premium paid for such protection is looked upon as an ordinary expense of parish administration. It may be said, then, that ordinarily some insurance protection is provided for every Catholic church property in the country.

"Conceding the foregoing point, I submit that deplorable conditions prevail with regard to the *adequacy* of insurance protection on Catholic church property and the *business methods* with which

---

[11] Canon 1279.
[12] Canon 1280.

it is obtained and written. Indeed, many of our pastoral administrators freely admit that they are ignorant of the very elements of
fire insurance. The sad result is that properties are, at times, in-
sured in excessive amounts which can never be collected in case of
loss, while, on the other hand, valuable properties which are monu-
ments to the sacrifices of generations of the faithful could be
destroyed in a few hours with no hope of obtaining, through adequate insurance, the financial means to replace them. The press
report, 'the building was partially covered by insurance,' is only
too often made of our Catholic church property. Wherever
such report appears, it is damning indictment of someone's
administratorship."[13]

All of these observations add up to the conception of the Catholic
church or chapel, not simply as a "meeting house" for the faithful,
but truly as the house of God. The living presence of Christ in the
Blessed Sacrament of the altar sets the tone and significance of
everything that adorns it and of every act that is performed within
it. Devotion to the sacred liturgy is not merely an attachment to
ceremonial, in the secular sense, but a reverent expression of faith
and the employment of all the faculties of man in the worship
of God. If creative talent, human treasure, and loving care are
expended upon the architecture, the adornment, and the upkeep
of the church, it is in the example of Christ who allowed the
precious ointment to be used for the washing of His sacred feet
and who rejoiced in the triumphant reception of the multitude
that "took branches of palm trees and went forth to meet him and
cried: Hosanna. Blessed is he that cometh in the name of the
Lord, the king of Israel."[14] The priest who makes his church, be
it simple or grand, a joy to behold, a place of reverence and prayer
to honor the Divine Presence, and who discharges his liturgical
functions with exactness and loving devotion is fulfilling one of the
most important duties of the active ministry.

---

[13] *Understanding Church Fire Insurance* (Washington, D. C. The Catholic
University of America Press, 1953), p. 1.
[14] Jn. 12:13.

"Because the Lord giveth wisdom: and out of his mouth cometh prudence and knowledge . . . Counsel shall keep thee, and prudence shall preserve thee" (Prov. 2:6, 11).

CHAPTER IX

THE PRIEST AND COUNSELING

I

ONE of the most difficult but most important tasks in the active ministry of the Catholic priest is the direction of souls through personal counseling. It is one thing to preach the Gospel from the pulpit and admonish the flock to a life of virtue. It is quite another to face the individual, to deal with his personal problems, and to give such practical advice as will bring order into his thinking and guidance to his life.

The Catholic counselor who simply depends upon his so-called "common sense" in the solution of human problems will sooner or later find himself in difficulty. Convenience and compromise with Christian morality are almost invariably the result of dependence upon natural reason alone. The seminary courses in philosophy and in both dogmatic and moral theology are calculated to provide the priest with the basic principles of judgment and action that conform to the teachings of Christ. To keep thinking with the mind of the Church, every priest engaged in counseling others and in directing their spiritual progress should regularly review his moral as well as ascetic theology. He should also keep abreast of current moral problems and orthodox thinking on these matters, by contact with the contemporary Catholic periodicals and other publications for priests.

To be truly effective and satisfying in this work, however, the priest must understand human nature intimately and be able to bring Christian principles into the definite focus of everyday living. The false assumption that one can solve all problems on the spur of the moment with the turn of a syllogism simply blinds the counselor to reality. A cold, theoretical, textbook knowledge may impress others with one's profound knowledge; but, by itself, it may serve also to fill them with fear and create a psychological barrier in the interview. The human personality is a complex thing and does not yield to oversimplification. Emotion as well as reason enters into the problems and outlooks of most people. Frequently, there are experiences, suppositions, and considerations that lie beneath the surface of consciousness which must be brought out into the open before real problems can be recognized and dealt with. One of the saddest things that can be said of a priestly counselor is that "Father is a very learned man: but I am sure that he doesn't know what I am talking about."

Some men are undoubtedly more intuitive than others and better prepared by native shrewdness and temperament, or by tact, to read the human mind and to interpret motives and patterns of action. Experience itself is a great teacher; and the maturing process of the individual priest is perhaps his richest source of preparation and wisdom. Understanding human nature is a long process and beyond the scope of this book. The idea that one must personally go through all kinds of experience to be able to counsel others, however, is quite false. This argument is sometimes used against marriage counseling by the clergy, who are celibate. It could be used with similar lack of validity against counseling in practically every other field and by practically every other learned profession, including lawyers, doctors, and social workers. The qualified counselor acquires knowledge by systematic study under competent teachers, by discussion, and by observation of himself and others, not by hit-or-miss methods, much less by a Dr. Jekyll and Mr. Hyde career.

To a sound knowledge of Christian principles and a realistic understanding of human nature must be added a third ingredient.

The priest-counselor must develop within himself those traits of human kindness that attract souls who are timid and confused, to inspire them with courage to unburden their difficulties and seek a solution for their problems. One's success in guiding others is largely dependent upon the mental and emotional attitudes of those who come for counsel and upon their personal regard for the counselor. In large part, it is his business to create a favorable, friendly, and relaxed atmosphere, in which people will be willing to talk out their problems, freely and frankly, and to accept indications and suggestions in a ready and willing spirit.

A spirit of annoyance or irritation can easily nullify whatever good there may be in one's advice or direction and render counseling ineffective. People will not even approach the priest who has a reputation for rebuking and censuring those who come to him for counsel. It should always be kept in mind that the more delicate the problem, the more difficult it is for most persons to reveal their secrets. What they need at such times is assistance, kindness, and an understanding spirit, not highhanded censure, contempt, or further embarrassment and humiliation. The counselor who is inclined to take unfair advantage of this situation and unleash his virtuous indignation upon those who seek his guidance should ever keep before himself the burning words of Christ to those who were about to stone the woman taken in adultery: "He that is without sin among you, let him first cast a stone at her."[1]

A fourth basic qualification for the successful counselor is a professional confidence in himself and ability to command the confidence of those who come to him for guidance. A diffident attitude or a feeling of inferiority and indecision becomes readily apparent to all concerned and is fatal to the purposes of the interview. This does not mean that the counselor should assume an attitude of superiority or overwhelm his clients or penitents with a display of knowledge and a flow of eloquence. On the contrary. But he should make it clear, by his general attitude and procedure, that the business at hand is serious and that his time is being engaged for the specific purpose of counseling, not for just a social call. The

---

[1] Jn. 8:7.

counselor who forgets his professional role and allows the interview to develop into an argument or water down to a pleasant social conversation is headed for trouble.

People will not communicate their intimate problems to a priest even in confession, or follow his directives as a counselor, unless they regard him as mature, qualified, and trustworthy. The confessional gives the assurance of absolute secrecy; but even counseling outside the confessional carries the responsibility of maintaining professional and sacred confidence. A spirit of levity on the part of the counselor or even a suspicion, on the part of the client, that the matter of the interview will become a matter of common knowledge, or possibly a source of comment and ridicule, is sufficient to end one's value to the person seeking advice or spiritual direction. The fact that a priest has a charming personality or that people seek his company on a social basis has nothing to do with their regard for him in matters of the soul or of deep personal anxiety. These factors may well be in his favor, but they must be combined with a recognized seriousness of purpose, reliable judgment, and consistency of priestly character, if they are to serve him as a counselor and spiritual guide.

2

The methods and procedures used in counseling vary considerably, depending upon the nature of the interview or hearing, the subject matter or problem, and the character of the individual involved. Thus, counseling in the confessional differs both in scope and freedom from the type of counseling that the priest may give in his office or parlor. With respect to the subject matter, it is obvious that moral problems have to be handled differently from problems of faith. Some anxieties arise from a simple situation which can be analyzed and dismissed in a single interview; others are more complex and may require repeated visits and an extended period of readjustment. Likewise, effective treatment may differ radically for persons of different age groups, mentality, sex, and temperament. Much will depend also upon how deep-seated the problem is.

The wise counselor will take all of these elements into consideration when he is counseling any particular case. Indeed, he will do well to size up the situation before he undertakes the responsibility of guidance or treatment, as the case may be. The first step in this procedure is to allow and encourage the consultant to speak freely and frankly and to open up the problem as fully as possible. Tears and tirades may have to be endured as part of the recital. This calls for an unhurried spirit and much patience on the part of the counselor; but it is only in this way that the real story comes out and the character of the person as well as the essence of the problem is revealed.

Many problems are solved simply in the process of relating them. In all cases, however, the individual should understand that the consideration of the difficulty, whatever it may be, and any positive advice that may be solicited, depends in the first place upon his own desire to be helped and his own willingness to tell the truth as it bears on the question. Insistent probing or premature interruptions by the counselor may cause a timid consultant to withdraw into himself, or a scrupulous one to become more confused. In some cases, shame or self-interest may induce the person to withhold vital information or to shade the story so as to give a partial and distorted conception of the facts. If, through tactless handling of a case, the consultant is frightened into silence or prompted to falsify the presentation of pertinent factors, the interview may end in failure and simply accentuate the anxieties and resentments of the consultant.

This is particularly true in the confessional. Especially in matters dealing with sex and with persons who are scrupulous, the penitent must be treated with the utmost consideration. The confessor should be extremely cautious and reticent about pushing the penitent into any description of physical acts dealing with sex. All that should be required is a statement that will reveal the distinctive nature of the act. If the penitent appears to be ignorant of the true nature of the act or confused on the problem, he may be asked whether he desires any clarification or elemental explanation that will help him. Explanations in the confessional should be strictly limited to essentials, with a word of advice and encouragement. A person who is badly confused or intensely scrupulous may be advised to seek consultation outside the confessional to reach the root of the difficulty. Anything like cross examination or extensive preaching in the confessional is subject to misunderstanding and resentment and may give rise to needless disturbance of conscience and mental peace.

In parlor or office counseling, where the consultant is looking for information or advice rather than pardon, as in the confessional, there is much more latitude of approach to a personal problem. Here, consideration of personality and temperament comes into view and may have a significant bearing both upon the nature of the problems and the solutions proposed. Problems of emotional disturbance may reveal a nervous or mental condition that lies at the base of the difficulty and that requires much more than routine counseling for correction.

If the consultant turns out to be simply a crank or troublemaker, the counselor should make it clear that he has no time to waste. In nearly every community there are persons of this type, for whom very little can be done except to discourage their visitations. Unless counseling serves a constructive purpose, in which personal problems are considered seriously and positive advice is solicited, it may degenerate into a sounding board for gossip and a source of annoyance to all concerned.

Whether one conference or several interviews are indicated will depend largely on the problem itself. A person who has become badly confused on matters of faith, for example, may require a series of instructions. Likewise for persons who have developed an erroneous conscience or bad case of scruples, repeated explanations and patient guidance over a period of time may be necessary. Counseling in marriage problems or premarital guidance often indicates the advisability of several sessions, possibly with both the husband or wife, or prospective partner. Family problems and problems involving broken homes and juvenile delinquency cannot be solved with any degree of satisfaction unless sufficient time is allowed in which to analyze the situation, to study the individuals concerned, and to lay the groundwork for such reforms and changes as may be necessary.

Two types of techniques are employed by professional counselors, the one known as *directive,* the other as *nondirective.* In the first, the counselor acts on the assumption that his own resources are superior to those of the consultant, who is in need of positive information, advice, or direction. In the nondirective method, the assumption is that the consultant is quite able to solve his own problem and needs only to be activated and encouraged to do so.

In both types of counseling, certain steps or procedures are indicated, although these may overlap to some extent. The difference in procedure appears in the factor of positive solution, namely, whether this will be offered by the counselor or be arrived at by the consultant after the problem has been examined. Whether these steps are combined in one interview or take place in separate, successive interviews depends on the nature of the problem and on various elements including the temperament, attitudes, and preparation of the consultant himself.

In the first step, the groundwork is laid by an introduction of the parties involved and a general outline of the basic or the apparent character of the problem. In all cases, it is important for the counselor to maneuver this interview so that the consultant understands he is acting on his own volition and is not a "captive audience," so to speak. If he has come reluctantly or under pressure from others, or as a referral case, he must be shown that the success of the interview or interviews will depend in large part, if not exclusively, upon his own desire to solicit help and get his problem solved. In nondirective counseling, it is essential that the counselor make it clear from the beginning that the responsibility for the solution of problems rest upon the consultant.

In the second step, the counselor proceeds to bring out all pertinent information about the consultant, by encouraging him to reveal his own character, circumstances, and reactions. If the problem is entwined with emotional elements, such as fear, confusion, discouragement, envy, hatred, or love, these should be allowed to come out, beginning with negative feelings and pro

ceeding toward the positive, even with the rehearsal of specific in-
cidents and experiences. In directive counseling, the counselor
suggests possible solutions or diagnosis as the case proceeds; in
nondirective counseling, the emphasis is upon self-revelation and
a more objective view on the part of the consultant.

In the third step, a more definite endeavor is made to view
the over-all problem or situation in a positive way. In directive
counseling, the counselor suggests preliminary solutions or diag-
noses as the case proceeds; in nondirective counseling, the emphasis is upon further self-revelation and the development of an
objective view by the consultant. In both procedures, however,
it is important that the consultant be induced to start working
himself on the evidence that he has adduced and prepare himself
to co-operate with the counselor in reaching the solution. The
method of suggestion by asking a question is often more effective
than making a positive statement or observation. The mere fact
of having to answer a question makes the consultant more aware
of his responsibility; and most people are more agreeable to solutions which they think they have worked out for themselves. In
this process of indirect suggestion and subtle insinuation, the
effectiveness of the counselor depends largely upon his own
knowledge of human nature, personality and behavior patterns,
and underlying motives.

In the fourth step, the solution, decision, or plan comes into
focus. By this time, the problem should be sufficiently outlined,
both in itself and in relation to the consultant's insight into
himself, so that a choice of alternatives — whether it be of action,
attitudes, interpretations, or principles — becomes more logical
and easy to make. If the consultant is now prepared to make a
wise choice for himself, so much the better. If he still needs encouragement or support, this is the time for the directive counselor
to assist by positive guidance and persuasion. In nondirective
counseling, the consultant begins to realize that the time has
come for him to face the facts squarely as he has presented them
and size up the situation for himself.

In the fifth step, the package is wrapped up, the solution is reached, the decision is made, and the case is concluded one way or the other. In all effective counseling, the consultant makes the plan or the choice his own. In the directive method, the counselor may have to be more positive in formulating the conclusion agreed upon; and in some cases, he may have to follow up by strengthening action or periodic checkup, to support the resolutions of the consultant. In the nondirective method, the consultant weighs the evidence he has produced and indicates what positive plans he has in mind. He has had an opportunity of talking over his problem with an intelligent counselor, who has helped him face a situation and analyze his problem; now it is up to him to act.

The important thing in counseling, whether directive or non-directive, is that the consultant be encouraged to use his own re-sources and understand that, in the last analysis, he is the one who must decide and act upon the decision. Unless he does this, the whole character of the interview or interviews is distorted. The consultant goes away resentful of what he regards as unacceptable demands or only half convinced of what has been agreed upon.

To achieve satisfactory results, it is obvious that ample time and opportunity must be given for a review of all pertinent phases of the problem. Hurried interviews, or even the impression of working under pressure, is often enough to nullify the purpose of the interview. Likewise, to arrive at a solution or to demand action prematurely is to assume that people act like machines. The fact is that they do not. The counseling procedure has not run its course or achieved its objective until the consultant and counselors are alike satisfied that they have brought the issue to maturity and there is nothing further to be done of a constructive nature except to decide and act. If the process breaks down, and repetition of any of the steps taken or even new approaches fail, one may have to withdraw from the case, refer it to others, or wait for a change of fundamental attitudes or situations.

3

A wide variety of problems may present themselves for con sideration and assistance of the priest counselor. Preparation for marriage, solution of marital problems and of family difficulties and sex questions, including those of deviation such as homosexuality, are frequently brought to his attention. Problems of alcoholism are familiar to every priest in parochial work. Vocational choices and adjustment to one's career or work are subjects of concern, particularly to adolescents and persons of temperamental instability. Various borderline mental disorders serve to complicate many personal problems, both real and imaginary, such as nervous tension or exhaustion, anxieties, obsessions, scruples, illusions, depressions, and criminal tendencies. Problems of finance, honesty, and professional ethics may come within the purview of the counselor. Difficulties of faith may complicate the picture and must be dealt with understandingly and sympathetically.

Early in the course of the interview, or as soon as the real nature of the problem becomes apparent, the counselor should decide whether he is competent to handle the case or whether he should refer the consultant to another. As a matter of fact, one of the most valuable services that a counselor can render is that of referral. In view of the wide range of subjects and problems that are brought to a priest for consideration and guidance, it is important that he possess a genuine appreciation of such service and a working knowledge of practical references. To leave consultants dangling in the air, so to speak, or to send them out with pious platitudes is unfair.

The prudent counselor should not hesitate to recognize and admit his own limitations in certain fields of counseling or attempt to give advice in matters beyond his competence. If the problem seems to arise from a physical condition or a nervous disorder, the priestly counselor should recommend consultation with a physician or medical specialist. If the difficulty indicates a mental derangement or maladjustment, tactful suggestion should be made for consultation with a psychiatrist; and under certain circumstances, it may be proper to advise the family of the individual so that they may take the needed action.[2]

---

[2] Cf. James H. VanderVeldt, O.F.M., and Robert P. Odenwald, M.D., *Psychiatry and Catholicism* (New York: McGraw-Hill Book Co., 1952), p. 211 sq.

The prudent counselor will make it a general rule not to accept responsibilities which are out of character with his legitimate role and which are likely to result in serious misunderstanding and embarrassment later on. In particular, the priest should be on his guard against giving advice in financial matters or in accepting funds for savings, investment, or distribution. Service of this kind should be referred to a bank or to a qualified investment agency. The counselor may wisely urge habits of saving and suggest budgetary procedures, but he will make a great mistake if he undertakes to become the depositary for his consultants. He may suggest the investment of funds in securities; but the minute he accepts funds for investment or even recommends a list of securities, he becomes responsible, in the mind of his consultant, for any losses that may be incurred. He may, under very special circumstances and with necessary safeguards, agree to assist in making restitution for someone; but when he agrees to act as the clearinghouse in the settlement of others' estates or in the distribution of allowances or the payment of debts, he immediately places himself in the middle of a potentially explosive situation and opens himself up to all kinds of criticism and trouble.

Precisely the same thing is true of attempting to give advice in legal matters. The ramifications of the law are many; and often an important decision may rest upon a technicality. The sensible procedure for the priest counselor to follow is to direct his consultants who have a legal problem to solicit the professional services and advice of a competent lawyer. In such matters as the drawing up of wills or even in the witnessing of wills, the priest should not allow himself to become involved in family disputes or legal contentions.

If the matter falls within his proper field and competence, however, he should be ready to work in all intellectual honesty with his consultant and give the best of his consideration and assistance. He must not dismiss the case with a solution that is based on the human race in general or marriages in general or scruples in general, but upon *this* individual person and *this* specific problem. Nor can he honestly treat a deep-rooted problem with an easy formula, such as administering the pledge to an alcoholic and telling him to go home and say his prayers.

4

It will be found, more often than not, that surface manifestations of a psychological character have deeper roots in the consciousness or subconsciousness of the consultant. It is the business of the counselor to assist in bringing these factors to the surface, where they may be examined as objectively as possible, assigned their proper value, and related to the solution of the case.

Thus in the counseling of children, it will often be found that erratic conduct serves as a kind of compensation for neglect or maltreatment, real or imaginary, at home or school or from playmates. The neglected child sometimes contrives bizarre and dramatic situations as an indirect way of gaining attention or of confusing and startling others into recognition. Phenomena as diverse as self-consciousness and delinquency may have their roots in the same home deficiencies. Consequently, the counselor must operate gently and patiently to bring out the sensitive truth; and at the appropriate time, he must insist that the parents and perhaps brothers and sisters join in the conference to understand the situation and to share in planning for the future.

Marriage counseling assumes a number of forms, depending upon whether it is in preparation for marriage or in examination of a problem within marriage. More and more, it is being recognized that simple doctrinal explanations of the sacrament of Matrimony or stern reminders of marital obligations are insufficient to cope with the complex personal problems of people in this generation. Solid preparation is necessary if marriage counseling is to prove genuinely helpful and effective. This is true particularly in more difficult cases where various kinds of neuroses or possibly physical maladjustments, in addition to confused or erroneous ideas, complicate the picture. The prudent priest-counselor will not rush in with ready advice or simplifications in such cases. He will himself take counsel and refer his consultants to qualified specialists.

He will also recognize the fact that deep-seated hostilities and alienated affections, which have developed over a period of time, cannot be healed in one easy lesson, but must be gently and profoundly studied by one of the two methods already outlined. The injured affections of persons who have been deeply in love are emotionally explosive; and the counselor must be on his guard against getting caught in the middle of a feud because of immature and naïve bungling. A tremendous amount of good can be done to remedy unhappy marital situations, providing the counselor is competent and knows what he is doing.

One of the most awkward and sensitive problems that may come to the attention of the priest-counselor is that of homosexuality, whether in or out of the confessional. In the case of children or youth who have stumbled into this situation and are not confirmed neurotic or psychopathic homosexuals, the priest can, with prudence and care, guide the individual back to self-discipline and normal living. Advanced and confirmed cases, particularly those combined with emotional instability, should definitely be referred to a psychiatrist. There are other considerations tied in with this problem which should make every counselor extremely cautious. Often, not only severe personality disorders but also secret social problems are involved, which only the most professional diagnostician and therapist can recognize and treat.[3]

Nearly every priest in pastoral work is confronted with cases of alcoholism in various stages which he is expected to assist. Within recent years, these have increased to an alarming extent, so that every counselor should be prepared to diagnose the problem and give positive guidance to the victims of this weakness or disease, as the case may be. While some individuals are biologically more prone than others to alcoholism, it will be found that the difficulty usually arises as a form of compensation for or escape from a personal problem. To unearth this problem and to assist the individual to adjust his attitudes and sense of values in a positive

---

[3] Cf. Alphonse H. Clemens, ed., *Marriage Education and Counselling* (Washington, D. C.: The Catholic University of America Press, 1951), p. 129; also *Psychiatry and Catholicism, cit.,* Chap. 22; and Agostino Gemelli, O.F.M., M.D., *Psychoanalysis Today* (New York: P. J. Kenedy and Sons, 1955), Chap. 3.

and mature spirit is precisely the task of the counselor. The administration of a pledge to an inebriate while he is still under the influence of liquor and filled with emotional remorse is generally a waste of time. A process of rehabilitation is necessary, gradual and sustained, with all the physical, social, and spiritual aids that a friendly, wise, and strong counselor can summon. The decision to reform, however, can be made only by the afflicted individual himself or herself.[4]

The existence of unfortunate early experiences and of distorted or heavily weighted mental patterns often underlies various types of morbidity which can be aided by counseling. One of the most frequent problems brought to the attention of the priestly counselor is that of scruples, which represent a curious combination of fear and indecision. The morbidly scrupulous person is obsessed by a sense of probable guilt, from which no amount of ratiocination or reassurance, remorse or contrition can deliver him. To render this more unbearable, the specter of divine justice constantly rises before the mind in the form of hell-fire. In other cases, the individual regards himself or herself as unworthy or unable to undertake various tasks and shrinks from the moral responsibility of failure or harm to others. Sometimes, the victim becomes the center of self-accusation for past deeds of carelessness, neglect, or omission, which conceivably might have caused loss, damage, scandal, or pain to others.

The source of many such problems may be found in a rigorous childhood training, in which sin assumed terrible proportions in every little act of mischief and the threat of hell became a dominant motive for virtue. With this kind of education, fear becomes the motive for action and the standard of moral valuation, even when reason struggles to free the mind from this slavery. In such cases, it becomes the task of the counselor to retrace the steps of moral training and to replace negative outlooks, fears, and spiritual anguish with motives of divine love, confidence, and abandonment to the goodness and understanding of the heavenly Father.

[4] Cf. John C. Ford, S.J., *Man Takes a Drink* (New York: P. J. Kenedy and Sons, 1955).

Mental patterns of many years' standing may be difficult to eradicate. The patient clings to old scars and wounds, almost terrified with the prospect of emerging into sunshine and health. The person who has associated God with a severe and overbearing parent from infancy will find it hard to conceive of Him as a merciful and loving Father. A person who has been taught religion in an atmosphere of repression and gloom will find it no easy task to make the adjustment to a positive and joyous view of faith. Nevertheless, to help the scrupulous person make these adjustments and discoveries and to inspire the spiritually sick back to health and happiness is the rewarding work of the priestly counselor. Perhaps a physical deficiency is involved, in which case consultation with a competent doctor ought to be indicated.

Similar problems may be confronted in persons who have become dejected through bereavement and grief, business reverses, poor health, disappointment, or discouragement. The counselor can notably assist in restoring mental health by proposing a more positive view of life, with stress upon the providence of God, the example of Christ, and the demands of personal responsibility. In nearly all such cases, the *nondirective* method of counseling is indicated. In other words, the consultant must rehabilitate himself and apply the discipline of his own will to what he necessarily recognizes as rational procedure and behavior.[5]

The experienced counselor will become familiar with the element of self-pity in many cases of morbidity and will recognize the fact that underlying much apparent helplessness there is a secret stubbornness and desire to nourish and even enjoy the mental illness. The cure or the solution of the problem, therefore, often comes with the revelation and recognition of shame, self-deceit, self-pampering, or cowardice, as the case may be. Strange as it may seem, the development of self-confidence and renewal of courage comes with the breaking of pride and the adoption of humility as a basic attitude. As a matter of fact, humility is the essential ingredient for all self-revelation. The counselor is com-

[5] Cf. Alfred Wilson, C.P., *Pardon and Peace* (New York: Sheed and Ward, 1954), p. 134.

paratively helpless unless or until he has secured this attitude in his consultant.

5

It must not be supposed, however, that all the work of the counselor is consumed in the diagnosis of cases that call for correction, reform, or straightening out. Much counseling is simply in the nature of advice or discussion which will assist the consultant to come to a decision regarding some future problem or course of action. The question may be the selection of a school for a boy or girl, or the choice of a career. It may involve advice relative to a religious vocation. Advice may be solicited on the continuance or breaking of a courtship. It may deal with an offer of employment or a change of position.

Sometimes the counselor's advice is asked in handling the problems of third persons. Parent-children relations, brother-and-sister disputes, husband-and-wife problems, employer-employee situations, and various social adjustments are brought in for discussion and advice.

In all of these cases, the counselor performs his best role as a good listener. The consultant should be encouraged to speak freely of what he or she has in mind, and to weigh the "pros" and "cons" of alternate courses of action. The counselor should fill in to assist the consultant to formulate direct questions which should be answered or to suggest considerations which may have been misunderstood or overlooked. Positive information or direction should be offered only when the consultant is ready to receive it, and then in a way which places the responsibility for the decision or conclusion upon the consultant.

Of course, one cannot predict or control what an individual consultant may do or report as a result of a counseling experience. Some people unburden themselves, with the false idea that the rehearsal of their point of view constitutes its justification and commands the agreement of the person who is patient enough to hear it. To the fullest extent possible, the counselor should make it clear that listening to a story or hearing a complaint or receiving a request does not mean that one agrees or assents to it. On the other hand, the mere suggestion of a course of action is enough to persuade some that they have been "pressured" or "badgered" into a decision, particularly if they later regret it. For this reason, the counselor should always be positive and insistent upon the point that although he endeavors to assist, guide, and inspire toward a better understanding and right solution of a problem, the free choice and responsibility for action remains with the consultant.

Having achieved reasonable satisfaction in the solution of a problem, the counselor should maintain his professional role and make it clear that the consultant must now stand on his own feet. One must guard anything like a permanent dependency or that kind of personal attachment which makes the counselor a life partner in the ailments or difficulties of his consultants. If the case warrants the return of a particular consultant from time to time, to report on his state or progress or secure additional assistance, this may be encouraged and required. But frequent and uninvited reappearances, particularly on an informal basis, give rise to the suspicion that an undesirable change in relationships is taking place. A kindly but firm indication should be made to avoid misunderstanding and disappointment.

The effectiveness of a counselor depends in part upon his knowledge, his experience, and his technique. Competence begets confidence. But it depends also upon his ability to take an objective view of the consultants' problems and to induce them to do the same. The unique position of the priest as counselor arises, of course, from his character as a spiritual father. When he loses sight of this factor and allows himself and his views to become personally involved with his consultants, his value as a counselor has ended and he opens himself up to problems which he may live to regret.

These observations are pertinent also in the priest's ministry as spiritual director of souls who are striving for a life of perfection, not only of those who are endeavoring to solve a personal problem or overcome a particular vice. St. Francis de Sales notes that a good director "must be full of charity, of knowledge, and of prudence; if one of these three qualities be wanting in him, there is danger."[6] Commenting on these qualifications, Garrigou-Lagrange writes: "Knowledge is required of the spiritual life and of the means which lead to union with God: prudence is essential for the practical application of principles to the individual being directed: fervent charity is required so that the director inclines his will towards God and not towards himself, leading souls to God and not to himself. This spirit of sincere and fervent charity is opposed to sentimentality which is merely a pretence of love existing in the emotions and hardly at all in the will."[7]

Especially for the direction of religious, the spiritual guide ought to acquaint himself with the traditional teaching of the great ascetical writers and masters of the spiritual life. Occasional review of the *Spiritual Exercises* of St. Ignatius, for example, is a powerful stimulant to clear thinking and right order in spiritual progress. While leading delicate souls toward greater purity of motive and the practice of contemplative prayer, the priestly counselor will carefully avoid the tolerance or development of scruples and of emotionalism. False premises or the encouragement of anything bordering on obsession or hysteria can lead one away from God more quickly than many people realize. "I should prefer spirituality to be unaccompanied by prayer," writes St. Teresa, "than not to be founded upon the truth. . . . From foolish devotions may God deliver us."[8]

The spiritual director must always keep in mind also that he is dealing with human beings, even when they are in the garb of consecrated religious. They have their passions, their sentiments, their mental troubles, and their problems of adjustment, which may be rooted in physical ailments and glandular hypertrophy, as well as in sheerly spiritual crises. The type of personal relationship established by the priestly counselor, his recognition of symptoms,

---

[6] *Introduction to the Devout Life* (London: Burns, Oates and Washbourne), Part I, c. 4.

[7] *Op. cit.*, p. 169.

[8] *The Complete Works of St. Teresa*, trans. of Allison Peers (New York: Sheed and Ward, 1946), Vol. 1 (Autobiography), p. 80.

and his ability in the discernment of spirits — whether of God, of the devil, or of human nature — are of the utmost importance in spiritual counseling. Whether he meets and solves the anxieties of his spiritual children, within the confessional or outside, or leaves them floundering and worse confused, will depend upon his acumen and preparation. Spiritual progress is impossible unless founded in sanity and a realistic conception of human nature. Ardent souls can be led to great heights of perfection and productive activity, or they can be misdirected into states of frustration, disgust, and even mental breakdown.

"With regard to the mentally ill," the authors of *Psychiatry and Catholicism* observe, "one must keep in mind two facts: the first is that many mentally disturbed persons are first observed by the priest; hence he is responsible for doing something about them. The second, and more important, fact is that the problem of the mentally disturbed very often concerns a moral or religious outlook on life. For these reasons, priests should have some knowledge of mental disorders, their diagnosis, and their therapy."[9] One may add that this knowledge is important, not only for the correct treatment or referral of the sick, but also for the timely curbing of dangerous tendencies, and further for the positive and upward direction of souls whose aspirations and graces may lead them to the highest spheres of supernatural faith, hope, and charity.

The ability of the priest to inspire others to grow in sanctity is undoubtedly the product of God's grace shining through his own life of virtue, of Christian love, and sacrifice. His own spirit of prayer and his own spiritual vision set the standard and pattern of those who recognize in him "another Christ." If to this he adds the technical knowledge and experience of counseling, he becomes truly a mature and competent master of the spiritual life, with power akin to that of the Apostles who were sent by Christ "to cure sickness and cast out devils," and to bring blessed happiness and direction to the souls committed to his care.[10]

---

[9] Vander Veldt and Odenwald, *op. cit.*, p. 210.
[10] Mk. 3:14–15.

"Feed my lambs . . . Feed my sheep"
(Jn. 21:15–17).

CHAPTER X

THE PRIEST AND THE PARISH

I

ONE of the most important realizations of the priest in the active ministry is the fact that his is a social mission and that he must deal with people in an actual social setting. While the seminary training in preparation for the priesthood develops a sense of spiritual principle and the corresponding habits of life, at the same time as it imparts the knowledge of Catholic dogma and morality, it remains incomplete unless it arouses a social consciousness and a desire to know the field of activity to which the levite will be called. In other words, every priest entrusted with the pastoral care of souls ought to know the social complexion of the diocese in which he will work and the nature of the parochial problems which he will have to face.

Within recent years, sociological surveys have been made of the Church, on national, regional, diocesan, and parish levels. Although these have been conducted within certain limitations and must be constantly expanded and revised to meet current situations, they have produced at least one beneficial effect, namely, that of enlarging the view of the clergy upon the extent of their task and of assisting in the organization of diocesan and parochial effort.

One of the great advantages of the Church in the United States is that it has, practically from the beginning of the republic, functioned along parochial lines. There has been a constant effort to define parochial boundaries and jurisdictions, even where there has been some overlapping as in the case of national or racial parishes. As a result, the priests have been in reasonably close touch with their people and have been able to define and deal with the specific problems of the souls, the neighborhoods, and the areas entrusted to their care.

Nevertheless, much remains to be done in the shaping of attitudes and in the development of information which will enable the individual priest to cope with the problems of his parochial assignment, to work harmoniously with his confreres in the diocese and to maintain a zealous and apostolic concept of his mission. Despite initial spiritual ideals, it is easy to fall into the attitude of classifying parishes simply as desirable or undesirable. For a fruitful ministry, as well as a satisfied and happy existence, the priest must face all parochial work, no matter where it may be, as a challenge to his vocation. Whether the parish be rural, urban, suburban, rich, middle class, or poor, it represents a field of extremely interesting and important activity for Christ.

The place to start in the development of this outlook on the ministry may well be in a sociological survey of the archdiocese or diocese itself. As priestly vocations appear in this country, the seminarian comes from a particular parish or neighborhood, if in a large city, or from a rural community or area, usually without more than a superficial understanding of the social structure and problems of the other areas or of the over-all diocese in which he will be called to work. For effective and co-ordinated activity, it is important for the priest to recognize the existence of rural areas even though the metropolitan see may be a large city. He must be aware of industrial concentrations, and recognize their special problems of labor organization, housing, immigration, language and assimilation. If racial problems exist, he ought to be acquainted with their origin, character, and directions. He should have some conception of population movements and trends, and the changes taking place in urban, downtown, suburban, and rural parishes. In a word, he ought to be able to make a plat of the entire diocese is well as of his own parish, and look at it analytically and strategically as in a planned campaign for Christ.

The place to begin this study is in the seminary. It is encouraging to note that more and more seminaries are incorporating sociological studies and surveys into their curricula. But it is essential that this interest remain throughout the active ministry of the priest as a directing and dynamic impulse to a larger and better understanding of the pastoral mission.

2

The primary purpose of the parish is to establish a spiritual community for the worship of God and the promotion of faith and morals in accordance with the teaching and under the authority of the Catholic Church. There are many secondary objectives of the parish which contribute to this primary purpose, and there are many other valuable purposes that a parish can serve. In weighing the many demands upon his time and attention, however, the parish priest will keep this primary norm and standard always in mind. If he finds that what he is doing or giving his major energies to is at variance with this objective or is simply a kind of pastime, his immediate obligation is to rechart his course.

When we speak of the parish as a spiritual community, we do not, of course, signify a religious order or community bound by a common rule and the vows of poverty, chastity, and obedience. Rather, we stress the fact that, in distinction to the civic or temporal community, this group of persons is held together for a spiritual purpose, the salvation of their souls. They are bound together, not for the purpose of building roads or administering public justice, or organizing business, industry, or recreation, but of hearing the word of God, saying their prayers, receiving the sacraments, and leading lives in accordance with the laws of God and the injunctions of Christ.

It is important to recognize, however, that the members of the spiritual community are the same persons as those who comprise the civic and temporal order. They are men and women, youth and children; the good and the bad; the friendly, the lukewarm, and the hostile; the stupid, the instructed, and the ignorant; the rich, the poor, beggarman, thief; the butcher, the baker, and the candlestick maker. They are all constituents, real or potential, of the Church. They are the parish.

It is with this human material, with all their virtues and vices, that the pastor and the parish priest must deal. To the extent that he regards himself as their shepherd, like Christ, and loves them and cares for them as his sheep, he will be successful. In the same measure as he welds together this community in the spirit of Christian charity and develops the love of God among his parishioners, he will be a good pastor. The priest who tends to be a recluse, who is afraid of meeting and mingling with people, who feels himself superior to the rest of men, or is annoyed with the prospect of having to deal with them, is headed for trouble in parish life.

It is not always easy to keep before oneself the primacy of the spiritual purpose of the parish. The numerous demands upon a priest's time for many apparently petty considerations, the business of keeping the parish financially solvent, and the attention to many aspects of parish life and organization of a material or social nature may cause the priest sometimes to wonder whether priestly ordination was necessary to do the kind of work he is called upon to do. Nevertheless, he must grapple with the problem of selection so as to place first things first. He must organize his time, so that his spiritual mission never becomes buried or obscured by commercial considerations or by a series of functions and motions which any club or secular agency might perform.

Some of the spiritual work of the parish priest is already cut out for him. His daily Mass, the Sunday sermon, confessions, and sick calls form the core of spiritual ministration in the average parish. Religious instruction of the youth, whether in the parochial school or in Sunday school, is an important part of his work. The presentation of special devotional exercises and the organization of pious unions, sodalities, and Holy Name Societies will involve special attention. Baptisms, marriages, and funerals are part of the parish service. Counseling those who call at the rectory for one cause or the other may consume considerable time, not only during the day, but also during the evening hours. All of these spiritual activities, which are centered principally around the church, and the priest's house, the school, and the parish hall or center, are of the essence of activating the Catholic spiritual community.

3

It is not enough for the priest to wait for the parishioners to come to him. The parochial clergy can never direct the parish from a swivel chair. It is important, indeed essential, for the pastor and his assistants to get out of the rectory and to learn the character of the parish and the spiritual problems of their people by a program of systematic visitations. To a limited extent, this can be done by personally visiting and inspecting different parts of the parish territory, by "spot" checks here and there, and by occasional social calls. But for a serious, comprehensive, and satisfactory understanding of the parish and one's parishioners, nothing can take the place of a census.

Censuses differ according to their purpose and the manner in which they are taken up. The so-called statistical census is satisfied with numbers, names, and addresses. The research census concentrates on specific kinds of information which can be tallied to present the picture of any given social problem or situation. Both types are useful for their purpose; and the latter can be expanded or modified indefinitely, with valuable results. But we are concerned here with a third kind, which may be designated exactly as the parish census.

"A parish census, in the strict sense," according to Rev. George A. Kelly, "means an official enumeration of all the Catholics residing in a parish, made by a priest or competent religious with a view to determining the moral and religious condition of the parish and with the intention of correcting existing moral evils."[1] In view of the spiritual conception of the parish, the various parts of

---

[1] Cf. *The Sociology of the Parish*, ed. C. J. Nuesse and Thomas J. Harte, SS.R. (Milwaukee: The Bruce Publishing Co., 1951), p. 236.

this description are worthy of comment. The object of the census is to secure a complete listing of all parishioners. This can be obtained with the aid of a religious community, such as the Parish Visitors and the Mission Helpers of the Sacred Heart, which specialize in this work. It may enlist the assistance, particularly in the preliminay stages, of the laity, through organizations like the St. Vincent de Paul Society and the Legion of Mary. The fact that the pastor has ordered the census to be taken makes it an official undertaking; and this is necessary to secure co-operation and authenticity. But ultimately, it is the priest himself who has the obligation of personal contact and acquaintance with his parishioners.

That the parish census is a matter of obligation, not simply a work of supererogation, is evident from the directive of the Holy See communicated to the American Hierarchy by the Apostolic Delegate:

To make the pastoral ministry by this means (the parish census) even more fruitful, the Sacred Congregation of the Council has instructed me to remind the Bishops of this country of their obligation to have parish priests keep an accurate and current census of the faithful entrusted to their care.[2]

Parish priests should be charged to take up a census in every parish and mission, no matter what the difficulties or the outlook.

The seriousness and success of the parish census will be measured in large part by the purpose for which it is taken. A census which is designed simply or principally to compile names and addresses for the envelope collection system can hardly be called a parish census. Inasmuch as there are easier ways of gathering such lists, the alleged census soon bogs down, and the census taker, after a few sporadic excursions into the parish, resorts to the simpler expedient of revising lists within the rectory from previous records or parish organizations. If the census fulfills its true objective of determining the moral and religious condition

[2] Most Reverend Amleto G. Cicognani, letter of the Apostolic Delegate to the Bishops of the United States, in T. Lincoln Bouscaren, S.J., *The Canon Law Digest* (Milwaukee: The Bruce Publishing Co., 1943), II, p. 147.

[3] *Ibid.*, p. 149.

of the parish, nothing short of personal investigation and "on-the-spot" inquiry will reveal the actual facts. If, as a result of the census, the parish priest is to undertake the correction of existing moral evils, he must know in detail just what these evils are.

There can be no doubt that the parish census, whether for an urban or a rural area, is no easy task. But its difficulty and disagreeable features are an indication of its necessity and value. For one thing, rapid growth of population has the tendency of removing Catholics from their priests and the Church. While definitive figures are not available to make any sweeping generalizations, it is clear that an increasing number of Catholics are in various degrees of separation or laxness so far as church attendance and reception of the sacraments is concerned. Even in areas with a dense Catholic population, the parish census is almost certain to dispel complacency on this point. Many nominal Catholics do not know their pastor or, for that matter, any priest. When to this lack of personal contact are added invalid marriages and poor instruction, it is easy to understand the development of lukewarmness and even hostility to the Church. These people must be contacted and known to be helped and to be restored to a feeling that they belong to their Church.

The procedure of the census is comparatively simple, but it requires considerable preparation, much patience, and persistence. The census should be announced in advance from the pulpit and the parish bulletin, as well as through the parochial organizations, and even through the local newspapers, where this is feasible. At the same time its purpose should be explained positively, so as to create a reasonable and favorable impression. A map of the parish should be drawn up and followed systematically, with a division of the labor if more than one priest or other census takers will conduct the census. Whether the census is to include non-Catholics as well as Catholics is for the pastor to decide. Special local conditions will give the answer; but it should be kept in mind that the first field of inquiry is the Catholic population, be they active or lapsed.

To get systematic results and establish a record, upon which subsequent action can be taken, a card form should be devised, preferably a 5 x 8 folding card suitable for filing. This may be designed as separate for every individual or as a family schedule, which will list the individuals involved. Both types have their advantages and disadvantages, but the family card results in a less bulky file and a more ready means of identification and comparative information. Samples of various cards are readily available from religious goods stores or priests who have been successful in this work.[4]

This card should list (1) names, addresses, and telephone numbers, (2) relationship to the head of the household, (3) personal description, age, color or race, and nationality, (4) education, including school, grade, and place of religious instruction for children, (5) religious affiliation, if in a mixed marriage, (6) economic status, including occupation, ownership or rental of home and its actual or estimated rental value, (7) observance of religious duties including the facts of Baptism, First Communion, Confirmation Easter duty, attendance at Sunday Mass, frequency of Communion, conversions in the family, and (8) description of marital status.

It is important to create a favorable impression if one is to secure good results. The purpose of the census should be explained in each case, and it should be made abundantly clear that the priest has come to learn and to help, not to pry needlessly or to rebuke The taker of the census can expect all kinds of reactions, some of them definitely unreceptive and antagonistic; but his reputation for kindliness and helpfulness will spread as he makes his rounds and will lighten his burden in the course of time.

It should also be made clear that the census is concerned with compiling essential information. Corrective action, if indicated must generally be deferred until later. This is particularly important, if the preliminary census is taken by a lay visitor or religious Moreover, it should be tactfully indicated that the visit is of an official character, not just a social call; and protracted visits with

---

4 Cf. *The Sociology of the Parish*, p. 245.

he acceptance of refreshments should be courteously avoided if
ossible.

Whether the census is to be taken all at once in a concentrated
ffort or spread throughout the year is for the pastor to decide.
Iowever, to retain its value, the census should be kept current.
A census once every five or ten years loses much of its value. In
changing population, vital records must be constantly revised.
Ioreover, an important function of the census is to keep the
riest in personal touch with his people — all of his people, not
ierely a few chosen friends. For this reason, it would seem that
ie census, once established, should be maintained on a perpetual
asis with a systematic program of visitations throughout the year.

As already noted, the purpose of the census is not completed
ith the assembling of factual data. With this information, the
al work has only begun. The census is a means toward an end,
amely, the correction of existing moral evils and the strengthen-
g of religious life in the community. Marriages will have to be
lidated, bad situations remedied, provisions made for religious
struction, the faith and the sacraments restored to lapsed Cath-
ics, and steps taken for revitalizing parish life. The value of the
nsus is not so much that it lists the parishioners but that it opens
the parish priest the realities of the social order and of the
iritual community in which he lives and makes it possible for
m to bring his ministry to the full flock of which he is the
epherd.

4

While the primary purpose of the parish is the organization of
vine worship and the infusion of Catholic moral principles and
iritual life into the community, it should not be assumed that
her objectives are of only incidental consideration. As human
ings in this life are not disembodied spirits, they must be dealt
th in the dimensions of the flesh and in the world of which
ey are a part. Faith is engendered and strengthened by instruc-
n. Good morals are developed and protected by the creation of
vorable environment and facilities for Christian social organiza-

tion and activity. The prestige and influence of the Church itself is reflected in the encouragement of initiative and leadership by the laity in all forms of legitimate human endeavor. And the Christian community itself benefits by the application of Christ's teachings to the realities of the economic, civic, and cultural order.

The general form these activities will take depends on a number of factors, such as the status of parochial development, racial and national considerations, economic and cultural levels, the percentage of Catholic and non-Catholic elements in the area, and its designation as an urban or rural parish. In all cases, the priest should be conversant with local conditions and direct a leadership for their betterment. Spiritual improvement is frequently dependent upon satisfactory material environment. The social message of Christ reaches into all departments of life. Justice and charity in practical fulfillment are as much a part of the active ministry as the encouragement of prayer and administration of the sacraments.

Basically, the priest works toward these objectives through the apostolate of teaching and instruction. Hence the great importance of a vital pulpit in which all the commandments are taught and their application is made pertinent to the real problems of today. This apostolate is further extended through the school, convert and instruction classes, study clubs, forums, and parochial libraries.

It is further exemplified in parish organizations with the specific objectives of developing spiritual life and of encouraging Catholic social living, particularly among the youth who ought to have facilities to meet one another. It may take the form of planned inquiry into economic and hygienic conditions and the organization of parochial agencies to assist the parishioners toward a better use of their natural resources. It should aim at the general improvement of their standards of living. All of these activities go hand in hand in the development of mission areas, so that the Church brings the benefits of a better life in this world as well as the hope of eternal salvation. The priest who preaches the kingdom of heaven and does nothing to combat crime, alcoholism filth, disease, delinquency, poverty, ignorance, and sloth in his parish is failing in essential and important aspects of his ministry.

In promoting the temporal welfare of his people as well as in providing material facilities for their benefit, the priest must, to repeat, keep in mind the primacy of the spiritual and the relationship of these things to the Christian personality and eternal salvation. This consideration will warn him, for example, against such mistakes as becoming involved in civil politics or political campaigns, even under the pretext of advancing justice. It will serve to steer him away from becoming involved or involving the parish funds in any kind of commercial enterprises, calculated to give employment to people or to raise money, even for the most pious of purposes.

The prudent priest must also recognize that there are limits to human time, energy, and resources. It is possible to spread one's energies too thin and to become engaged in so many varied activities that one's life becomes a series of mechanical motions and one lives in a state of constant exhaustion. Personal and parish activities should be studied both in themselves and in perspective with the general good. It is far better to concentrate on the essential matters and to develop a few important activities which reach into the heart of the community than to become distracted with numerous secondary demands.

Within these cautions and limitations, however, and always with the counsel of the Ordinary of the diocese, the zealous and resourceful priest will find it possible to do much in raising the living standards of the poor, in directing the potential of the prosperous toward the common good, and in encouraging the formation of a Catholic consciousness and leadership of benefit to the entire community. In the city parish, he will take an interest in the conditions of labor, work for the establishment of recreational centers for children and youth, and assist in raising the standards of home life. In rural parishes, he will familiarize himself with the Catholic, secular, and governmental agencies and techniques for improving farm production, soil conservation, marketing, and credit. He will devote his attention to the problems of good housing, good roads, and modern living. He will not be afraid to plead the cause of the unprivileged, the racial minorities or depressed groups, and to assist the immigrant and the displaced persons in their adjustment to new environment.

He will, moreover, encourage his parishioners to participate in civic affairs. Instead of letting them drift or take a passive or subordinate position, he will encourage them to join and aspire for a directing voice and leadership in school boards, adult education, local politics, the public library, lecture courses and cultural events, the newspapers, and general activities of public opinion and influence. Through his own teaching and example, he will assist others to combat bigotry and prejudice positively. This is Christian charity in action.

5

The question of parish boundaries and jurisdictions is comparatively simple, being determined by diocesan authority. This may be complicated, however, by national and racial problems and even occasionally by the fact of Oriental rites within the area In all these problems there is only one safe and sound basic rule namely, the norms established by Canon Law and administered under the direction of the bishop.

The overwhelming majority of parishes in the United States are territorial in nature, that is, they are determined by assigned physical lines of demarcation. The territorial parish may be composed predominantly of parishioners of a single national background, or it may include those of various origins and even of different races. Most parishes today include persons of man European backgrounds represented in the great melting pot of America — Irish, Germans, Polish, Italians, French, English, and numerous others. Urban parishes, particularly those in the near "downtown" areas, frequently have parishioners of various race including Negroes, Latin Americans of Indian and Negro admixtures, Chinese, and other Orientals. Unless these people have been specifically exempted from the jurisdiction of the territorial parish, for one reason or the other, it is not only the right of the pastor to require their conformity to parish regulations but also his duty to minister to them and to see that they are given all their rights as parishioners in the fulfillment of their duties.

In a parish which is composed of homogeneous national and racial elements, this is comparatively simple. If the parish is made up of national groups of recent European origin, linguistically, temperamentally, and economically diverse, the pastor may find himself confronting a situation which calls for the utmost tact and patience. He must learn to conquer prejudice and antipathy within himself and carefully avoid acts which give evidence of discrimination in favor of or against one group or the other. It should be part of his Catholic message, at the same time, to develop a spirit of Christian tolerance, understanding, and co-operation among the various national groups within his jurisdiction.

The problem of national origins is sometimes met with the establishment of juridical national parishes. There are a number of such, not only in the large cities but also in various rural areas. The rapid concentration of immigrants of the same origin and speaking a language other than English, requiring in many cases the importation of clergy of the same nationality, has made the juridical national parish a special organism, with its own particular rights and duties. It is distinguished from a territorial parish which happens to be composed of a predominant nationality. In fact, it may cut across a territorial parish and draw its parishioners from an entire city or area, even after its original national concentration has been dispersed.

Since 1918, the establishment and change of national parishes — Germans, Poles, French, Latin Americans, and any other groups — has been reserved to the Holy See. As these various groups become absorbed more and more into American life and lingual barriers disappear, the tendency is for the national juridical parish to diminish and disappear. In reality, it represents only one stage of society in transition. Attempts to enlarge upon such entities artificially, or even to prolong the distinction between national groups beyond the second or third generation, are bound to result in alienation and leakage from the Church.

While the priest in charge of a juridical national parish should follow conscientiously the prescriptions of Canon Law and the directives of the Ordinary in the conduct of his work, with full respect and devoted service to his people within these norms, he should also recognize the changing character of his flock and not put nationalism above their Catholic faith or attempt to identify the two. Excessive nationalism produces an insular and exotic condition, holds back parishioners from legitimate development, and has even been responsible for religious splintering and schisms.

Whether a national parish is territorial or juridical, the priests in charge have an obligation of providing a devoted and intelligent service. Priests assigned to Italian or Mexican parishes or neighborhoods, for example, should learn the languages of their parishioners and be prepared at least to hear confessions in the vernacular. They should make every effort to conserve the cultural values of European and local backgrounds and make people proud of their heritage, not ashamed of it or hesitant to admit their origins. The Catholic Church is universal, and one of its glories is that it is a loving mother to all nations.

Special problems arise when racial factors are involved. The comparatively few Chinese parishes are more or less national in character. Most Catholic Indians are included in missionary churches. A growing population of Latin Americans with Indian blood, such as Mexicans and Puerto Ricans must be provided for both in the large centers and as migrant farm workers. The largest and most rapidly expanding group, however, are the Negroes.

Negro Catholics may belong to a territorial parish of mixed character or in a predominantly Negro neighborhood. Or they may be assimilated into an exclusively Negro parish, which is actually if not *de jure*, the equivalent of a national parish. According to some canonists, the exclusively Negro parish is personal rather than national,[5] unless membership "is determined essentially in view of the racial characteristics of the parishioners, and only

---

[5] Clement Bastnagel, "Is a Parish for Colored People a National Parish" *The American Ecclesiastical Review*, CVIII (1943), p. 383.

modally by means of any territorial consideration."[6] This is a question which the priest may safely leave to the determination of the Ordinary.

The practical problems confronting the priest in a mixed Negro parish are largely of a social nature. In various ways, they differ from one section of the country to another and assume various modalities within given areas, cities, and neighborhoods. In a transitional society, composed of heterogeneous elements and evolving under the same basic guarantees, the prudent priest will avoid brusque statements and hasty action. Overzealous champions of racial equality may hurt the cause they wish to advance. The only sound position for the Catholic priest to take is that of Christian charity, recognizing the fundamental dignity and equality of all men in the sight of God and working patiently for human justice and harmony.

The way of progress in this field is through education, not argumentation which serves only to increase emotional tensions and prejudices. But education itself, through the principles of Christ, must be followed by positive action in accordance with the norms of the Church. If, for example, there are Catholic Negroes within a predominantly white parish, they have an obligation to send their children to the parochial school; and the pastor has the duty to admit them. Opposition on the part of some white parents is no reason why he should swerve from the path of duty. He will find that children are often far more understanding in this matter than their elders; and quiet determination to what is right will bring about a peaceful and truly Catholic solution of the problem. The trend today is definitely away from segregated racial parishes. The Catholic priest and Catholic people should take the leadership in facing reality and of living with it in a positive, Christian spirit.

6

In establishing the parish unit, it is certainly the mind of the Church that the faithful should regard it as the center for

[6] *Ibid.*, p. 384.

the fulfillment of their religious duties.[7] The parish church serves for the baptism of their children, the regular hearing of Mass, the reception of the sacraments, marriage, and burial. It is to the parish priest that they normally turn for spiritual guidance and consolation. In return, he is entitled to their loyalty, co-operation, and material support. The pastor is, moreover, endowed with certain jurisdictional rights, as laid down by Canon Law, in respect to marriage and other matters within the limitations of his parish.

This does not mean that the parish is to be regarded as a kind of walled city or enclosure. On the contrary, it is only one, correlated unity within the body of the diocese, as the diocese is one correlated unity within the body of the Church. It is possible for the priest in his concern for the preservation of pastoral and parochial rights, to develop a shortsighted and localized view of Catholicism with a high and mighty conception of his rights and privileges far beyond the facts. In this sense, "parochialism" has come to designate a narrow-minded and petty point of view which loses sight of larger values.

A parish priest may find it necessary, from time to time, to remind his parishioners of their duties toward the parish and to insist upon his essential prerogatives. But an unyielding attitude on all requests for exemptions and special considerations may result in ill will and gain him the reputation of a tyrant. There are occasions when parishioners may wish to be married by another priest who is a relative or close friend of the family. They may ask for another to baptize their children for sentimental reasons. They may ask for a special priest to officiate at a funeral service. On all occasions, the pastor may stand on his rights and refuse permission. But if he is wise and considerate, he will lean toward friendly and paternal compliance and rise in parochial esteem and affection.

Similarly in interparochial and extraparochial activities. The parish priest who is ready and eager to co-operate with his fellow

---

[7] Cf. Rev. John B. Fee, *Parishioners' Handbook* (Philadelphia: Jefferies and Manz, 1955).

priests in a community endeavor and to encourage his parishioners to co-operate with common causes is never the loser. It is possible to look with a jealous eye upon such endeavors as "taking money out of the parish," as distracting attention from parish life, and generally as evidences of disloyalty and disruption. The fact is that parish life breathes new vigor and vitality when it looks out to the world beyond itself. The pastor or the parish priest whose teaching and example stimulates this larger conception of Catholic life and action has truly grasped the significance of the parochial unit in the Church.

"That you also may have fellowship with us and our fellowship may be with the Father and with his Son Jesus Christ" (1 Jn. 1:3).

CHAPTER XI

THE PRIEST AND PARISH SOCIETIES

I

THE leadership of a priest may be exerted in numerous ways. The good teacher and preacher is a leader, as he points out the paths of truth and action to his listeners. The writer, similarly, leads by the influence of his pen. Personal example, through devotion and sincerity of effort, provides inspiration for those who come within its radius. But for consolidated influence and the enlargement of action, there is probably nothing to compare with a well-directed social organization.

There are many things that the priest can do by himself, and many things that only the priest can do. But good organization among the faithful can notably supplement and extend the work of the clergy and indeed intensify practically all activities of the apostolate. The pastor who tries to do everything by himself soon finds himself working in a vacuum. The priest who knows how to enlist the co-operation of others and who is willing to entrust responsibility to his co-workers, both clergy and the laity, will achieve results far beyond his personal dimensions.

Organization simply for the purpose of organization, of course, is a waste of time and can degenerate easily into mischief. Unless a Catholic society serves a definite purpose in conformity with the needs of the Church or of the parish, it has no reason for being or for consuming the energy of the priest. Specifically, all parish organizations should have as their great and final objective the sanctification of souls and the increase of public worship, whatever their intermediate purposes or activities may be. If this is kept in mind, they will flourish and strengthen Catholic life. If it is lost sight of, they will wither away or degenerate into abuse.

Parish societies may serve a variety of useful purposes. Their special character and organization will conform to their particular reason for being. Thus one group, such as a sodality or nocturnal adoration society, may be formed primarily for prayer and development of the spiritual life and personal sanctification. A familiar and appropriate type of parish organization is designed specifically for religious service, such as altar and rosary groups or ushers for Sunday Mass and other church functions, as well as the Holy Name Society and sodalities for spiritual development.

An important field with various ramifications for organized parochial activity is that of education. This may take the form of a parent-teachers association, with the object of promoting better understanding on the part of parents with the school problems of their children and better relations with the teachers and school authorities. It may appear in the organization of study club groups or in the promotion of forums for adult education in a better understanding of Catholic principles and current issues. Or it may concentrate on instruction in Christian doctrine and defense of the faith.

Some of the most worthy parochial societies are those which have as their special object a work of charity, such as the St. Vincent de Paul Society. Under this general heading may be included organizations for various activities of social welfare, such as providing day nurseries, aiding unfortunate and delinquent youth, as in the Big Brother and Big Sister groups, or staffing recreational and training centers in underprivileged areas.

Some societies devote themselves to the raising of funds for church or school, for welfare causes, or for the home and foreign missions. They may function through personal sacrifice and contributions or by appeal for aid through benefit socials and similar projects. Through the generosity of such groups, many a parish has been kept alive and many a worthy cause and worker for Christ has been sustained.

A number of parochial societies have been developed to improve the economic condition of the parishioners. Credit unions, co-operatives, insurance plans, and various agricultural organizations have thus been developed in communities, under parish direction, to raise the level of the people and help them through difficult times. In some places, union organization of labor has been fostered under Catholic auspices, and training for Christian leadership has been provided where otherwise Communistic and violent elements would be in control.

Some parochial societies are devised primarily for social purposes, to bring Catholic people together in friendly relationships and wholesome recreation. While it may be argued that it is not the priest's business to provide such facilities and activities for the people, there can be no doubt that opportunities for Catholic boys and girls to meet one another under favorable circumstances will do more to promote Catholic marriage and develop a Catholic community than all the sermons that one might preach against mixed marriages.

2

All of these objectives are good and in harmony with the work of the priest so as to justify his time, attention, and guidance. But, since no one has boundless time or energy at his disposal, it is advisable to consider parish societies in their order of need and importance. It is possible to spread oneself so thin over a wide range of activities that no one of them rises to any genuine significance or success.

In some cases, it will be found that the various organizations are simply a regrouping of the same people, in more or less closed circles, drawn together by various interests and deriving a sense of importance from the fact that they hold office or membership in several societies. In other cases, the societies calling for time and special attention are small groups that might well combine their efforts or ask themselves whether the particular benefits they seek are not already available. It may be pleasant, for example, for a small coterie of ladies to gather on Sunday afternoons for particular devotions and a special conference from their chaplain or moderator. But if this is all they have to contribute or offer to Catholic life, the busy priest ought to ask whether they cannot derive the same and greater benefits from the Sunday Mass and parish sermon. Needless multiplication and duplication of efforts result simply in a drain on one's energy and distraction from activities of prime importance.

In examining the status of parochial organizations or in contemplating reorganization or new societies, it may be well to take a perspective view of the situation. Catholic organizations may be not only parochial and local, but also regional, national, and international in scope and affiliation. Moreover, they may be classified as ecclesiastical or lay in character, depending upon their nature and authorization. It is important to keep these distinctions in mind for the proper functioning of the societies which one may establish or be called upon to direct.

An ecclesiastical society has been defined as a "free union of the faithful established or approved by ecclesiastical authority for the exercise of some work of piety or of charity not prescribed for all the faithful."[1] Ecclesiastical societies are divided into third orders secular and pious unions. The latter embrace sodalities and confraternities. If instituted by the Pope, ecclesiastical societies are designated as papal societies; if by a bishop, they are diocesan. Ecclesiastical societies in general are governed by Canon Law and enjoy a kind of corporate existence within the law with juridical protection and privileges defined by official norms.

Third orders, such as those of the Franciscans and Dominicans, may be founded only by authority of the proper authorities of the respective religious superiors so authorized. Papal societies are governed by special regulations administered by the arch-

---

[1] Thomas J. Clarke, *Parish Societies* (Washington, D. C.: The Catholic University of America Press, 1943), p. 3.

confraternity or union in Rome. It may be noted that the Code of Canon Law requires the establishment of two confraternities in each parish, under diocesan responsibility, namely, The Confraternity of Christian Doctrine and The Confraternity of the Blessed Sacrament.[2] In the case of diocesan societies, such as the Holy Name Society, the Sodality of Our Lady, and other diocesan unions, it is essential that the parish unit be established or approved by the Ordinary to carry the rating of an ecclesiastical society. For a Sodality of Our Lady to gain this privilege, it must be affiliated through the national office of the Sodality for aggregation to the Roman *Prima Primaria*. Otherwise, it is merely a pious union, not a Sodality of Our Lady in the official sense.

Lay societies may be established by either the clergy or the laity, but they are distinctive in that they are governed and directed primarily, not by ecclesiastical authority, but by the laity. If they have chaplains or priests as moderators, these hold office, not by ecclesiastical regulation, but by election or appointment of the members. Many parish societies belong to this category, even though they may have been formed under the direction of the pastor. Many other lay societies cross parish boundaries and are regional or national in scope either by organization or affiliation.

Familiar examples of parish lay societies are professional groups of lawyers or doctors, First Friday clubs, study clubs, young people's clubs, and dramatic groups. Among national lay societies may be cited the Knights of Columbus, Catholic Daughters of America, Ladies of Isabella, the Catholic Order of Foresters, the Catholic Central Verein, and various Catholic organizations of similar character. Many parochial and regional groups are affiliated with national federations such as the National Council of Catholic Men, the National Council of Catholic Women, and the Catholic Youth Council. These federations assist in forging parish and local participation in diocesan and national councils and bring together the benefits of wide experience and representation.

In selecting and setting up societies within the parish or in

---

[2] Canon 711.

co-operating with Catholic organizations on a broader basis, the priest may be governed by a number of considerations. For re-vitalizing the parish in its various aspects, providing necessary and useful services, and bringing the parish more closely into the general life of the Church, careful study should be given to the selection of those societies, whether ecclesiastical or lay, which most fit particular needs. Care should also be taken that the so-ciety is established in full conformity with the authority governing ecclesiastical societies and in accordance with such other pro-cedure as may be required to make the organization authentic and recognized.

3

In addition to serving a definite purpose, with an over-all spir-itual motive, Catholic societies must conform to sound adminis-trative principles if they are to succeed. A group of people, an assembly, or a following does not constitute a society or organiza-tion. Basic rules, constitution, and bylaws or the equivalent are necessary as a pattern for procedure and action. Offices must be established in accord with agreed principles, and the rights, duties, and responsibilities of officers must be fixed and respected. A society in which the officers are only nominal, while the pastor or priest does everything, from conducting the meetings to sweeping out the hall, is merely a space-filling device and a captive audience.

It is true that some of the more numerous and popular societies are of a "mass" type with a nominal membership and light enroll-ment requirements. In many even of the more selective organiza-tions, officers may be proposed by a nominating committee, and the priest in charge may have to exercise a certain control over the nominees and keep factional elements well in hand. But in all cases, the officers must respect their position and be permitted to exercise their true functions if the organization is to be vital and make a real contribution to Catholic life.

There is sometimes an inclination on the part of the priest, be-cause of his privileged position, to regard the faithful in too paternal a spirit. The result is that people, treated like children, fail to develop maturity and leadership, and persons of real competence are repulsed. If a group is worth organizing for a constructive purpose, its potentiality can be realized only to the extent that it operates in a mature, organized manner.

Sometimes the disinclination of the priest to grant real authority to parish societies and their officers springs from the fear that they will abuse their position and meddle in affairs that are beyond their competence. This can be avoided by clearly defining the purpose of the organization and strictly limiting its authority through definition of the constitution and bylaws. In other cases, there may be a reluctance to grant freedom of expression or action, lest unruly factional disturbances arise or individual troublemakers cause turmoil. This can be avoided by insistence upon correct parliamentary procedure at all business meetings and the creation of a formal, businesslike atmosphere which all will respect. Every priest who is a chaplain, moderator, or adviser to an organization should become competent in parliamentary procedure and insist that the chairman and officers be likewise prepared before they undertake to conduct and control meetings.

Difficulties may arise when the priest himself stimulates factional strife by acts of discrimination and favoritism or by affecting, unwittingly or otherwise, to favor first one side, then another. In all matters of policy, the thing to keep one's eye on is "the good of the order" and the purpose of the organization. Human elements, personality clashes, and outside interests and considerations should be kept to a minimum; and this can be done by the teaching and example of the priest himself. Petty bickering and backbiting should be strictly discouraged. The members should be reminded, from time to time, of the Christian principles of charity, justice, and service, and of the adage "in union there is strength."

Largely dependent upon the type of leadership exercised by the priest, the Catholic society will assist its members in their spiritual growth and personal maturity. His failure, weakness, or duplicity will succeed in pulverizing the group or reducing it to an un-Christian spectacle of recrimination and intrigue. The fact that people are Catholics or that they allege good intentions is no proof against the weakness of human nature.

The failure or inefficiency of many Catholic organizations can be traced to an altogether different cause, namely, a lack of active interest and support by the clergy. Whatever one may say about the responsibility of various groups for their own affairs, the fact is that Catholic people look to their priests for inspiration and guidance. Where this is lacking, discouragement, frustration, and resentment are the result.

Even a cursory interest is better than none. If one cannot be present for the entire meeting of an organization, one can at least drop in for a moment and say a word of encouragement and appreciation. Most parish societies feel that they are contributing time and effort for the benefit of the parish. Many of the members, particularly the officers, may make considerable sacrifices unselfishly for the cause. They need some evidence from the pastor or the priest in charge that their efforts are known and appreciated. Whether the society is cultural, charitable, devotional, or fraternal in character, it has a right to expect this.

Sometimes criticism is voiced of certain Catholic groups because their meetings are dull and a waste of time. If such is the case, the priest should ask himself what he is contributing by way of suggestion or assistance. Most Catholic organizations, like all similar groups, need guidance and at least an occasional sparking of effort. The chaplain who consistently misses the meetings of the groups for which he is responsible ought to examine his conscience and ask whether it is not part of his business to help in the formulation of a program of action. The pastor who allows his societies to drift might well question himself whether their indifference and mediocrity are not simply a reflection of his own inertia.

This is a matter to which the priest in the active ministry should give earnest consideration. It is indeed discouraging for the cause of Catholic Action, whether the event be a lecture, a play, a benefit, a social, a "mixer" for the youth of the parish, or planning for the community welfare, to find that the pastor and the priests of the parish are absent and possibly even contemptful of community effort.

One of the great benefits of parochial and Catholic organizations, whether ecclesiastical or lay, is that they provide an opportunity for the priest to meet the people on a human, personal basis. This kind of contact develops loyalty and provides a stimulus to action in both men and women. Even the bowling club and the sewing circle, which bring Catholics together, may be a source of strength for the parish. People who would otherwise never meet their pastor can do so in the friendly, relaxed atmosphere of a group; and probably more good is done in this way than we have any idea of.

The priest who is willing to work with his societies, to take them seriously, and inspire them by his example is truly serving the cause for which he was ordained; and, incidentally, he is combating by the most effective method the possible specter of anticlericalism.

4

A handicap which many parishes and Catholic societies face is the lack of a satisfactory meeting place. Fortunate indeed is the parish that has a center where the various groups can meet under favorable auspices and conduct their business or recreational activities. Every parish should aspire to possess such a facility. In some areas, it may be practical for adjoining parishes to work for a common center or to utilize the facilities of a fraternal group such as the Knights of Columbus.

The plan for such a center will depend in large part upon the finances of the parish. Such planning may include a gymnasium which can be used also as an auditorium, a library, and one or more smaller meeting rooms or offices. Many such centers have been established, so that the pastor who has such a center in mind should have no difficulty in securing suggestions and practical plans.

In general, however, it is a mistake to regard such centers as profitable ventures or places for commercial enterprise. Thus, while the parish center may be appropriately available and needed for social events and dances for the youth of the parish, it should not be turned into a "dance hall" or skating rink to serve the area. While it may be properly used for charitable benefits for the parish, or neighboring parishes, it should never become the repository for slot machines and other gambling devices. While parish suppers and refreshments may be served with its facilities, it should never become a place for dispensing alcoholic drinks. Nor should it become simply a lounging place for people to idle away their time or a kind of poolroom and cards-and-smoker den for people who should be at home or at work.

To avoid such abuses and even the appearance of competition with legitimate commercial enterprises, the parish center or clubhouse should be governed by definite regulations and conducted accordingly. This means the observance of definite hours, proper conduct, and the speedy elimination of unruly elements. All events should be duly authorized and properly supervised; and those using its facilities should be made to understand that expense and responsibility are involved in the project. Otherwise, even with the best of intentions, a clubhouse will soon become a shambles, and those in charge of it will regret the day they became involved.

These same observations apply to clubhouses, hotels, or centers which may be owned or operated by fraternal organizations and other groups under Catholic sponsorship or auspices. The fact that they are Catholic is no assurance that they are proof against human frailty or exempt from the necessity of strict accounting and good business procedures. The reaction of injured innocence or righteous indignation when questions are raised about temporal matters may be an indication that an investigation is overdue.

The only way to maintain high and desirable standards and to avoid embarrassment is to insist upon (1) the determination of definite objectives, (2) setting up of programs and schedules in conformity with these objectives, and (3) regular supervision of the premises and activities in accordance with these standards.

This calls for considerable thought and planning and the assumption of responsibility on the part of those who are designated by office or appointment in charge of activities. Illegal activities, private interests, roughhouse elements, and the provision of facilities simply for people to "hang around" should not be tolerated. The chaplain, moderator, or pastor ought to regard it as part of his duty to insist, kindly but firmly, on these principles.

Similar attitudes should govern the handling and accountability of funds in all organizational activities. The only safe rule to follow is to establish sound collection payment and accounting procedures from the beginning. The responsibilities of the treasurer should be set forth exactly and all routines should be outlined in practical form, with provision for a regular audit of funds and accounts. This need not be elaborate, but it should be adequate. Any professional accountant or bank can give preliminary advice on these matters, and systems can be devised to meet the needs and scope of the organization.

A bank should be designated as depository, and regular financial statements should be made available for audit and report. No one, even of the highest spiritual qualifications, should be given unlimited custody of funds. The history of slipshod methods, dissipation of savings in bad investments, unsecured loans, thefts and inefficient management, all point to the necessity of competence and controls in every enterprise where money is involved.

Nor should any Catholic organization be allowed to become the private venture or auxiliary enterprise of any individual, tied in with his business or commingled with his or her personal finances. Almost invariably, this experience ends unfortunately either through neglect, discrimination, misuse, or defalcation. If the treasurer or business manager agrees to contribute facilities and services to the organization, these should be clearly outlined and identified as such and not be confused on the accounts either of the organization or of any private business enterprise. These observations are not intended to question or reflect on the honesty of anyone. They follow sound principles of administration, readily recognized by qualified and experienced administrators.

For orderly procedure and record of all societies which operate under a constitution and bylaws, it is important to keep minutes of all business meetings in a special book for this purpose. This is essential, of course, for organizations which have been incorporated under civil law. The secretary should be instructed how to keep minutes and to write resolutions in correct form, and the minutes should be signed by the responsible officers. Minutes should be kept current and be available for inspection by authorized persons; and the minute book should be held in a safe and secure place. These records belong to the organization, for custody by the designated officer, and are not the private property of any individual.

The deliberations of the governing body ought to be respected with confidence, and the decisions of majority vote should be adhered to until legally revoked. Responsible members and officers are not going to express themselves honestly and freely if they have reason to think that their confidential opinions, expressed in a closed meeting, will soon become common property of the community. A responsible organization or board of directors is not going to take itself seriously if its decisions can be ignored or dismissed as nonexistent. The priest who is chaplain or moderator must keep this in mind if he expects to receive continued cooperation from his societies.

5

In dealing with the human elements in organizations, the best rules for the priest to follow are prudence and tact. These are more easy to state than to spell out in detail or to follow. Some priests are better equipped than others, by natural endowment and personality, to deal with individuals and groups. Experience itself is the best teacher. In general, however, it is better to lean to the side of kindness than of severity. People are repelled by a domineering attitude. On the other hand, leadership calls for decision. A straddling and evasive attitude on the part of the priest indicates weakness and fear.

These principles are pertinent, regardless of the type of organization. Different kinds of problems arise in organizations of men or women, and in mixed groups, whether of children, youth, or adults. But people respond in the same general patterns to the same general treatment. Fair and square dealing meets with corresponding reaction even though it means the application and acceptance of a rebuke or penalty. Impartiality always merits respect, even from those who are seeking special favors.

It is important, in dealing with irksome problems, to guard against "losing one's head" or indulging in personalities. There may be times when stupidity and insolence tempt the priest to psychoanalyze others in public. Impertinent arguments may urge him to invoke his sacerdotal rank and squelch offending members. An apparently unfair decision may send the young levite in charge of an athletic team out to the floor or field with murderous designs upon the umpire. All of these reactions are proof that the priest himself is human and in need of education in restraint and in Christian social living; but this is one of the purposes of organizational activity.

Patience and tolerance are also requisites in the priest who is interested in the survival of his societies. Childish pranks and even malicious destruction of property can be expected wherever there are children's groups. The abuse of privileges, introduction of liquor, and occasional fights are not uncommon in connection with social events and dances for young people's clubs. Factional disputes and political soreness and recriminations often occur in men's organizations. Gossip and backbiting are found in women's societies. Family rivalries and petty arguments are often incidental to mixed groups.

The simplest way of disposing with these problems is to dissolve the organization. But a still simpler solution would be to have no organizations in the first place. The mature and wise priest will be prepared to face all of these problems patiently and to deal with them individually as part of the human scene and a challenge for the application of Christian principles. People develop in perfectly human ways, often by the method of trial and error, mistakes and repentance. And no organization should be made to suffer because of the indiscretion or sins of some of its members. Positive correction is better than the methods of general denunciation and extinction.

One thing Catholic societies should never lose sight of is that they are Catholic in character and direction, designed primarily for a public exemplification of the faith and the development of Christian virtue. To the extent that they serve these purposes, they justify their existence. This does not mean that their programs are necessarily devotional or always religious in character or that a religious atmosphere must dominate all of their activities. Their underlying or final purpose may be exemplified in the variety of ways already outlined — educational, charitable, fund-raising, service, and social, as well as devotional.

It is a mistake to settle anything like a puritanical spirit upon their proceedings, as if this made them more religious, or to impose religious symbols upon a gathering of general character as if this were necessary to safeguard virtue. Catholic organizations should flourish in an atmosphere of easy cordiality and of civilized social intercourse appropriate to the occasion. Repression, suspicion, and gloom are as alien to healthy Catholic organizations as they are to the spirit of the Catholic religion itself. When Christ said, "Where there are two or three gathered together in my Name, there am I in the midst of them."[3] He was undoubtedly thinking of numerous Catholic organizations which extend the influence of the Church far beyond the confines of the Sunday pews, and He was giving the assurance of His blessing to the priests who are devotedly serving in this apostolic work.

6

Question may be raised as to proper attitudes and policies of the priest toward lay societies and organizations outside the jurisdiction of the parish. These may be divided into Catholic organizations, nonsectarian or secular groups, and societies which have been banned by the Church for Catholics.

With respect to Catholic organizations, there can be no doubt

[3] Mt. 18:20.

that, given the right kind of leadership and furnished with desirable objectives, and a good program of activity, they can and do contribute much to the strengthening of Catholic life and influence in the community. If their membership is national in scope, they are capable of much good on a national scale. Whether they actually achieve these goals depends to a considerable extent upon the support, encouragement, and guidance which they receive from the clergy.

The record of the Knights of Columbus, of the Catholic Daughters of America, the Ladies of Isabella, the Catholic Order of Foresters, and numerous other Catholic lay organizations in the United States is indeed impressive evidence of the value of such groups to the Church. For one thing, they provide a social outlet and source of contact for Catholics with fellow Catholics, which naturally produce a sense of security and strength. Their basic requirements for membership and their religious programs definitely encourage compliance with Church law, reception of the sacraments, and better instruction in the Catholic faith. They have contributed liberally to educational and charitable Catholic enterprises, both on local and national levels. And they can be called upon at any time to demonstrate their solidarity with the Church in upholding sound principles of patriotism and the defense of civil rights. The extent to which they engage in other works of Catholic Action, such as cultural programs for their own members or for the community at large, depends principally upon the type of leadership within the organization; but this, in turn, depends in considerable measure upon the interest and indications of the bishops and priests to whom they turn for guidance.

It may even be noted that for lack of such organizations in various Catholic countries, laymen particularly have turned, for social, business, and political reasons, to societies banned by the Church. No ambitious person likes to live in a social vacuum. If the Church does not provide, approve, or favor Catholic lay organizations, one can naturally expect that men and women of gregarious instincts will turn elsewhere. Under these circumstances, even in a traditionally Catholic country, the Church may witness a slow but sure attrition of its potential lay support and the development of hostile leaders through affiliation with lodges which it is forced to condemn.

Even Catholic groups which are left severely alone by the clergy or which, for one reason or the other, are the object of constant criticism and bickering can go off in strange tangents. Unless the watchful eye and helpful hand of the Church are in evidence, and a friendly disposition of the priest is manifest, undesirable elements may seize hold of important offices and swing the organization far out of line with its original purposes and Catholic character. A positive and co-operative policy on the part of the priest may be, not only helpful, but decisive.

With respect to secular social, professional, or civic organizations, circumstances may differ from place to place. In general, however, the Catholic laity should be encouraged to participate and even aspire to a position of leadership, far more than they actually do. "For instance," as John J. Kane notes, "in a national or regional meeting of a professional or learned society, with the probable exception of law and medicine, Catholic lay people are apt to be scarcer than the proverbial 'hen's teeth.' If a simple question is raised, for instance, how a certain subject is handled in a Catholic school, a timid laity may look around for a cleric to answer it. If erroneous statements are made about Catholicism, outside the theological area, some lay Catholics immediately go on the defensive. If a priest is present, they expect him to reply, yet in such situations a layman's answer is apt to be much more effective simply because the spokesman is a layman."

"Actually," he continues, "there is a common Catholic proclivity to avoid such meetings entirely. The residues of separatism still operate, and it is true that Catholic organizations tend to parallel nonsectarian organizations. There is good reason for the existence of separate Catholic organizations, but there is no reason for Catholics to separate themselves from nonsectarian organizations. To the extent that they fail to join, attend, and exercise some leadership in nonsectarian associations and meetings, ignorance of Catholics and Catholic thought will abound. Absence of Catholics from groups and meetings creates two impressions among non-Catholics. They tend to believe, first, that Catholics are forbidden to associate themselves with such organizations and, second, that no one but a priest would have the necessary training or ability to participate.

"What is true of professional and learned societies is less true, but not untrue, of many types of community enterprise. In terms of their numbers in the population, the Catholic laity simply does not exercise proportionate leadership."[4]

The Catholic priest in the modern world should keep these observations in mind, particularly if he is inclined to take a suspicious view of Catholics who actually do participate and achieve some distinction in these groups. Moreover, he should ask himself what he is doing to strengthen the preparation of a Catholic laity which can share his apostolate with him in a world which asks questions and does not respect timidity.

With reference to forbidden societies, of course, there is only one answer. It should be made perfectly clear that a man cannot be a member of the Masonic Order, the Knights of Pythias, or the Oddfellows, for example, and remain a practicing Catholic at the same time. This does not mean that Catholics should regard every Mason as their personal enemy or as a personal enemy of the Catholic Church. On the contrary, many individual members and officers of such organizations are friendly disposed and do not look upon their fraternal order membership as of more than social in character. Indeed, local lodges and chapters of societies forbidden to Catholics often contribute to Catholic charitable and cultural causes. Nevertheless, the principle is clear and the prohibition against membership by Catholics has been imposed by the Church for good reasons which everyone versed in history and theology should know.

In the case of local organizations which appear to share affiliation with these orders or which stem from a non-Catholic religious group, great caution and prudence should be observed. In case of

---

[4] *Catholic-Protestant Conflicts in America* (Chicago: Regnery, 1955), pp. 218, 219.

doubt, the Ordinary of the diocese should be consulted. But where Catholics are inclined to join such organizations, the priest should ask himself what he is doing to provide for his people, either by guidance into desirable groups or by the formation of a more active Catholic life and organization. In the last analysis, positive action is what counts, and it is the responsibility of the priest to recognize values and to show the way, through a realistic attitude, an understanding of the modern world, and farsighted counsel.

CHAPTER XII

THE PRIEST AND EDUCATION

I

ONE of the first and most important of the duties of the priest is to teach. This follows directly from the injunction of Christ to His Apostles: "Going therefore, teach ye all nations. Teaching them to observe all things whatsoever I have commanded you. And behold I am with you all days, even to the consummation of the world."[1] In the beginning, the Apostles taught on the street corners and in the market place. Following the example of Christ, they probably taught also in the synagogues until they were driven out. St. Paul in Athens taught in a schoolhouse. In the course of time, schools were formed for the teaching of Christian doctrine, first in the secrecy of homes and in the catacombs, then more openly in churches and public classes.

The rise of the Church, particularly as exemplified in monasticism, both of the East and of the West, was identified with education. It has been said truly that the Church conserved the ancient culture and civilization of the Greeks and Romans at the same time as it preserved the Holy Scriptures of the Jews and taught the doctrine of Christ. Churches and schools went hand and hand, as the great teaching orders of the Middle Ages flourished. Universities were founded, from Bologna to Oxford. In the missionary activity of the Church, likewise, schools followed shortly after the initial preaching of the Gospel. Catholic

---

[1] Mt. 28:19, 20.

culture has always appealed to the whole man, bringing mankind into knowledge of better living, developing the arts and crafts, and stimulating the production of both literature and science.

The priests of the Catholic Church have always been respected as men of learning. Their acceptance and leadership in society have been due primarily to their spiritual message and example, but their exemplification of sanctity has been founded upon an enlightened faith. This follows logically from the fact that faith, in the Catholic conception, is an act of intellectual assent, which in turn requires instruction. The priest, therefore, must himself be educated in the theology of the Catholic religion before he can instruct others. And as theology enters into and draws from all phases of life in the application of its truths, the priest is drawn into all phases of learning and, as teacher, is required to face all levels of instruction.

One of the basic questions, raised over and over again, is whether the priest, notwithstanding his own broad preparation in the humanities, should devote his teaching efforts to anything outside the strict lines of theology and possibly of philosophy. Why, for example, should he be called upon to teach mathematics or to pursue research, as a career, in the physical sciences, or give his time to instruction in history or literature? These are subjects, it is argued, which the laity can teach pre-eminently well, without diverting or wasting the theological preparation of the priest, who should confine himself to the teaching of religion.

There is no easy answer to this problem. The fact is, however, that numerous religious orders, such as the Jesuits, Dominicans, Benedictines, and Vincentians have devoted themselves to the teaching of youth and to the organization of colleges and universities for instruction in all branches of learning. In many dioceses, the secular clergy are placed in teaching positions, covering all subjects in the curriculum, in the preparatory seminaries. In not a few places they conduct and teach in high schools and colleges. Diocesan as well as religious priests hold distinguished posts in leading Catholic universities throughout the world and have achieved eminence as historians, mathematicians, scientists, musicians, artists, and writers in various fields of knowledge. From this, one might well conclude that a teaching career is by no means inconsonant with the priesthood. Even more, the Church evidently regards teaching as an important phase of the priestly apostolate.

In large measure, this activity stems from the general attitude and policy of the Church toward education. The Catholic position is that education is not simply the imparting of information of a factual nature but also the relating of this knowledge to the spiritual destiny of man and the formation of Christian personality and character. This task calls for teachers who are imbued with a correct theological and philosophical background and who can bring to their teaching an integrated understanding of all subjects in this light.

The problem of the Church, therefore, has been an organized approach toward providing Catholic education. Hence the development of the various religious teaching orders, both of men and women — priests, Brothers, and Sisters. So far as the individual secular priest is concerned, his place in an active teaching career arises from the need of the Church in any given place and his own personal inclination and preparation. An intellectual clergy, with opportunity to teach in higher education, is a source of strength for any diocese.

"Wise encouragement and help," writes Pope Pius XI, "should be given to those members of the clergy, who, by taste and special gifts, feel a call to devote themselves to study and research, in this or that branch of science, in this or that art: they do not thereby deny their clerical profession; for all this, undertaken within just limits and under the guidance of the Church, redounds to the good estate of the Church and to the glory of her divine Head, Jesus Christ. And among the rest of the clergy, none should remain content with a standard of learning and culture which sufficed perhaps, in other times; they must try to attain — or, rather they must actually attain — a higher standard of general education and learning. It must be broader and more complete; and it must correspond to the generally higher level and wider scope of modern education as compared with the past."[2]

This does not mean that the Church is unwilling to encourage the formation of lay teachers. On the contrary, the recognized need for qualified lay teachers, both in the Catholic and the public schools, is constantly increasing. The extent to which Catholic schools which are conducted by priests or religious can avail themselves of the services of Catholic lay teachers is a practical matter, involving financial considerations. With the increase of student registration, it is probable that more and more of the laity will be required to supplement the work of the religious and to fill posts of specialized learning and skills in Catholic schools.

In any event, it is of the utmost importance that the Church, through its religious, priests, and bishops, maintain a position of inspiration which will show unmistakably its esteem for education and its desire to develop leaders in every field of learning. From this will proceed naturally the recognition and growth of a strong intellectual and teaching apostolate among the laity.

2

The first teaching obligation of the priest in parish or missionary work is, of course, that of religious instruction. In this work, the pulpit and the classroom share the honors. With respect to the former, a number of indications have been given in the chapter on preaching. The classroom presents a distinct opportunity as well as numerous problems which call for special consideration.

In parishes and areas which do not have parochial schools, the responsibility for teaching Christian doctrine to the children falls directly and even personally upon the pastor and his assistant priests. In the actual organization of the instruction classes, whether in Sunday schools or other arrangements, qualified auxiliary lay teachers may be used. A Confraternity of Christian

---

[2] Encyclical *Ad Catholici Sacerdotii* in *The Popes and the Priesthood* (St. Meinrad, Ind.: Grail Publications, 1953), p. 62.

Doctrine may be organized with great advantage. Young men and young women of the parish, or Catholic teachers and parents, may be trained to conduct sections of the classes. But it is the priest himself who must personally supervise this work and see to it that his charges are all properly prepared for their First Communion and Confirmation.

In some communities, where a parochial school is not available, a small group of Sisters, either living in a community house or sent out regularly from another school or headquarters, may be the answer to competent religious instruction. This has been tried with considerable success, and may be adapted to local conditions. Time may be designated on Saturdays or on Sunday mornings between Masses. Where local civic laws and authorities permit, released time may be granted from public school class schedules to allow religious instruction; and this opportunity should by all means be taken. But, whether the instruction is given by religious or laity, the priest himself should supervise the project and check the outcomes.

The so-called "penny catechism" still remains the most satisfactory basic text; and from the standpoint of exact definition and remembrance, there is probably nothing that can take the place of learning its answers by rote. At the same time, the broadening of general experience makes it imperative that the memory be strengthened by a fuller explanation adapted to the eager mentality of the child. Many changes and improvements in teaching texts and methods have been devised within recent years for religious instruction. It is not enough to give simply the bare bones of the creed. A rich and human understanding of the Catholic religion is necessary for the requirements of today. Every phase of Catholic thought and life should be expounded — moral as well as dogmatic principles, the art of the Church, liturgy, music, literature, and a sense of the Church's social mission — all related to divine truth.[3]

The informed and zealous priest will fill his auxiliary teachers

---

[3] Cf. Thomas C. Donlan, O.P., *Theology and Education* (Dubuque: Wm. C. Brown Co., 1952), Chaps. 7, 8, and *passim*.

with enthusiasm for their task and encourage them to improve their own preparation and teaching methods. For the children, the catechism class will no longer be a dreary and restless hour, held together with stern discipline, but a refreshing and enlightening experience from which they will wish to learn more and more. The achievement of these results, of course, requires considerably more than a background of theological training. It calls for education and study of techniques in religious education, a serious and professional regard for the task, and careful preparation for each class. Moreover, there must be a steady advance in levels of instruction. Youth in the high school or children in the elementary grades are not satisfied to hear only a repetition of the same things they heard practically from the kindergarten.

It is important, whether there is a parochial school or not, to make provision for the religious instruction of students in the public schools. This is often a difficult and ungrateful task, partly because of the indifference of parents and partly because of the various interests and irresponsibility of the children. But the fact is that in the over-all picture, there are more Catholic children in the public than in the parochial schools; and these are the people most in need of religious instruction if they are to conserve the faith. Ways and means should be found to reach them in every community. The parish priest should become acquainted with the public schools in his area, with the school boards, their administrators, their teachers, and the parents. He should co-operate in every way possible, both as a citizen and as a man of God, to help them maintain high standards in their service for the education of youth. An aloof and hostile attitude will profit nothing; a friendly and co-operative understanding will make him an honored leader in the community and will enormously increase his influence.

3

There can be no doubt that, however effective the instruction in the catechism or religious instruction classes may be, in the Sunday school or in a released-time program, nothing can compete with the Catholic school in the formation of the Catholic mind and character, except, of course, the good Catholic home. The reason for this is that religious education, as already noted, means the integration of all knowledge into a conception of the meaning of life with God as its goal.

The living example of the religious teacher and the conscious relation and motivation of all activity to the salvation of one's soul is the unique contribution of Catholic education. This is not simply a religious veneer laid upon secular education, but the subtle and constant blending of time with eternity, that makes Catholic education distinctive. For the Catholic trained mind, education is not merely a collection of bits of information like so many scattered pieces of colored stone or glass, but the development of a guiding wisdom which brings these elements into a great pattern and reflection of the Divine Plan.

The curriculum of the Catholic school, while it may resemble that of the public or secular school and, indeed, include the same subjects, as required by the standard accrediting agencies, is guided by a radically different basic concept. This concept is the unfolding of knowledge as a revelation of the mind of God and the relating of all knowledge to the honor of God and the salvation of one's soul. This is a social as well as individual concept, inasmuch as it views society as working co-operatively toward this objective and as held together by the bonds of justice and charity.[4] It is a dynamic concept, inasmuch as it regards the process of salvation, not as a passive acceptance or condition, but as the development of all one's powers and talents for the greater glory of God.

To make these ideas operative requires more than pious motives and good intentions. The Catholic school, whether on the elementary, high school, collegiate, postgraduate, or graduate level, cannot fulfill its purpose unless it is provided with the essential

---

[4] For an application of this principle to the elementary grades, confer: Sister Mary Joan, O.P., and Sister Mary Nona, O.P., *Guiding Growth in Christian Social Living,* a publication of The Commission on American Citizenship (Washington, D. C.: The Catholic University of America Press, 1952).

physical equipment and staffed with qualified teachers. Inasmuch as Catholic education, in most secular states today, receives little or no financial support from public taxes, it must look to the private generosity of the faithful as well as to the dedicated sacrifice of religious teachers whose contributed services constitute a veritable living endowment.

With regard to parochial schools, different plans are followed in different places. In some, the school is supported, at least in part, by the tuition of the students. This is often reinforced by the proceeds of charitable bazaars and contributions from parish funds to make up the deficit. In others, no charge is made for tuition, the entire parish being taxed for the upkeep of the school and teachers. There is much merit in the latter plan, which follows the same principle as general taxation in support of the public schools. The principle for this procedure is a sound one, namely, that education is a public investment for the welfare of the entire community; hence all should contribute toward it, as toward any other public benefit, the unmarried and the childless as well as those whose children are sent to school. This principle is certainly valid as applied to the parochial elementary school, since the civil law requires elementary education. To a large extent, it is valid also for the parochial or interparochial high school. In other words, to the extent that facilities are available, every Catholic child should get a Catholic education, and the Catholic public should pay for it, to the extent that public funds are not available from other sources.

The same argument cannot be used to the same extent in support of Catholic higher education. While college and university education are desirable, they are not requisite for the average person, nor required by law. The students attending school on these levels should be expected to pay their way, even though the school may make provision for a limited number of scholarships for deserving students. It is important to recognize, however, that, with few exceptions, the Catholic college or university cannot sustain itself on student tuition and fees alone. Nor can it give scholarships indefinitely from its largess. The fact is that tuition and fees cover only a part of the costs of maintaining a college, and indeed only a fraction of costs of postgraduate and graduate studies.

The practical question of Catholic higher education, therefore, comes down to this: If the Church wishes to maintain an educated Catholic laity and leadership, it must pay for it. If Catholic education is expected to prepare teachers, scientists, professional men, and leaders whose activity will radiate Christian principles and enhance Catholic prestige, then the Catholic public must give to the cause.

The Catholic priest who is truly interested in Catholic education will do well for the cause to familiarize himself with the facts. It is possible, in the fairly set pattern of the seminary, to lose sight of the needs and requirements of education for the laity. Unless one makes an effort, the priest may never grasp the meaning and importance of postgraduate and graduate studies, and may unconsciously develop a kind of contempt for advanced educational work and research, which are really the advance guard for the preservation and development of the faith.

One does not have to be a profound thinker to recognize the truth of these observations in the lessons of history. Largely because of the loss of a dynamic conception of Catholic education and failure to provide for Catholic higher education of the laity the nineteenth century witnessed a wholesale defection of the intellectual classes from the Church in practically all the Catholic countries of both the Old and the New World. By the year 1889, when The Catholic University of America was founded for higher education, practically every Catholic university of Europe and Latin America had been taken from the Church and given over to hostile hands.

To recover from these losses and to develop a strong, enlightened Catholic leadership, priests and people alike must recognize the importance of Catholic education from bottom to top and be prepared to support it. The problem and needs are becoming greater and greater. But there is no other way if we are going to survive.

4

For the priest in active parish work, the maintenance and opera
tion of a school involves numerous details of a practical character.
Reduced to their most common denominator they all spell the
word "service." Some of this service is physical in character, some
educational, some social, and some spiritual. Much tact is required, and much patience is necessary, not only in providing
conditions satisfactory to the instructional staff but in meeting
the problems of children and parents alike.

With respect to physical plant, it is often difficult for the
parish to erect even an elementary school that will match the
facilities of the modern public school. Nevertheless, careful planning will produce an economical structure to meet all standard
requirements. Adequate provision should be made for the physical
needs of the teaching and student personnel, as well as for
satisfactory instructional arrangements. Ample provision for recreational purposes, due regard for hygiene and safety, and adequate toilet and rest facilities are basic.

The same care should be given to providing decent living
conditions and services for the religious in charge of the school.
The convent or house occupied by the Sisters ought to be large
enough to give them reasonable privacy and comfort. Crowded
and run-down domestic conditions create tensions and dissatisfaction even among the saints. If one desires a school with a bright
and happy spirit, it is essential to provide living conditions,
however modest, that are geared to produce happiness and contentment in the teachers. The pastor who finds himself in
possession of a fine large house for himself, while several teaching
Sisters are required to share one or two rooms, should lose no
time in providing them with satisfactory domestic quarters.

Similar observations may be made relative to the support of
the teaching Sisters. It is understood that the religious orders
take the vow of poverty. Nevertheless, they must clothe themselves and eat and secure the various necessities for decent and
cultured living. The financing of the parish school should take

this into consideration. There may be times and circumstances in which workers for the Church have to sacrifice and live on meager rations. In run-down parishes or in newly opened areas and mission territories, life may be on a hand-to-mouth basis. The good religious will rejoice in this opportunity to share in the sufferings of Christ. But in a settled community, with comfortable standards of living, where the demands for service are also high, there is no reason why the teaching Sisters should have to conduct raffles or take up penny collections, under one pretext or the other, to keep themselves in the necessities of life. Their daily bread and all that this implies should be provided as part of their agreement with the parish, so that they may be free to give their full time and energies to their work.

The establishment of satisfactory spiritual services is also important. The life of teaching religious derives its inspiration and strength from its spiritual source, Jesus Christ, physically present in the Blessed Sacrament of the Altar and spiritually present in the confessional. Without any question, daily Mass and Holy Communion must be provided, regularly and punctually, and care should be taken that regular and satisfactory opportunity is given for confession, all in accordance with the norms of Canon Law. Due consideration should be given also to the spiritual exercises which are special to the religious community.

Consideration and kindness ought to set the policy and pattern of all the priest's dealings with his teaching Sisters. A spirit of friendly co-operation and the establishment of definite, positive policies will practically assure a satisfactory school. Antagonisms, negative criticism, suspicions, and continued misunderstanding between the rectory and the convent are almost certain to be reflected in a bewildered and unsatisfactory school.

The pastor is primarily responsible for the maintenance and operation of the school. But the active teaching and administration are the business of the religious community which he engages for this purpose. Therefore, excessive intrusion and interference on his part may be as embarrassing and annoying as an attitude of unconcern and neglect. The exact point of vigilance and active

participation is not always easy to determine and is certainly beyond the scope of this book. In general, however, it may be noted
that the principal administrator of teaching and discipline in
the school is the religious superior. The pastor or his delegated
assistant should conduct the official business of the school directly
with her, not with the Sisters under her direction or with the
students. He should confer with her personally, on an adminis-
trative basis, not by indirect communications or innuendos or
by the unfair method of criticism to members of the parish. If he
has praise or blame or directives to offer, he should do so in a
friendly, positive manner, and in line with established policy
and program, never as the result of rumor, whim, or temperament.

These principles apply, not only to matters of curriculum and
teaching program, but to discipline, recreation, and extracurricular
activities of the school as well. On matters of major policy, of
course, the priest should be consulted, and he should be prepared
to handle difficult cases of final referral. He should be alert to
the educational standards and requirements of the school; and
he should exercise reasonable vigilance over the discipline and
morals of the student body, not excluding the problems of mari-
juana, liquor, and sexual deviations. But he should never, by an
inconsistent and shifting policy, get himself into the position of
having to make every decision for the principal or having to
back her up on every occasion by a show of authority.

The question of the extent to which the priest should participate personally in the athletic games, picnics, and social events
of the school is largely a matter of good judgment. He should
encourage and assist in the development of a rational program
of extracurricular events and stimulate interest by making a personal appearance. But he will be prudent to avoid situations
in which he becomes personally involved as a contestant and
runs the risk of sacrificing or diminishing his priestly character
and respect.

In dealing with parent-teachers associations and various lay
auxiliaries of the school, the priest will welcome the intelligent
interest, co-operation, and assistance of all concerned. If their

function is one of good relationships with the school or better understanding of Catholic educational problems, his best course of action is to assist them in drawing up a program of conferences, interviews, and special events with these objectives in mind. If their purpose is to assist in the financial support of the school, he will guide their efforts. But it is important to direct all these activities so as to avoid any tendency on their part to usurp authority in conducting the school or in the financial control of its operations.

In setting the entrance requirements for the parochial school, one must keep in mind the prescriptions of Canon Law as regard Catholic education. As Catholic parents have an obligation to give their children a Catholic education, they have a corresponding right to send them to the local parochial school, whether they be rich or poor, black, white, yellow, or red. The question of race, and possibly of social position, may be raised in some localities. There is only one standard, even if some parents withdraw their children as a result of its application.

5

The problem of higher education for Catholics involves many problems, which are solved on a diocesan rather than on a parochial basis. Comparatively few parishes are able to support a Catholic high school. If satisfactory physical and scholastic standards are to be maintained, interparochial co-operation is usually necessary; and any program of high school development, to carry weight, requires the support of the bishop.

Needless to say, the responsibility of providing Catholic college and university facilities comes within the purview of the dioceses and of the religious communities and orders dedicated to this task. Nevertheless, every parish priest has a responsibility in reference to the higher education of the young men and women under his jurisdiction. In the first place, it is his duty to remind parents and students alike of the importance and indeed their moral obligation to select a Catholic college or university, if this is possible. In the second place, it is his duty to keep an eye particularly on the youth of the parish who, for one reason or the other, do not go to a Catholic college but select instead a secular institution for higher studies.

In the past, various views have been expressed as to the correct attitude and policy regarding Catholics in non-Catholic or secular high schools and colleges. According to one view, these students are blameworthy and are not entitled to any special consideration. Indeed, to provide special Catholic facilities for them has been considered as equivalent to encouraging their choice. On the other hand, it is important to take a realistic and considerate view of the facts. A Catholic high school or college is not available in many places or within the means of many Catholic families or individuals. In some instances, Catholic institutions do not offer the vocational training, professional courses, or specific opportunities desired. In many cases, there is probably little reason for the individual's selection of a secular rather than a Catholic school. But it must be remembered that if all eligible Catholics were to apply for admission to Catholic schools, the majority of them would be turned down for lack of space.

All these considerations seem to point clearly to the fact that special provision must be made for Catholic students in secular schools. Chapels, chaplains, spiritual directors, religious and cultural courses, and organized recreational facilities are urgently needed for these people. Planned service and activity will save and strengthen the faith of thousands and broaden the influence of the Church in secular areas. Neglect and antagonizing of these students will certainly result in a large defection and the loss of many potential leaders. In addition, special consideration and encouragement should be given to the Catholic members of the faculty, administration, and general staff in these institutions. Rich spiritual dividends will result.

6

One of the most important and least appreciated phases of Catholic education is adult education. We endeavor to take our children through the elementary schools and, so far as possible, through high schools under Catholic auspices. The more fortunate few get a Catholic college education. But the vast majority remain at age fourteen throughout life so far as Catholic intellectual and cultural development is concerned. As a result of this gap, the Catholic mind is largely inoperative in society, the impact of Catholic literature is restricted to a comparative few, and the outlook of the average Catholic on events of the day does not differ significantly from that of his non-Catholic associates even in matters where Catholic interests are at stake.

The key to this situation may possibly be found in the basic Catholic conception of existence, which regards this life as a kind of moral testing ground for eternity. While this conception is fundamentally in conformity with the doctrine of Christ, it is subject to various modes of application. A passive and constricted application is inclined to act on the principle "sufficient for the day is the evil thereof." Simple faith and a good life are the basic formula. Into this view there may be injected an indifference toward worldly wisdom and a suspicion that ambition for intellectual growth and cultural improvement, beyond the minimum requirements for social life, are somehow the work of the devil or at least a dangerous tendency. On the other hand, a dynamic application of the principle results in the full development of the human personality, the growth of knowledge and talent, artistic expression, higher physical standards of living, social progress and leadership, in accordance with the moral law; and all with the motive of serving God.

It is this latter application in which we are interested, for the salvation and revitalizing of society. Unless definite steps are taken for the progressive formation of an alert, informed Catholic mind beyond the elementary formation of the child, the Church can expect the same loss of the intellectual classes as occurred in the Latin countries during the nineteenth century and the bewilderment of the laboring classes that exists in many Catholic countries of our own twentieth century.

The Catholic home and the school must co-operate in stimulating a dynamic conception of Catholic culture in the mind of the child and the youth, so that he emerges from his formal training with a love for books, a power of discrimination based on Catholic principles, and a desire to keep growing. But even more than these centers, it is the parish priest who holds the strategic position of developing a sense of values and of setting up the standards. The priest who is himself a man of culture and who takes pains to assist in the intellectual and cultural growth of his people throughout their mature adult life is performing a service of apostolic character second to none.

"The dignity of the office he holds, and the maintenance of a becoming respect and esteem among the people, which helps so much in his pastoral work," in the words of Pope Pius XI, "demand much more than purely ecclesiastical learning. The priest must be graced by no less knowledge and culture than is usual among well-bred and well-educated people of his day. This is to say that he must be healthily modern, as is the Church, which is at home in all times and all places, and adapts itself to all; which blesses and furthers all healthy initiative and has no fear of the progress, even the most daring progress, of science, if only it be true science."[5]

A program of adult education adapted to the average parish may take various forms, or it may be a combination of activities. The three general lines most recommended are the establishment of a parochial library, the organization of a lecture series or forum, and the formation of study clubs. These three supplement one another, and, if planned on a co-ordinated basis, will produce the maximum desired results. The experience of parishes, schools, and clubs which have conducted successful adult education activities should be consulted, both for projects and methods.

It is important to keep in mind that the distinctive purpose of Catholic adult education is to make better known Christian principles, Catholic literature and cultural expression, and representative Catholic views on leading topics of the day. Some parishes, individually or by interparochial co-operation may be able to expand their programs, so as to include numerous activities, from

[5] *Ad Catholici Sacerdotii, loc. cit.,* p. 61.

the teaching of languages to the social arts including ballet and folk dancing. But it is possible to spread one's efforts too thin and depart from the real objectives that call for primary attention. There are numerous worthy activities that are better left to secular and commercial agencies.

A parochial library is one of the most rewarding and easily managed of adult-education projects. It should be conducted on a businesslike basis, with a simple card index and borrower's card system. Rules for the borrowing and return of books should be established and strictly enforced. Almost any place will do for the display and lending of books. If a special room is not available, the vestibule of the church will serve efficiently between Sunday Masses or at established hours during week nights. It is important that the announced schedule be adhered to. A librarian or librarians should be available to give service and check books in and out.

There are numerous services for the selection of Catholic books. Among book clubs may be included the Catholic Book Club, the Catholic Literary Foundation, the Thomas More Book Club, the Spiritual Book Associates, the Catholic Family Book Club, and the books clubs of the Catholic Digest and the Maryknoll Fathers. The catalogs of Catholic publishers and book reviews and advertisements in the leading Catholic periodicals help one to keep abreast of worthwhile Catholic literature. Novels, biography, history, current events, religion, philosophy, morals, Catholic reference works, and self-help, all fall within the range of the Catholic library. The selection of books should normally be limited to approved Catholic authors unless the particular book is of special interest and value to Catholics.

It is sometimes argued that, instead of establishing a Catholic parochial or interparochial library, more good would be accomplished by introducing Catholic books into the public libraries. There is much merit in this consideration. However, experience has shown that, with few exceptions, non-Catholics will not ask for Catholic books; and Catholics need to be educated specifically in Catholic reading. The priest and the parish librarians will perform a valuable service in directing Catholics to the public library for needed books and references of special character and in co-operating with the public library for an interchange of services. But their first and distinctive contribution is the creation of a Catholic library service and the development of an awareness of Catholic books and a taste for Catholic reading by Catholics.

The success of the Catholic parish library depends in large part upon its contemporary character and the sustained interest of the priest. It is a complete delusion to think that one is establishing a parish lending library by transferring to it castoff volumes from the shelves of yesteryear. Antiquated novels, old travel books, and dusty theological tomes or black-covered spiritual works are not going to attract readers. People are interested in new books, books with a modern appearance, style, and flavor, books that others talk about and that deal with problems of a personal and con-temporary character. These have to be renewed constantly and many have to be discarded when they have served their purpose. A static library is a dead library. A living library is one in which the books get off the shelves and keep in circulation. This means new acquisitions as well as a weeding-out process.

It is not enough to set up a library and wait for people to come. The parish library, like everything else that expects customers, must be constantly advertised. The simplest and most effective advertising is from the pulpit. If the priest takes into the pulpit one or two books each Sunday, or even occasionally holds one up with the title and recommends it, there will be no difficulty in putting it into circulation or creating interest in Catholic reading. If this were done throughout the nation, there would be a veritable renaissance of Catholic literature and the creation of a tremendous Catholic influence upon society. This is positive ac-tion, the type that gets results. If people should be warned against bad literature, then they should be guided to good literature. And if it is assumed that bad literature is a real threat, then it should be evident that these same people are capable of reading good books and magazines.

The problem of financing a parish library is often regarded as a sufficient deterrent to action. Yet, the answer to this problem is comparatively simple. A good parish library can be started with as little as fifty to one hundred dollars. Most parishes can afford this. It might be suggested that the pastor or priests of the parish make a monetary contribution to the cause from time to time or contribute good books from their own libraries when they have finished reading them. It may not be too much to ask regular patrons to give a dollar or two once a year, and to pay their fines cheerfully when books are overdue. They have no difficulty in meeting these requirements in the lending library in the corner drugstore. In a word, if the parish library is worthwhile, it is worth supporting.

In conjunction with the library or independently of it, a lecture series or forum is worthy of serious consideration. Planned as a series of book reviews or conferences on current topics, or as a combination of both, a lecture program is capable of broadening the spiritual and cultural perspective of the parish and of raising the prestige of the Church among all elements of the community. Catholics are made aware of the fact that Catholic thinkers are giving study to current events and that the Catholic faith is a living force capable of facing life's problems in every field of thought and action. Contact with Catholic writers and speakers, both of the clergy and of the laity, is a valuable experience in itself and an effective means of introducing Catholics and the general public as well to a further interest in their writings and activities.

Planning a lecture series requires careful thought, for programing, advertising, and financing. The program should be variegated and speakers should be selected who are thoroughly qualified and prepared. The Catholic lecture series or forum may deal with literary, international, sociological, travel, philosophical, and inspirational subjects; but it should carefully avoid partisan politics or crusading issues. Advertising should never be sensational, and it should carry the definite seal of ecclesiastical approbation, even though the Church need not endorse all the personal opinions of the speakers. The best advertising and evidence of support is the personal appearance of the priests at the lectures. Unless the parish has sufficient funds to provide a subsidy, fees for membership or admission should be charged, and the speakers should be paid a proper honorarium. To assure the success of such a venture, the entire Catholic community should lend its support, rather than breaking off into little competitive groups each with its own project.

A further extension of adult education is the organization of study clubs. For the development of a mature and progressive grasp of Catholic principles as applied to specific problems, the study-club group or groups provide a most effective and practical plan of action; but it should also be understood that this calls for intensive work. In some cases, the groups may be organized along professional lines, as doctors and lawyers, or with sections of businessmen, workers, nurses, or simply mixed groups. The groups should be kept small so that everyone participates, and meetings should be held at stated times and places on definite schedule. Usually once a month or once every two weeks is sufficient, so as to give adequate time for preparation. For intensive study and possibly most satisfactory results, weekly meetings are advocated. Meetings may be held in the rectory, the parish center, or the homes of the participants. It is not necessary that the priest in charge should attend every meeting; but he should make at least an appearance from time to time to show his continued interest and a guiding hand.

The success of the study club depends in the first place upon a carefully planned syllabus. Subjects for study may include Church history, social problems, the liturgy, missiology, dogma and morals, international problems, Catholic literature and art, and any number of variants. The syllabus should list the particular phase of the subject for each meeting, to be developed in one or two papers. An outline of suggested development, with references to be consulted should be part of the syllabus. The papers should be assigned at the beginning of the season, so that ample time is allowed for their preparation. Discussion follows the reading of the papers at each meeting. The time should be strictly limited, so as to avoid fruitless arguments. If refreshments are served at the end of the meeting, they should follow a modest pattern; otherwise, the study club may wash out in needless social competition.

There are various ways of securing syllabi for courses of study. The priest in charge may develop a syllabus on a subject with which he is familiar, possibly using a basic text with collateral reading. The National Catholic Welfare Council and the National Councils of Men and Women have prepared syllabi on a number of subjects. A teacher or expert in the community may be willing to draw up a course. In all cases, emphasis should be laid upon Catholic principles; otherwise there is no particular reason for sponsorship by a Catholic or parochial group.

The second factor in the success of a study club is the preparation of papers. It may be that some members of the group are qualified to report extemporaneously. In general, however, the written paper is the only sure evidence of study and preparation. Even if most of the paper has been copied from other sources, it will make a contribution and provide material for fruitful discussion. When there is a tendency to depart from this method, the subject is lost sight of, guesswork and personal prejudices take the place of facts, and the group realizes that their time is being dissipated in casual conversation.

The third factor of success is objective discussion pointed to the particular phase of the subject assigned for the session. One of the benefits of the study club is to teach people, not only to express themselves, but to listen to the views of others without becoming angry or excited. It is marvelous what weird conceptions of Catholic doctrine many good Catholics have, and it is interesting to note how they differ in matters of applied judgment. Insistence upon tolerance for the views of others is the beginning of learning. At the same time, it is important to hold the discussion to the subject at issue. Otherwise, it will inevitably gravitate to favorite personal themes that have little to do with the matter in hand.

Organization of study clubs is simple. The host or hostess for the evening serves as chairman. The priest moderator or executive secretary delegated by him carries the over-all responsibility for the continuity of the group, the distribution of syllabi, and helpful hints.

This is only one form of study club. There are many other forms, in which the priest may act as a teacher or various experts may be invited to present different phases of the subject. But unless there is some group participation and opportunity for the members to express themselves personally, the element of study is likely to be lost sight of, and the development of a dynamic appreciation and leadership is thwarted.

In many ways, an adult education program is a capstone of Catholic education. It provides continuity in Catholic cultural development and conserves and strengthens the intellectual potential of the parish. Catholics respond readily to this opportunity and learn from it to take the leadership in all community activities. Catholic belief and practice assume a social as well as personal significance, and the Church gains enormously in prestige and influence of solid character.

"The true Christian, product of Christian education," declared Pope Pius XII, "is the supernatural man who thinks, judges, and acts constantly and consistently in accordance with right reason illumined by the supernatural light of the example and teaching of Christ."[6] The priest who recognizes this truth and who devotes his time and energy to the apostolate of Christian education can truly say that he has applied the injunction of St. Peter: "Sanctify the Lord Jesus Christ in your hearts, being ready always to satisfy everyone that asketh you a reason of that hope which is in you."[7] Toward this fulfillment, all Catholic education must be directed, on all levels, from the kindergarten to graduate studies. Nothing less can satisfy the command of Christ, "Going therefore, teach ye all nations."

[6] *On the Christian Education of Youth* (Washington, D. C.: National Catholic Welfare Conference, 1936), p. 36.
[7] 1 Pet. 3:15.

"And other sheep I have that are not of this fold: them also I must bring. And they shall hear my voice: and there shall be one fold and one shepherd" (Jn. 10:16).

CHAPTER XIII

THE PRIEST AND THE MISSIONARY CONCEPT

I

IN THE constant renewal as well as the expansion of the work of the Church, there is no principle of action more vital or energizing than the missionary concept. By missionary concept is here meant that view of the Church as in the beginning or initial phases of its work, with the challenge of a society which is still largely unconverted.

It is recognized that this definition does not apply, *de jure,* to the Church in countries where ecclesiastical organization has progressed to the establishment of regular dioceses and parishes. As a matter of fact, in many areas where the Church has been in existence for an extended period of time, even though the Catholic population is reduced numerically, the idea of being considered mission territory could be proudly rejected. Nevertheless, if we may be permitted to use the expression "missionary concept" as explained above and not as necessarily restricted to areas which are still classified officially as under missionary jurisdiction, the principle may be effectively applied everywhere.

The reason for this assertion is simple. The missionary starts out with the realization that his first task is that of converting the people to the Catholic faith. This may have to be accomplished in several steps, breaking down antagonisms, winning confidence, and giving material and medical aid as well as spiritual instruction and counsel. In the course of time, if the mission is successful, a Catholic community is developed around the nucleus of a church or chapel with possibly other facilities such as a school, a hospital, and an orphanage or house of refuge. This is still only the beginning. The missionary recognizes the fact that his work must go on with the objective of bringing all within his assigned territory to the faith of Christ, "Who will have all men to be saved and to come to the knowledge of the truth."[1] So far as he is concerned, this work is never completed.

In the course of time, the growth of the Church in mission territory may be such as to require parochial and diocesan organization. Native vocations and local Catholic institutions flourish. The local Church acquires a permanent status and gives proof of ability to sustain itself, justifying the termination of its missionary status and its incorporation into the full juridical life of the universal Church.

Does this mean that the Church in the given area has now reached its saturation point? Does this signify that the populace is now so confirmed in the faith that routine instruction and administration of the sacraments are sufficient to hold all the gains that were achieved during the missionary era? The answer to both of these questions is clear. As a matter of fact, the Church never has and probably never will reach a point where everyone in a given area is a practicing Catholic. Moreover, history has demonstrated wholesale defections from the Church in countries and regions where it had been firmly entrenched. We have only to open our eyes to witness large-scale defections from the Church today. In short, the assumption that full juridical establishment of the Church ends the need for further missionary activity is the worst of delusions.[2]

Carrying these observations one step further, we may say that the Church remains vital and continues to grow only to the ex-

---

[1] 1 Tim. 2:4.
[2] Cf. Emmanuel Cardinal Suhard, *op. cit.*, pp. 147, 148.

tent that it retains the missionary concept. The day that it relaxes its efforts in the feeling of security and confidence that its work has been done, dry rot and retrogression set in. This is true of nations, dioceses, and parishes alike. The priest who regards himself simply as an administrator of an established parish and is quite satisfied to provide spiritually for the good Catholics who have been born to the faith is performing only a fraction of his apostolate. And while his heart may burn with zeal for the conversion of heathens far across the sea, who have never heard the message of Christ, his own area may be filled with souls who know not Christ, who are falling away from the Church, or who are in deep-seated hostility to Catholicism.

The priest who is thoroughly and actively imbued with the missionary concept will take stock of the situation around him, in his own parish and diocese, as well as in more remote sections of the country where Catholics are few, and in the far-off mission countries. He will recognize a missionary challenge within his own jurisdiction and go to work as a missionary in his own right, at the same time as he pleads assistance for the missionaries in primitive and pagan lands.

2

For genuinely effective local missionary work, a program and plan of sustained effort are vitally necessary. Conditions may differ radically from place to place, so that methods as well as degrees of aggression may have to be varied and modified. But the objectives and means for the achievement of these objectives remain basically the same. These objectives may be outlined as follows: (1) the creation of a friendly attitude in the community toward the priest and the Church; (2) general clarification of the purposes and doctrines of the Church, making Catholic faith and practices better understood in the community; (3) bringing back lapsed Catholics to the practice of their faith; (4) conversion of non-Catholics to the faith; (5) general raising of the moral and cultural standards of the community.

The means, particularly in the well-established parish, are principally good example and instruction. With respect to the first, it is hardly necessary to observe that as spiritual uplift is the stock in trade of the priest, any public or even publicly suspected deviation from the straight and narrow path on his part will weaken and even nullify his work. People rightly expect sanctity in a priest, even though he may be a thoroughly human and jolly individual. The minute he shows feet of clay, so to speak, they see not only human weakness but insincerity and hypocrisy as well. It is certainly true that to command respect and exercise leadership in any community, the priest must practice what he preaches.

The creation of a friendly attitude in the community is largely the result of tact and service, together with personality factors which engender friendly reactions. In solidly Catholic areas, the priest inherits a tradition of respect and cordiality from his people. All he has to do to maintain this is to conduct himself like a priest and treat his parishioners considerately. But in non-Catholic communities or in mixed communities, where Catholic life is not always burning brightly, the priest may find attitudes of indifference, misunderstanding, prejudice, bigotry, hostility, and outright intolerance. Under extreme circumstances, he may find himself living in a social vacuum, shunned even by his own parishioners. Under these circumstances, he may have to work long and hard simply to show that he is a law-abiding citizen and an agreeable person to know. A cordial greeting, a pleasant manner, kindness and willingness to help others and to be of community service eventually win over fair-minded people. The word goes around that the Catholic priest is really a human being. In the course of time, the favorable attitudes which he engenders personally are bound to relieve tensions against the Church and to open the way toward open-minded inquiry.

Clarification of the purposes and doctrines of the Church begins normally in the pulpit. One cannot overemphasize the importance and power of consistently good sermons. Positive, explanatory, and inspirational preaching can do more than practically every other medium at the disposal of the priest to gain respect for the Church and to attract an increasing congregation. People are hungry for a solid spiritual message. Indifferent, lukewarm, and lapsed Catholics gain new impetus, and non-Catholics are drawn irresistibly to the teaching of the Church, by the force of sacred eloquence.

There are numerous other avenues of making the Catholic faith and practices better understood in the community. Opportunities are now available locally and even nationally for appearance on radio and television broadcasts; and in many places the Church is offered special facilities for programs over the air. These opportunities should be seized and acted upon to produce the best possible impression. Priests are frequently invited to address luncheon and dinner groups, clubs, and gatherings as special occasions of a civic, cultural, business, or general character. In some instances, the demands may be more than one has time to meet, or circumstances may render acceptance inadvisable. In general, however, the competent and tactful priest should accept these invitations, even at a personal sacrifice, and give the best he has in him.

If there is any doubt as to the propriety of his appearing before a non-Catholic or mixed audience, the priest should consult the chancery office or bishop, and unhesitatingly abide by official decision. Special prudence must be exercised when he is invited to participate in a panel representing different religious faiths. If clearance is given for him to speak, he will be careful to keep his presentation on a positive, informative, gentlemanly basis, animated by Christian learning and charity. While there have been celebrated and possibly fruitful public debates on religious issues by Catholic churchmen in the past, one may seriously question the advisability of engaging in this kind of polemics. If permission to speak under non-Catholic, general, or interdenominational auspices is denied by the bishop, the matter should be quietly but definitely explained as a matter of policy. Cowardly, evasive, or false excuses never help the Catholic cause.

Occasionally, the secular newspapers may be used with propriety to advertise a Catholic Church service, to report a special sermon or event sponsored by the Church, or to explain the position of

the Church on a particular issue which may have caused misunderstanding or misapprehension in the community. In the past,
different points of view have been expressed on the value or
desirability of publicity in this form. Within recent years, it has
been recognized that the injunction of Christ not to hide one's
light under a bushel but to place it so that it may shine before all
men, may be applicable in this important medium.[3]

An excited attitude, even under provocation, and sensationalism
must be strenuously avoided. The temptation to leap into print
with a sarcastic, vitriolic, and abusive pen should never be in-
dulged. But a friendly co-operation with the newspapers, whether
it be in the form of a news item, the rectification of an error, or
even a firm insistence upon fair dealing where the Church has
been placed in an unfavorable public position, all appear to
come within the sphere of good public relations, subject of course
to approval by ecclesiastical authority.

The maintenance of good personal and public relations, whether
with the press, the civil government, or the community at large,
is of the greatest importance. A priest's motives may be as pure as
the driven snow. He may work himself to the bone, unselfishly,
for the cause of religion. And yet he may acquire a queer reputation, because of his failure to take time out to make social contacts,
to give fuller public explanation of his activity, and to cultivate
the friendship of those who are able to shape public opinion. The
Church may be engaged in charitable, educational, and spiritual
work of the highest character and value to mankind; but unless it
has a program of deliberate information to the world about all
this, it may suffer false accusation and be persecuted for its pains.

It should be pointed out that the priest cannot carry on all of
this work alone. He needs the assistance of the laity, both Catholic and non-Catholic. In some instances, an organized group of
representative Catholic men, such as the Knights of Columbus,
under prudent direction can perform valuable service in "fronting,"
so to speak, or representing the Church, where the personal appearance or activity of the priest might be inappropriate or un-

---

[3] Mt. 5:14–16.

acceptable. One of the primary objectives in any local public relations program for the Church should, in fact, be the development and utilization of a strong and intelligent Catholic lay leadership, both of men and women, in the community. In some places and circumstances, it may be helpful to engage the advisory services of a professional public-relations agent, whose experience and technique can be used to advantage in many ways. And in the process of developing good will and friendly co-operation, the priest will welcome the expression of friendship and the offer of assistance from the non-Catholics in the community. The growth of such spirit is in itself an evidence of missionary progress and of the activity of divine grace.

3

The mission of bringing back lapsed Catholics to the practice of their faith is one of pressing importance in nearly every parish. An extensive literature has grown up on this subject to show the leakage from the Church. Although there is considerable difference of opinion on the validity of the statistics advanced, the fact is that many Catholics start weak in the knowledge of their faith. Many become weak in its practice. Many abandon it altogether, and not a few adopt an attitude of positive antagonism to it. After one or two generations, the children often lose all contact with the Church and all sense or remembrance of the religion which their forefathers may have conserved, with great sacrifice, for centuries.[4]

Who are these lapsed Catholics, and how are they to be found and identified? Some are well known as a result of their civic prominence. Others are recognized as the result of a dispute with the pastor, a marriage outside the Church, and a dramatic repudiation of Church membership. Others are not so well known or they are not known at all. Coming from another community, they leave their past affiliations behind them, or they become lost in their new environment. Laziness, mixed marriage, divorce, a bad moral situation, excessive attachment to the pursuit of business and the

---

[4] Cf. John A. O'Brien, *op. cit.,* Chap. 8.

almighty dollar, a mistaken conception of social advancement, poor instruction, confused thinking, or resentment over a real or imaginary injury — any or all of these factors may enter into the picture. In some cases, the family friends or business associates can identify the individual who has lost the faith or stopped going to Mass and the sacraments. In other cases, the individual successfully conceals the fact from all except himself and God.

Perhaps the most effective way of bringing lapsed Catholics back to the faith is through the assistance and prodding of friends and associates. This is an apostolate for the laity, which is deserving of the utmost encouragement and commendation. Persons are frequently willing to confide in friends and sometimes in total strangers before carrying their problem to a priest. Shame and fear are powerful deterrents against reconciliation. Many lapsed Catholics have never known a priest personally, and they do not know how to come back. The guidance of a tactful friend may make the way easier.

A systematic and large-scale missionary program of action, however, is best inaugurated through a parish census. This process, which has already been described, discovers and tabulates the facts. With the contacts thus established and the causes of defection analyzed, the priest is in a position to go to work on each case individually and to enlist such assistance from family, friends, or associates as appears most effective in the circumstances.

There is no quick or easy formula for rehabilitation. Where loss of faith is deep-seated and of long duration, mental patterns and attitudes may create stiff resistance and loss of all interest. In the case of marriage with a divorcee, the problem may be one that only prayer and possibly only death can solve. Many lapsed Catholics will never return to the faith. Nevertheless, even the most hardened cases are worthy of consideration and a challenge to one's missionary zeal. And from a general, sustained program of action, many will return gratefully to the Church, who otherwise would have lived and died away from it.

For mass action in attracting Catholics of all kinds of spiritual condition and need, the parish mission may be recommended on an annual or biennial basis. The dramatic appeal and vigorous approach of a good missionary preacher often stir weak and lapsed Catholics to make another attempt. The opportunity of clearing one's sins in a general confession to a priest who is a total stranger in the community may make a return easier. The chance of "making the mission" for a spiritual revival can easily be held out to many who do not feel that they are ready to resume their full status as Catholics or to assume the responsibilities that this implies. This effort, with the aid of God's grace, has been the cause of innumerable good resolutions and many practical fulfillments of conversion and reversion to the Church.

It should be recognized that such good results of a mission are no guarantee of perseverance. Emotional instability as well as weakness of the flesh and other factors enter into the spiritual life of most persons. Before the first fervor of the mission has worn off, steps must be taken to establish continued spiritual contacts to steady and strengthen these people. Enrollment in a parish society, or activity, the promise of monthly or regular Communion for a year, and some kind of personal visitation or check by the priest at reasonable intervals may be indicated to sustain their spiritual regeneration. This is another reason for keeping the parish census current.

A busy parish priest may argue that this could take a disproportionate amount of his time. As an antidote to this argument, it is necessary only to recall the figure of Christ the Good Shepherd, who represents Himself as leaving the ninety-nine sheep to rescue the one that was lost. This theme occurs over and over again in the lessons of Christ to the Apostles. The story of the prodigal son exemplifies it. And the Master Himself has said, "There shall be more joy in heaven upon one sinner that doth penance than upon ninety-nine just who need not penance."[5]

The conversion of non-Catholics to the faith generally involves different psychological and spiritual processes than the return of persons who may be described as lapsed Catholics. In the case of the latter, there is a realization, however rudimentary or

---

[5] Lk. 15:7.

atrophied, that one belongs to the Church. There is at least a basic understanding of the doctrines of the Church and a mental pattern of acceptance, so that returning to the practice of the faith is something like coming back home, not going to a strange and foreign land.[6]

In the case of the convert, there may be a painful process of having to demolish, one by one, the deep-rooted hostilities of Protestantism to the Catholic Church or the long road of grasping, one by one, the articles of Catholic belief. The prospective convert is a lonely, courageous soul. His or her decision may have the effect of cutting off from friends and of being ejected by one's family. Consequently, the priest who undertakes the task of instructing and bringing converts into the Church assumes a difficult role, one fraught with responsibilities. In a way, he is like a parent who brings a new child into the world. He must share the pains of spiritual gestation and be prepared to assist his spiritual children in the process of learning to walk by themselves. He will be rewarded by the grateful appreciation of those whom he has brought into the joys of the faith; and he must be prepared for the disappointment of those who fail to receive the gift of faith or who, having apparently received it, let it slip from their grasp.

There are two general ways of handling the matter of converts. One is to wait for applicants who desire instruction in the faith and to take them on an individual basis. The other is to organize a course of instructions for prospective converts and inquirers alike, to run in series during the year, and to conduct the course on a group or class basis.

The first method is the answer to a demand for instruction by non-Catholics preparatory to marriage with Catholics. Some come for instruction, not because they wish to become Catholics, but simply because diocesan or parochial regulations oblige them to become acquainted with their basic obligations in contracting marriage. Some of these people may come in a hostile mood and never abandon their attitude of resistance. Others may present

---

[6] Cf. John A. O'Brien, *op. cit.*, Chaps. 6, 7.

themselves, with little or no preparation, but with their minds well disposed and practically determined to become Catholics even before they realize what this entails. Occasionally, a person asks for instructions to complete a long process of reasoning, which may have started from the example of a Catholic husband or wife or from a chain of reading and thought. Obviously, there must be variations in the human approach and in the type of instruction that is offered to these people. For this reason, there is much to commend in the method of individual instructions.

On the other hand, this procedure is not likely to attract converts in any large number. There are many non-Catholics who would welcome an opportunity to meet a priest and receive a course of instructions; but they are fearful of approaching him on an individual basis, and they are by no means certain that they will wish to become Catholics. If offered an opportunity of attending a class with others, under no pressure or feeling of being conspicuous or obligated, they probably would register for the course. Such, at least, has been the observation of most priests who use this method. There is no question but that planned and organized group instructions have been extremely fruitful in bringing converts to the Church. Those who decide to take the final step are given some private instructions to provide for their individual problems and difficulties which may not have been solved to their complete satisfaction in the regular class instruction. Some may not progress this far; but at least they have had the benefit of correct instruction in the Catholic religion, and this in itself is missionary achievement.

The record of conversions achieved by numerous priests using the group method on a scheduled and advertised basis during the year is truly phenomenal. It illustrates again that the missionary concept of priestly work is quite as important and effective in established parishes and Christian communities as it is in the pagan hinterlands.

The most satisfactory method for instructing converts still remains that of the catechism. The priest takes lesson after lesson and explains each question and answer. The members of the class, or the individuals under instruction, are required to memorize the answers and in turn explain more fully what is meant. In this way, one is reasonably certain that the instructions are understood and that the converts will later on be able to defend themselves and give a reason for their belief in detail. Collateral reading may be given, but this should be gradual so as not to confuse the basic issues or to be above and beyond the grasp of those under instruction.

Much of the success of convert and inquiry classes depends on the way they are conducted. The first rule is punctuality and regularity. If the priest cannot be depended upon to keep his appointments, he cannot expect sustained interest in his classes. The second rule is positive clarity. It is important to divest oneself of theological terminology, so far as possible, and make sure that the individuals or class understand the meaning of each lesson. A period should be allowed at each session for questions, but the questions should be confined to the matter at hand. Toward the end of the course, an opportunity should be given for a wider range of questions. The third rule is positive charity. In answering questions, one should never exhibit annoyance, impatience, or a sarcastic manner. This principle is basic in all pedagogy. The priest, however, must always keep in mind that he is not simply a classroom lecturer, but an apostle calling souls to Christ. This task requires the utmost patience, kindness, and a truly Christlike spirit in the priest.

Simultaneous with the articles of faith, the persons under instruction should be taught their prayers and the methods of prayer. The process of conversion, and even basic instruction in Catholic belief, must be pointed toward a personal approach to God. Simply learning what the Church teaches is no different in kind than a lesson in philosophy, comparative religion, history, or any other subject. The individual under instruction may adopt various attitudes toward the instruction and assignments. He may remain passive; he may be secretly hostile and resistant. He may become interested and even fascinated by what he learns. But until he recognizes that what he is searching is truth that involves the salvation of his immortal soul and a way of life ordained by God, he is not ready for conversion. The priest also must pray for the blessing of God upon his work, in the realization that divine faith comes not as the automatic result of intellectual preparation or even of good will, but as a free gift of God.

Before bringing anyone into the Church, upon completion of the course of instructions, the priest should carefully determine whether the prospective converts are fully and properly instructed. Special precautions should be taken if the individuals have been referred from another source, with the assurance that they have already received instruction and are practically ready to be received into the Church. It may turn out that the previous instruction has left a number of serious gaps. One must not assume that the unprepared person will naturally adjust himself to the faith and pick up the loose ends of instruction after formal profession as a Catholic. It is possible that the exact opposite may happen; and after a period of unsatisfactory floundering around, the apparent convert may abandon the Church.

It should also be reasonably clear that prospective converts are prepared to take the step of their own free will, to fulfill their new obligations, and to persevere even against serious obstacles. In the case of conversions which have been prompted by the consideration of marriage with a Catholic, one may agree that many or even most of these persons would not have taken instructions except for this circumstance. But it may also be pointed out that many persons would not be Catholics except for the circumstance of birth into a Catholic family. Many converts have been attracted to the Church by admiration for a priest or the friendship, kindness, and good example of Catholics. The important thing in determining readiness for acceptance into the Church is, not the circumstance of interest, but the fact of the earnest desire to become and remain a Catholic.

In cases of marriage, marital complications, or other situations in which personal adjustments of a basic character may be involved, all problems should be faced squarely and honestly prior to the decision. These matters should be clearly explained during the course of instruction, so as to avoid possible misunderstanding. Conversions with a qualification will not last.

Where it may be appropriately done, the ceremonies of formal conversion should be solemnly and joyfully celebrated, individually or collectively as the circumstances may indicate. While there may be some variations in procedure, as in the ceremonies of baptism and abjuration, the idea of group reception has much to commend it.

After conversion, with Confession, First Communion, and Confirmation, steps should be taken by the priest to keep close to his converts. Particularly during the period of adjustment, they need a kindly and strengthening hand. Intellectual and moral questions will arise on which they require advice. They will wish further direction on good reading. And if their conversion has created a difficult home, social, or business problem, they may need good Catholic friends to tide them over.

4

In communities or areas that can be clearly designated as mission territory, the missionary concept is identified with the full-time occupation of the priest. In some instances, the first objective of the priest may be to search out the Catholics of the area and organize religious services for them. This situation is common in vast areas of the United States, where the proportion of Catholics to the total population is less than that in India or China. In these localities the priest usually endeavors to establish a church in the central community from which he proceeds on alternating weeks to take care of one or several missions or outposts. The chapel for such missions is often the parlor of a Catholic family in which an altar may be set up temporarily and the faithful of the area may gather to hear Mass.

It is not uncommon, however, to find similar situations within the confines of many large metropolitan sees. Within one or two hours' drive of a number of major cities with strong Catholic populations, it is possible to find villages and rural areas in which the Catholic Church is on hardly more than a survival basis, and the local priest leads a veritable pioneer existence between his parish and his missions. In many cases, he must add the roles of housekeeper, cook, plumber, carpenter, and gardener to his pastoral duties.

Under these circumstances, where Catholics are distinctly outnumbered and constitute possibly the barest fraction of the total population, three problems of the priest become accentuated. The first problem is that of physical existence. Where Catholic families or individuals are poor and scattered over a wide area, their ability to provide support for the pastor or missionary is strictly limited.

In consideration of this fact, any hope of success in mission territory must be reinforced with financial aid from the outside. Simply to let a priest forage for himself under such circumstances is to invite disaster. In the case of diocesan clergy, aid may be sought in the form of loans or outright subsidies from the Ordinary, who shares primary responsibility for any parochial or missionary assignment within the diocese. With the approval of ecclesiastical authorities, the more prosperous parishes may come to the assistance of their less fortunate sister parishes or extend facilities for the priests of the latter to solicit funds for the maintenance of the outlying pioneer parishes and missions.

A device used with considerable success in missionary areas is the mailing list for the solicitation of funds on a national basis. When authorized by the bishop of the diocese or territory, this method is certainly justified; and priests and laity alike ought to answer deserving appeals with at least a modest offering. One has only to experience the distress and apprehension of a hand-to-mouth existence to share the appreciation of the missionary for any response. At the same time, it is obvious that such individual appeals must be controlled to avoid needless multiplication and abuse.

The missions conducted by religious orders are usually financed from the resources of their own organizations. The problem of the religious orders, however, is essentially the same as that of the dioceses with mission problems. As a result, they are obliged to resort to the same type of appeals for assistance. The history of the Church in many countries has been evangelization by the religious orders, then consolidation into dioceses with the diocesan clergy gradually assuming the direction of parishes, while the religious orders remain in charge of schools and other institutions and move into new missionary fields. The missionary history of the religious orders is one of great devotion, self-sacrifice, and adjustment for the welfare of the Church as a whole.

For an organized and large-scale approach to the problem of financial support, the Propagation of the Faith has been organized with international headquarters in Rome. Numerous missionary societies have been organized on national and regional basis, both for local and foreign missions. In the past, the Church in the United States has been the beneficiary of generous aid, both in personnel and money, from Europe and Latin America. In fact, were it not for this generous assistance, the Church in America might never have risen to its present eminence. For graphic illustration of the effects of lack of support for a missionary program, one has only to read the story of the southern states, where thousands of Catholic immigrants were lost to the faith.

Of outstanding service in providing aid to the home missions on a national scale, the Catholic Church Extension Society has proved of blessed relief and assistance to the struggling Church and impoverished priests from coast to coast. Chapels, churches, vestments, schools, rectories, mission equipment, and direct financial aid have been provided, with funds solicited by this great Society. It is no exaggeration to state that without the aid of the Catholic Church Extension Society, churches now flourishing in many dioceses would never have existed and possibly millions of Catholics in this country would have been abandoned.

The second problem of the missionary is one of human relations. The priest may be convinced that he brings the word of God and a desire to be only of benefit to the community. But others may not share this view. Anti-Catholic sentiments, weird, distorted ideas about the Church and the clergy, and the antagonism of entrenched interests may all combine to make the local reception anything but friendly. Even where the feeling is inclined to be open-minded and favorable, there is an expectancy that the priest must prove himself one way or the other. In other words, the priest must take the initiative, introduce himself to the local authorities, make his intentions clear, show himself in public, and endeavor to create a friendly atmosphere, before he can work in a new territory.

The establishment of a friendly atmosphere with the local powers and persons of influence is of the utmost importance. One may stand on his civil rights and appeal to the laws and the courts, but all this can be a costly and even futile process if opposition is experienced at every turn on the human level. Unless one is liked or at least tolerated, opposition can take numerous forms, from an undefinable social vacuum, to legal technicalities and zoning restrictions, refusal to sell property, weasel interpretations of building schools, and traffic regulations, arson, and calumny. On the other hand, a friendly attitude and a willingness to help will make all the difference, not only in matters of critical importance but in day-to-day existence as well.

There is no hard and fast rule for achieving these objectives. Temperaments and situations differ, and what might be prescribed for one individual and community would not be feasible for another. There may be circumstances under which the priest has to defend himself and the cause he represents with full vigor and challenge. There is a difference, however, between the Church Militant and the Church Pugnacious. If an open issue and battle lines of controversy are drawn, it is usually better to let others become excited. A quiet attitude of instruction, letting the facts stand for themselves, with a continued positive program of service, is generally the best policy and one that will eventually appeal to fair-minded, normal people.

Once the way has been cleared for safeguarding the basic rights and clearance has been given for action on a long-range com munity basis, steps must be taken to provide for consolidation of the Catholic population and to broaden the field of evangelization. The approach and program will, again, depend upon local conditions and state of development.

In what may, for lack of a better word, be described as primitive "grass-roots" conditions, the missionary may have to begin by street preaching or gathering a congregation of any kind into an available enclosure. This method has been used from time immemorial and under vastly different circumstances. It was the method regularly used by Christ, as exemplified in His sermon on the Mount. St. Paul preached in the open on the Areopagus at Athens. Missionaries have preached in the fields, under trees, and in the streets to the heathens of many lands. The Catholic Evidence Guild explains Christian doctrine today on improvised platforms in Hyde Park, London, and in many American city parks. Street preaching or Catholic instruction is given every year by priests and Catholic laymen in the public squares of cities and hamlets in the Southern areas of the United States where the Catholic Church has been known only by hearsay. Chapel cars and automobiles have served the same purpose.

It is difficult to state precisely how effective this method of evangelization is. Question may be raised as to its advisability under certain circumstances. Prudence and competence are necessary to avoid both eccentric display and unfortunate reactions. Nevertheless, the important thing is that a start must be made somewhere. Commenting on the words of the prophet Joel, "For whosoever shall call upon the name of the Lord shall be saved," St. Paul asked, "How then shall they call on him in whom they have not believed? Or how shall they believe him of whom they have not heard? And how shall they hear without a preacher? . . . Faith then cometh by hearing; and hearing by the word of Christ."[7] The missionary who is eager to get the word of Christ to the people cannot wait until, by some miracle, the unbelievers to whom he has been sent have assembled in his church.

---

[7] Rom. 10:13–17.

Even more important in the work of developing a Catholic community is the education of the young. Not until the missionary has secured at least the rudimentary elements of a school to instruct the children in the faith can he be assured that his efforts have taken permanent root. Adults may be slow to adopt a new faith, and parents who are lax in the practice of their Catholic religion often find it difficult, even under urging and persuasion, to realize their full obligations. But if they are willing to allow their children to secure a Catholic education, there is hope for the new generation.

It is from this renewal of the human race from generation to generation that the missionary concept of the priest's career derives its substance and significance. Mankind is never fully converted to Christ, nor is the established faith a guaranteed and confirmed reality. Only by constant effort are the young instructed, the weak made strong, the lapsed brought back, and the ignorant enlightened. And to these tasks, united by the universal charity of Christ, the Catholic priests throughout the world join efforts, by prayer, good works, and generous aid where needed, that there may be "one fold and one Shepherd."[8]

An essential part of the missionary program of every priest should be to point out to his people the beneficent influence of the Church in its missions throughout the world. The work and charity of the Church for the poor, the sick, the young, the aged, and the underprivileged around the globe is truly staggering. This story should become better known.[9] Youth everywhere should be encouraged to study the work of the foreign and home missions through such organizations as the Catholic Students Mission Crusade. The annual collections for the missions should be an occasion to stimulate the knowledge, enthusiasm, and generosity of the faithful for this great cause. Mission auxiliary groups ought to be encouraged for the sending of funds, books, religious articles, and general assistance to the missions. Protestant missionary groups

[8] Jn. 10:16.

[9] Cf. Joseph Schmidlin, *Catholic Mission History,* translation edited by Matthias Braun, S.V.D. (Techny, Ill.: Mission Press, S.V.D., 1933).

have given a tremendous example of zeal and organization. Catholics, whose very name means *universal*, can certainly do no less.

From the missionary concept of parochial life, communicated by the pastor to his people and operative in a better understanding and spread of the Catholic faith, there ought to result a general raising of the moral and cultural standards of the community.[10] This follows from the principle that the divine law is the fulfillment and clarification of the natural law, which makes for orderly and civilized living. The material standard of living in any area or community is governed by a number of factors, some of them beyond human control, such as climate and natural resources. Other factors, however, are subject to human control, such as government, housing, hygiene, transportation, education, and recreation. Depending upon the right use or abuse of power, a community progresses or it suffers. Depending upon the encouragement or discouragement of good leadership and talent, the world moves ahead or it stagnates and corrupts. It is certainly part of the mission of the Catholic Church in establishing the kingdom of Christ on earth to apply its power, its leadership, and its talents to a practical conception of the Gospel for better living in every sense of the word.

---

[10] Cf. Paul Hanly Furfey, in *The Sociology of the Parish, cit.,* Chap. 12.

"Bear ye one another's burdens: and so you shall fulfill the law of Christ" (Gal. 6:2).

CHAPTER XIV

THE PRIEST AND SOCIAL WELFARE

I

"RELIGION clean and undefiled before God and the Father," wrote St. James, "is this: to visit the fatherless and widows in their tribulation and to keep oneself unspotted from this world."[1] In pursuit of this definition, the work of the priest is evangelization, not by word alone, but by the deeds of Christian charity. Exhortation must be accompanied by an active ministry of social work and welfare, to bear one another's burdens.

In the first stages of missionary approach and development, the principal work of the Church is often that of social service. Medical assistance, the rescue of abandoned infants and children, caring for the aged, and even providing food and the other necessities of life are all an important part of missionary activity. These tasks are an evidence and exemplification of Christian principles, which give reality and proof to the preaching of the divine word. But, even after the Christian community has been established, the need continues for Christian social charity; and it is to the Church and to the priest that the community looks for leadership.

One has only to scan the newspapers to recognize the scope of this need and the dramatic character of the social disorders of our age in even the most advanced of so-called Christian communities. The unfortunate and vicious by-products of poverty,

[1] James 1:27.

disease, broken homes and divorce, alcoholism, juvenile delinquency, prostitution, and crimes of various kinds are evidence of the need of personal aid and social adjustment. The persistence of economic injustice, with constant dissatisfaction and forms of violence in industrial relations, interracial strife, unfair social discrimination, and deterioration of areas and neighborhoods point to human misery which cries for relief and remedy.

It may be argued that these problems are the business of the State and of the civil authorities responsible for the enforcement of law and order. In a number of encyclicals and other public pronouncements, the popes have repeatedly emphasized the duty of civil government, by legislative as well as relief measures, to secure decent living and working conditions as a protection for all and to safeguard the rights particularly of the weaker elements of society.[2] Sociologists and public-spirited leaders everywhere have stressed the importance of civic recognition of the problems of social welfare and of organized provision through law, taxation, and public welfare service to raise the standards of the so-called underprivileged elements. As a matter of fact, local and national governments in practically all modern states have taken advanced and even elaborate steps to protect the laboring classes and to offer financial assistance and various services to the unfortunate and indigent.

There is a limit, however, beyond which the State should not be expected or even permitted to solve the problems of social distress. Complete dependence upon civil action and monopoly by the State over the administration of charity can easily result in a mechanistic conception of society and the development of bureaucratic autocracy which gives rise to greater problems than those which it attempts to solve. If human liberty and dignity are to be safeguarded, then the responsibility for better education, personal counseling, rehabilitation, and constant vigilance, as well as for emergency relief, must be shared by all who have any interest in the safety and progress of the community.

[2] Cf. Pope Leo XIII, Encyclical, *On the Condition of Labor,* and Pope Pius XI, Encyclical, *Forty Years After,* in *Two Basic Social Encyclicals* (New York: Benziger Brothers, 1943).

Moreover, to the extent that social ills have their roots in spiritual causes, the Church has a duty to aid in the solution of these problems. It is of the utmost importance to recognize the fact that the struggle for human existence is not simply one of animal instinct, nor can it be brought under social control merely by statistical evidence, technological improvements, mechanical regulations, or economic distribution. Man is a combination of body and soul, with moral as well as material needs and aspirations. In reply to the devil who urged the Son of God to command that stones be made bread, Christ replied in the inspired words: "Not in bread alone doth man live, but in every word that proceedeth from the mouth of God."[3] Failure to comprehend the significance of man's spiritual nature in the solution of his social problems will result in the same bad situation as created by similar failure which has given rise to those problems. It is a primary mission of the Church to keep this truth burning bright and to hold it aloft as a guiding light to all engaged in social work, whether on a public or private basis.

Related to this principle, upon which the ultimate success of social welfare must stand or fall, is that of motivation. It is quite true that pious hopes and religious intentions, by themselves, cannot put bread into a man's mouth when he needs it or put a distressed family or community back on its feet. It is possible also that bungling methods may sometimes spoil the efforts which are inspired by spiritual motives. Nevertheless, the whole conception of Christian charity, which gives it life and meaning, is the love of neighbor for the love of God. The second commandment "Thou shalt love thy neighbor as thyself" stems directly, in the teaching of Christ, from the first Commandment "Thou shalt love the Lord thy God with thy whole heart and with thy whole soul and with thy whole mind and with thy whole strength."[4]

With this motive underlying social welfare and with this integral spiritual conception of human nature, the Catholic priest has, not

---

[3] Mt. 4:3, 4; cf. Deut. 8:3.
[4] Mk. 12:30, 31.

only the right, but also a positive duty, to aid in the solution of social problems by study, investigation, education, personal services, agencies, and material assistance. Armed with spiritual power, sustained with spiritual motivation, and adequately prepared by knowledge of what he is doing, he can be a tremendous force in a society which needs the work of God as well as daily bread.

The challenge of social welfare does not start or stop with desperate and dramatic instances, even though these may be humanly necessary to arouse and spark interest and effort. The work of the Church, whether by itself or in conjunction with secular agencies, extends to the daily, normal living of all of its members and includes a program designed to assist the entire community to lead a better and more abundant life. Its action is not of an emergency or occasional nature but is based upon the constant example of Christ, the Good Shepherd, regularly concerned with His flock, but ready to go after those that have strayed from the fold, and others that should be brought into the fold, that there may be "one fold and one Shepherd."[5]

2

Social work and assistance may be viewed in three steps or phases. The first is relief of an immediate nature. The second is an investigation of the causes of distress and an endeavor to correct the source of trouble or to provide a more permanent solution of the problem. This phase may include also the adjustment or rehabilitation of individuals, families, or areas, after the basic correction or remedy has been effected. The third phase is the development of a program or plan for the permanent betterment and maintenance of the community.

The logical starting point for a systematic program of parochial social welfare is the parish census. After a personal visitation of all sections of the parish, with the data thus compiled on an individual or family basis, the pastor will find himself in the best position to analyze the local situation and deal with the various de-

---

[5] Jn. 10:11–16.

mands for assistance. He may find that some of the most deserving cases would not otherwise have come to his attention. This information, moreover, will provide him with the material for the long-range positive program of community conservation and development referred to above.

The most familiar form of need appealing for social assistance is that of poverty; and a most elemental evidence of Christian charity is that of almsgiving. There has been a supposition that social welfare is necessary only in poor communities or among the poor in more prosperous areas. But it is clear, from the observations already made, that social problems cover a much wider area than those of financial need. The fact is that prosperity is no guarantee against social disintegration, vice, crime, and human misery. There is abundant evidence that drink, divorce, sexual looseness and deviation, juvenile delinquency, and personal disintegration exist among the rich as well as among the poor. Consequently the concept of social welfare must be broadened to include the whole range of problems with a social character or impact. Priests in the so-called "run-down" parishes or blighted neighborhoods may be confronted with a larger number of cases which stem from poverty; but those in charge of more elite areas may be surprised at conditions which an honest parish survey sometimes reveals.

There has always been a tendency on the part of certain elements in society which are prosperous and law-abiding to feel that the most effective way of dealing with persons in need of social assistance or correction is to refer them to the appropriate institution. This might be an orphanage, an asylum, a hospital, a home for the aged, or a jail. Obviously, all of these institutions serve helpful and necessary purposes. Considerations of both justice and charity make institutional service an essential part of organized social welfare.

Institutions are designed specifically to provide services which are not practical or available in the family setting of a home; but they should not be substituted for an obligation which belongs strictly to family care and personal responsibility. Even granting the advisability or necessity of institutional referral in any particular case, one must always keep in mind the problem of personal and social adjustment. The individual must be helped to help himself. His dignity as a human being must be safeguarded to the fullest extent possible. Christian charity is fulfilled, not simply by a mechanical solution which removes needy, afflicted, or maladjusted persons from public sight, but by the healing arts which restore them to competence, health, decency, and self-confidence.

The aim of social work should be to help people live normal happy lives in an average community or at least under conditions which approximate those of pleasant family and community organization. Under some circumstances, this may be difficult. Insanity, advanced addiction to drugs, desperate alcoholism, hopeless disease, pronounced criminal tendencies, and the like may render personal rehabilitation practically impossible. In some cases, environmental factors may have deteriorated to a point where they cannot be improved or where the nature of the case renders what might be called normal living out of the question. But even in these cases, the essential dignity of the individual must be kept in mind and safeguarded.

The solutions of sterilization, contraception, euthanasia, and similar operations designed to end crime, poverty, and suffering by immoral means are constantly advanced by scientists and sociologists with a mechanistic conception of society and of the human personality. Eternal vigilance is necessary to guard against and counteract these tendencies, which are to be found in the most highly civilized as well as in the most primitive society.

The responsibility and activity of the Church in social teaching and welfare exists, therefore, in every field and area and on every social level. Particular problems may differ from place to place; but the basic needs of human beings are the same everywhere, and the principles of Christian charity are universal. With this profound conception of social work as identified with his sacred ministry, the Catholic priest is a tremendous force for good, gratefully recognized and accepted in his community.

3

The pastor who stirs no farther than his desk or front door will probably receive numerous appeals for money and aid of various kinds. His instincts of pity, motives of Christian charity, normal powers of human appraisal, and limitations of resources will guide his responses to these appeals. But for any kind of constructive social welfare, co-operative action is necessary. The priest who attempts to do everything by himself, ignoring or rejecting the organizations and agencies which are available in this field, is unfair both to himself and to the cause he is trying to serve. As the works of social charity are organized on a civic and diocesan as well as parochial and merely local basis, the prudent pastor should also co-ordinate his personal and parochial efforts with those of the larger bodies of action to which they are logically or physically related.

Effective parochial work, in the first place, requires at least some planning, experience, and possibly professional skill. For this reason, it is recommended that parishes, particularly those of mixed social and economic character, organize a conference of the St. Vincent de Paul Society. An active group of this kind, meeting regularly, under the direction of the pastor or delegated priest, serves to study and process various appeals for aid. One of the rules of this society of laymen is that members go in pairs when visiting poor families and others in need of assistance. By personal visitation, they gather the facts that lie behind human misery and suggest adjustments to correct or improve the situation. An alert group will uncover deserving and serious cases that otherwise might never come to light or at least not be brought to the attention of Catholic authorities. They assist in raising funds for charitable purposes. By counsel and example, in the spirit of their saintly patron, they recover many souls for Christ.

The examination of a typical report by this Society is sufficient to convince one of its value. Thus in one community, 32 out of a total of 38 parishes reported 289 members with St. Vincent de Paul Conferences. The annual report of the president showed 6565 family visits made in the course of a year. During this time, 4193 persons in 1040 needy families were assisted. Positions were secured for 69 unemployed, 37 persons were enabled to return to distant homes, 31 couples were aided in validating irregular marriages, 95 baptisms were arranged, 60 children were enrolled in parochial schools and 82 in Sunday schools. Eighty-two persons were helped back to their religious duties, and a total of 3485 books, magazines, and papers were distributed. From poor boxes, weekly collections from members, and other sources, the Society spent for the benefit of the poor, practically without overhead expense, a total of $80,041.26. In addition, summer-camp facilities were provided for 100 children.[6]

One of the distinctive and basic features of this Society is precisely that it works with a spiritual motive and aims to restore the spirit of Christ in the homes of those to whom it brings aid and comfort. Its members regard this volunteer work as an apostolate for the salvation of their own souls as well; the Church has richly endowed their activities with spiritual blessings.

Other groups of men and women, such as the Big Brothers and Big Sisters, perform a grand service particularly in the protection and rehabilitation of youth exposed to bad environment and the experience of crime and vice. Several religious communities are likewise dedicated to works of social service in parishes, either on call or in permanent residence.

In more difficult cases and in large parishes, particularly those of an industrial or blighted social character, the services of a trained social worker may be indicated. It is important to recognize the fact that, over the years, a vast body of knowledge and experience has been developed and organized in social work, the same as in the fields of nursing, medicine, and other professional and vocational areas. The trained, professional social worker brings to welfare work a background of understanding and a skill in the recognition and solution of problems that is invaluable where something more than routine attention and Christian compassion are required.

---

[6] Washington, D. C., 1955.

The fact that the professional social worker commands a salary should be no cause for wonder or alarm. In the words of Christ Himself, "the laborer is worthy of his hire."[7] The doctor, the professional nurse, and even the priest lives by salary or equivalent in the offering of those who are served. These observations may appear superfluous and impertinent to some; but to others they may be helpful for a correct appraisal of the services and worth of the professional, trained worker in social service.

Within recent years, the Catholic Church has recognized the importance of this field of training; and schools of social work have been established in a number of Catholic universities. The need for prepared experts who are, at the same time, thoroughly imbued with Catholic principles is becoming increasingly evident. In the direction and technical guidance of diocesan charity bureaus, in planning community social welfare projects, in drawing up programs of youth and recreational development, coping with problems of delinquency, family rehabilitation, public health, and the co-ordination of agencies in this vast field, the Catholic-trained social worker performs a truly essential and apostolic service.

The average parish probably has little or only occasional need for a trained social worker, except on a consultative basis. In problem areas, however, these services may be highly valuable, particularly on an interparochial or co-operative basis, where serious problems common to the area call for community consideration and action. In such cases, of course, diocesan authorities should be consulted, so as to insure a concerted plan of action.

Many problems of social assistance cannot be handled effectively except on an organized and institutional basis. In such cases, there is nothing to do but look for the appropriate institution to which the individual may be committed or the family be referred. Institutional care requires an even larger co-operative effort, with the pooling of funds and technical skills as well as administration on a large scale. Most Catholic institutions are operated by religious orders and communities, ranging from homes for orphans and the aged to asylums for the mentally ill, homes for detention and cor-

---

[7] Lk. 10:7.

rection of delinquents, hospitals, and educational guidance centers for the handicapped, schools for the deaf and blind, and services for the part-time care of children. Nevertheless, there has been a definite trend toward the co-ordination of these various activities under the heading of diocesan Catholic charities, and in most dioceses a concerted drive is made annually, under the direction of the diocesan charity bureau, to provide necessary funds for their support.

It is the duty of every parish priest to know his diocesan charities, to contribute liberally to them, and to encourage his people to do likewise. The principal sources of revenue for these institutions are public funds, responsible relatives, who recognize their duty to assist in the support of children and old people under institutional care, community funds and chests, and private contributions. Under the last categories, every Catholic has a responsibility to give generously according to his means.

Other services also must be supported in the nature of welfare agencies. Food, clothing, education, shelter, and recreation must be provided for children under full-time care in institutions or foster homes. Day nursery and settlement care is needed to enable working mothers to keep their children under protection and to provide off-the-street programs for older children. Maternity care for unmarried mothers as well as for poor married mothers must be provided. The training of mentally and physically retarded children calls for special facilities. Bureaus are necessary to help immigrants adjust themselves and to prevent them from falling into dangerous hands and from becoming permanent public charges.

All of these services, and many others, are possible only by organized, co-operative effort. In some instances, the individual priest may be required to establish his own welfare agencies and may indeed be a pioneer in devising ways and means of meeting a particular social problem. But if his plan requires funds for its support, he must turn to the parish as a whole, to the larger community, to the diocese, or to the country at large for his finance. It was by comparable steps that Father Flanagan developed his

Boys' Town. Numerous welfare agencies and services have similarly developed from private and parochial enterprise to meet a specific need. But with their growth, they have become assimilated into larger bodies, with combined administration and improved techniques, for efficient and economical operation.

With improved and enlarged facilities for research, new fields of service and special programs of assistance are being developed in social welfare, both in the Catholic and general agencies of social welfare. X-ray services for the detection of tuberculosis is but one of these developments. The administration of hearing tests in the schools, therapy classes for hard-of-hearing children, special schools for blind and deaf children, and the production of braille aids for the blind may also be mentioned. Remedial reading programs have been inaugurated, of great benefit particularly in the less privileged metropolitan areas. Free milk and lunches are provided in many schools, where the children are in need of such assistance. In-service training, for both institutional and casework personnel, and the organization of facilities for field training of public health nurses are likewise part of the larger plan for social welfare adopted by organized charity. In many of these activities, Catholic and public agencies, as well as those of various religious and fraternal groups, have learned to co-operate in the interests of exchanged experience, appropriate referrals, better finance, and the avoidance of needless duplication.

Every priest engaged in the active ministry — parochial, educational, missionary, as chaplain, or in administration — should make it a point to keep himself informed on all of these developments. They enter vitally into his work. The saving of souls is a far bigger task than a routine administration of the sacraments and an elementary teaching of Christian doctrine. It involves an understanding of the whole human person, body and soul, and of the entire community, with its misery as well as its contentment. And the administration of Christian charity, as one of the works of the mystical body of Christ, requires an intelligent understanding, full co-operation, and generous support of Catholic institutions and agencies on a diocesan and national as well as local basis.

It is important also for the parish priest to be well informed on the existence, the services, and the activities of public centers and other agencies in this field. There are a number of reasons for this. Catholics, who are also taxpayers, are entitled to the same assistance and services which are supported by public funds as all others. Catholic institutions which serve as agencies for the care of dependents, delinquents, and others committed by public law are entitled to reimbursement by public welfare funds, and should apply for these payments to carry on their work. Much can be learned from methods and procedures of these various general and private welfare bureaus and workers as well as from their spirit of zeal and dedication. At the same time, the priest ought to keep in touch with the various agencies to which Catholics may apply for assistance, as a precaution against advice and practices contrary to Catholic faith and morals.

4

It is obvious that social welfare worthy of the name cannot be satisfied with merely almsgiving to vagrants or with occasional doles and baskets of food to needy families at Christmas time. Nevertheless, in some cases, the immediate need or situation is so desperate that action must come first and questions later. Hunger, disaster, and suffering cry out for immediate aid on humanitarian grounds alone; and Christian charity in such emergencies cannot wait for the deliberations of legislators or the diagnosis and statistics of experts. "For I was hungry," said Christ, "and you gave me to eat: I was thirsty, and you gave me to drink: I was a stranger, and you took me in: naked, and you covered me; sick, and you visited me: I was in prison, and you came to me."[8]

Any program of social welfare must give consideration to emergency physical relief before it can proceed farther. The soup

---

[8] Mt. 25:35, 36. For a general survey of objectives and methods of social work, confer: Arthur E. Fink, *The Field of Social Work* (New York: Henry Holt, 1949); Marguerite T. Boylan, *Social Welfare in the Catholic Church* (New York: Columbia University Press, 1941); Mary J. McCormick, *Diagnostic Casework in the Thomistic Pattern* (New York: Columbia University Press, 1954).

kitchen, the mission relief station, and temporary shelter for the "down and out" in the slums and on "skid row" all serve a useful and meritorious purpose. Even the dregs of humanity are still human beings, brothers and sisters in Christ. If, in extreme cases, one cannot find a better motive to serve these poor creatures, one may reflect on the consideration that much crime originates in desperate need. Any act of kindness under these circumstances may serve to protect the community from theft and violence. This is true even though the nature of some cases is such that continued alms and assistance are the only form of practical help. Some people are congenital beggars and impostors, incapable of permanent improvement or reform, whose strongest appeal is in their nuisance value.

But in all cases of continued need, particularly where the individuals or families involved are residents of the community, a reasonable investigation should be conducted as soon as possible to determine the cause as well as the extent of distress. If justification for continued aid is established, measures should be taken for the correction of the situation. Some encouragement and friendly advice, together with the offering of temporary aid, is often enough to rectify a situation and enable the victims of misfortune to get back on their feet. In other cases, the immediate problem may be only the surface manifestation of a deep-seated and chronic condition.

Very often, in such circumstances, one situation leads to another, and various factors may become inextricably tangled together. The difficulty may arise from a defect in character or it may result from environmental factors and other external considerations. Moral problems are often caused by economic and social conditions. The shiftlessness and squalor obvious in many poor Negro communities and neighborhoods, for example, are too easily ascribed to a defect in the Negro character, whereas they may actually reflect the low level of educational standards and of economic justice and opportunity. Negroes who are given opportunities for education and decent remuneration show themselves quite capable of ambition, leadership, and domestic and community pride. Offered the guidance and inspiration of religion worthy of the name, their moral and civic life immediately improves. In these respects, they are no different from any other race or people.

In the diagnosis of social misery and disorder, it is a mistake to make sweeping generalizations, particularly of the sort that absolves the individual from blame and lays the responsibility upon society and social environment. Many persons have only themselves to blame for their sad plights. Nevertheless, an examination of the causes of trouble leads most frequently to family backgrounds. The family is the natural unit of society. When the family fails in its obligations, for one reason or the other, to provide a decent living for its members, to create an atmosphere of friendly domestic relations, and to exercise reasonable vigilance over the household, society begins to face mounting problems.

Juvenile delinquency, as exemplified in destructive gangs, theft, drunkenness, sexual looseness, and perversion, is usually the product of unsatisfactory home life. It may be the reflection of a broken or disrupted home, with alcoholism in the picture. Both parents may be found at work, unable to supervise their children. It may be the result of the neglect of overindulgent parents, or of parents so engrossed in their own interests and pleasures that they take their children for granted. Juvenile delinquency, as already noted, appears in prosperous as well as in impoverished families.

The broken home or the deserted home may itself lead to various trails. Unemployment, mismanagement, insufficient income, incompatibility, personality defects, alcohol, or extramarital adventures may account for the unhappy situation. And these in turn may point to faulty education, lack of a sense of personal and family responsibility, a sense of frustration and self-pity, or an inadequate income or unjust economic situation.

Where misery originates in the maladjustment of individuals or families to the realities of existence, their rehabilitation is usually a matter of re-education, counseling, and vigilance. Unfortunately, the solution for marital and family financial problems offered by many secular counselors is that of divorce, sterilization, or contraceptive birth control. There is need for increasing Catholic bureau and counseling services, in marriage and family problems, if Catholics at least are to be spared this kind of advice and kept on the positive path of virtue and Christian reconciliation.

Where the problem originates in economic and environmental factors beyond the control of the individual, action may have to be taken by organized effort to secure social justice. The struggle for a living wage, decent working conditions, and reasonable security for the laboring and also for the so-called "white-collar" classes has been an uphill fight, as history testifies. This has been complicated, not only by the greed and shortsightedness of many employers, but by the vandalism and "racketeering" of many labor leaders as well. The Church's stand on these matters has been reiterated in numerous documents, notably the encyclicals *Rerum Novarum* of Pope Leo XIII and *Quadragesimo Anno* of Pope Pius XI, with which every priest should be familiar. The bishops have repeatedly called attention to the moral principles involved in industrial relations and economic and financial problems.

The priest who is called upon to face these problems in the course of social welfare has no alternative other than to plead for and champion the cause of justice. It is important, however, that those who speak for the Church on social justice be prepared to practice it themselves. Those who engage in a crusade for economic and industrial reform should be thoroughly armed with facts as well as qualified with a knowledge of principles and endowed with great prudence. Front-line participation, particularly in labor disputes, should never be undertaken by priests except after consultation with and approval by ecclesiastical superiors.

5

The maintenance and temporal betterment of the community may appear to be outside the proper sphere of the Church or of the individual priest, with a spiritual mission to fulfill. Yet, body and soul are joined together, and the spiritual life is so closely linked with temporal and material activities and conditions that one cannot ignore the one while tending to the other. Indeed, it may well be asserted that an essential part of the ministry of the Church is to work for the physical betterment of mankind in every sphere, at least indirectly, and to assist the community to adjust itself with a temporal objective in mind.

A case in point appears in the problem of interracial relations and in the impact of diverse immigrant, national, and racial groups upon an area. Many factors, undoubtedly, have been at work in the movement of these elements toward the metropolitan centers, with the consequent deterioration of urban neighborhoods. Industrial and commercial demands, importation of cheap labor, lower cultural standards of certain groups, and depreciation of real-estate values have created a dilemma for many people and induced them to flee from their old homes to newer sections and suburbs. In many instances, with improved financial position and facilities for commuting to work, others have of their own choice moved farther out in the metropolitan periphery.

While one of the results of this movement has been the further growth of the large cities and the creation of new real-estate values, it has created large "blight" areas, with run-down parishes and social conditions of the most primitive and objectionable character. Something must be done to halt this endless process of flight and of progressive social instability and deterioration.

Part of the problem arises from the failure or refusal of established elements of society to accept the coexistence of diverse elements in a neighborhood. This becomes particularly acute when different races are involved. Prejudice and emotion are sometimes fanned to a high pitch even among those who consider themselves good Catholics. This condition, if allowed to proceed unbridled, may be responsible for mounting tensions and the neglect of social responsibilities. This directly intensifies the problem.

To stem this tide and to protect the very foundations of Christian society, the Church must take a more active initiative in planning for the future. The development of a more realistic and Christian attitude toward social opportunity and integration is indicated on the one hand. On the other hand, a more vigorous campaign for the evangelization and Catholic education of immigrant, migrant, and racial elements is imperative. The conservation and rehabilitation of neighborhoods for better living thus becomes part of the social and spiritual mission of the Church, of the greatest importance.

The same considerations are applicable to life in the rural areas. It has been noted that the largest concentration of Catholics in the United States is to be found in the large cities. In part, this has been due to the first gravitation of Catholic immigrants. But there has also been a large-scale migration of Catholics in the second and third generations from the farms and smaller communities to the metropolitan centers. The results, as reflected in population statistics and Catholic influence, may be regarded with apprehension. Steps have already been taken by the Catholic Rural Life Conference and other agencies to study this situation and strengthen Catholic life and solidarity in the farm areas.

This type of planning, designed for better personal and community living, should not fear to enlist the support and co-operation of all elements, non-Catholic as well as Catholic. Nor should Catholic leaders hesitate to support any community measure, no matter by whom originated, which conforms to Christian principles and is planned to alleviate human misery and improve living standards and human relations. Participation in community chests, support of medical research against disease, contributions to causes such as the Red Cross, assistance to underprivileged children, and the encouragement of projects for better community recreational facilities are all recommended for consideration. Catholics should not only appear in the lists of contributors but should also aspire for positions of leadership in these movements; and the priest should encourage his people in these endeavors.

In dealing with problems of social vigilance and reform, the Church may have to take cognizance of legislative measures and tendencies in the civil order. Some proposals are definitely worthy of support. Others are questionable. Still others are clearly in conflict with sound morality and are hostile to the interests of the Church. Before taking sides on these issues, especially if partisan politics are involved, the individual priest will be wise to consult with his Ordinary. He should avoid any involvement of the Church in public controversy unless authorized or directed to do so.

Careful thought should be given also, before launching private programs of moral and social correction. Priestly zeal and indignation may lead one to vigorous criticism, denunciation, and suppression of current evils and abuses. But one must be on his guard against first impulses of a reforming character. It is possible to consume one's best energies in fighting peccadillos and to identify oneself with fanaticism in crusading against current fads and styles. One may expect to be criticized and attacked the moment he assails any form of vice, if it touches someone's ease, pleasure, convenience, or pocketbook. But it is best to reserve such attack for matters that really count, and then to organize the attack in the most dignified and effective manner, with the support and co-operation of responsible and respected elements of the community, as a reasonable assurance of success.

In general, social planning and reform should be positive. Even when certain evils must be denounced and suppressed in a community, a positive solution or substitute should be offered or at least suggested. If bad theater or movies have to be named and exposed, action should be indicated for clean and equally attractive entertainment. If immoral, suggestive, or irreligious literature and periodicals must be singled out for attack, this campaign should be accompanied with a program and practical provisions for reading of an uplifting, informative, and orthodox nature. If youth are warned to stay away from certain places, and danger zones are to be marked for extinction, immediate steps should be taken to secure recreational centers where young people can go with security and approval.

This, to be sure, places a special responsibility and burden upon the priest and possibly also upon the parish, institution, or community that he represents. But there is no other way in which he can function honestly and conscientiously. The social mission of the Church is a positive mission. The message of Christianity is not simply a combination of restrictions but a way of good, gracious, and joyous living.

In the words of Jacques Maritain, "Catholic action does not remain on the purely spiritual level; of itself it demands passage to the social level. In all countries where it does not suffer constraint, Christian social action is par excellence its mode of action. . . . The Church has established in the speculative order a doctrinal firmament of principles and truths dominating every social and economic subject. Practically, she gave her faithful the mission to enter her own pastoral ministry in order to bring into the social life and the treatment of social problems, through Catholic action, the testimony of Christ and an apostolic zeal for the salvation of souls and the expansion of the Kingdom of God."[9]

"I am the way, and the truth, and the life," said Christ.[10] "I am come that you may have life and may have it more abundantly."[11] In helping and inspiring mankind to achieve that more abundant life in this world as well as in the next, the Catholic priest finds his own life and his work.

---

[9] *Scholasticism and Politics,* translation edited by Mortimer J. Adler (New York: Macmillan Co., 1940), pp. 202–204.

[10] Jn. 14:6.

[11] Jn. 10:10.

CHAPTER XV

THE PRIEST AND PAROCHIAL RECORDS

I

AMONG the various responsibilities imposed by Church Law upon the priest engaged in the parochial ministry, none is more carefully laid out than that of keeping the parish registers or records. The reason for this is that every member of the Church has a particular juridical status which must be recognized and respected, quite as much as his civil status as a citizen. Membership in the Church is acquired by Baptism. Definite social position is established by Matrimony. Other relationships, rights, and duties are established by the reception of the sacraments of Confirmation and Holy Orders. The general spiritual status of a Catholic is of more than passing importance throughout his life, and the fact of death is in itself a matter of the greatest juridical consequences.

At times, it may be necessary for one to prove the existence of his juridical personality as a Catholic. One's freedom to marry or one's marital status may require proof or documentation. Proof of death may be an essential factor relating to the rights and duties of others. All of this implies the existence of records whose authenticity cannot be impugned and which are available for inspection and transcript by those who have a right to this information.

The keeping of these records, which actually reflects the administration of the sacraments, as in the case of Baptism or Matrimony, or the discharge of some other phase of the care of souls, devolves upon the pastor or the priest with equivalent jurisdiction. This is clearly set forth in Canon 470 of the Code of Canon Law, and is spelled out in considerable detail in many other canons of the same Code.

Five books are explicitly named in Canon 470, namely, the Registers of Baptism, Confirmation, Marriage, Death, and the *Status Animarum* or spiritual condition of the parishioners. This canon places upon the pastor the responsibility of keeping these records as accurately as possible. All of these books are to be inscribed according to the usage approved by the Church or prescribed by the Ordinary, and maintained in a safe place, open to inspection by the bishop and carefully guarded against falling into unauthorized hands. It is further indicated that at the end of each year the pastor is to send an authentic copy of the parish records, except the book on the *status animarum* to the Episcopal Curia or Chancellery. The fulfillment of this precaution, which points to the importance of safeguarding all official records, depends, of course, upon practical considerations and the injunction of the bishop.

It is not our intention here to enter into all details or technicalities involved in the keeping of parochial records. What must be stressed, however, is the importance of keeping them accurately, safely, and in permanent form. The basic purpose of these records is to establish proof of juridical status. These records, as well as certificates or transcripts drawn from them, are designed to establish a fact. Because they are made by the priest acting as a designated official and in the form determined by law, they have the nature of public ecclesiastical documents.[1] Hence the vital importance of conscientious and correct inscription and transcription of these records, as well as their safekeeping and control.

These observations are primarily pertinent to the ecclesiastical status of the individual, but they may also bear upon his status in civil law. If the entries are maintained in proper form, they are recognized as admissible evidence under the rules in common law jurisdiction in the United States of America. A baptismal

---

[1] Canons 1813, 1814. Cf. Rev. James J. O'Rourke, *Parish Registers* (Washington, D. C.: The Catholic University of America Press, 1934).

certificate, duly signed and sealed, is generally sufficient to establish place of birth and citizenship. It is obvious that the absence, loss, or confusion of these records may work considerable hardship, embarrassment, and harm.

Standard books, with tabulated columns and other desirable features in conformity with official regulations, are available from Catholic church goods vendors. A few principles, however, should govern their selection and use. The books selected should be kept exclusively for their one specific purpose. They should be in bound form, not loose papers, loose leaf, or detachable certificates. A good quality linen paper should be selected, and the binding should be substantial, in view of the length of service expected. The pages should be numbered, as a further precaution against fraudulent substitution, and an index should be provided for ready and permanent reference.

The inscription should be entered in permanent quality ink. These records should last for a century or longer. All writing should be perfectly legible, so as to avoid misunderstanding; and abbreviations, particularly those of an arbitrary or cryptic character, should be avoided. Room should be left for later additions. Thus, the Baptismal Register should leave room for later entries indicating marriage or Holy Orders, as these additions may be of the utmost importance later on.

Custom regulates the language to be used, whether vernacular or Latin. A safe rule is the use of the vernacular, except for confidential notes, which may be put in Latin. If corrections have to be made, erasures and cancellations should be avoided. Instead, a marginal note should be added, or a new record may be imposed with cross reference, with the signature or initials of the person making the correction.

All entries should at least be witnessed by the signature of the pastor. According to Church legislation the obligation to maintain parish records and to issue certificates as transcripts from them devolves personally and as a grave obligation upon the pastor. This authority devolves also upon those endowed with parochial powers, including the quasi pastor, administrator, or substitute

pastor. Curates are not so empowered, except by delegation of
the pastor, letters of assignment by the Ordinary, or determination
by diocesan statutes. Competent commentaries allow the curate
to presume the pastor's permission in cases not covered by the
provisions of Canon 476.

The time to enter records is promptly after the fact. It is
advisable to make entries directly in the appropriate register.
Notes made on scraps of paper are easily lost.

The parish records should be kept under lock and key or the
equivalent. In other words, these registers should be regarded as
confidential and carefully maintained as such. Moreover, they
should be kept in a place secure against theft and fire. Failure
to take this precaution has been responsible for the loss of
many parish records, with consequences easy to imagine. A
substantial, fireproof, and protected safe in the sacristy of the
church or in the rectory should be standard equipment.

The pastor has the right and duty also, as official witness in
matters pertaining to his office, to secure a parish seal.[2] This
may be either of the paper embossing type or an ink imprint.
The seal is used, in addition to the pastor's signature, to fortify
the authenticity of parochial documents and to complete the
certificate or statement.

Certificates or transcripts, drawn from the parish registers,
should be signed by the pastor or delegate, as indicated above,
and impressed with the parish seal. Properly drawn, these certificates are authentic and official documents.[3] Scrupulous care
should be observed in the issuance of such certificates, to make
certain that the transcript is accurate.

In the matter of baptismal certificates, requests may be received from time to time, to modify dates of birth or to change
names or to omit any further references which may appear in
the record. In no case can falsification be justified. By his
signature and parochial seal, the pastor acts as a notary and
testifies to the truth of his statement when he inscribes original

---

[2] Canon 470, § 4.
[3] Canon 1813, § 4.

records or draws a certificate from his parochial books. Whether it is necessary to include notations beyond those relating directly to Baptism depends on the purpose of the certificate. If the certificate is desired in connection with marriage, then it is necessary to include annotations that may be found in the baptismal record relating to the marital status of the individual. If it is sought merely to establish birthplace, date, and nationality, or to secure a passport, for example, such annotations are unnecessary. In all cases, however, certificates should be dated, so as to avoid the possibility of their being used for other purposes beyond a reasonable time limit.

Certificates are generally given in the vernacular, unless they are requested for countries speaking another language, in which case Latin is used. When certificates are sent from one country to another, the Sacred Congregation of the Council requires the signature and seal of the Ordinary. Recognition of the authenticity of such certificates also pertains to the bishop, not to the pastor.[4]

If legitimate custom approves, a proportionate fee may be charged for the issuance of a certificate. A charge should not be exacted of the poor or of those who cannot afford to pay for this service.

2

The Baptismal Register may be regarded as the principal and in many ways the most important of the parochial records listed in Canon Law. Basically, it records the names of the persons baptized, the minister of baptism, parents, godparents, place, and date of baptism.[5] If the Baptism has been administered outside the proper parish church, the parochial register of the parish must be inscribed with the record. If Baptism has taken place in a parochial church other than the one proper to the recipient, with due permission or just cause, the record of Baptism is to be inscribed in the registry of that parish.

The name of the minister of Baptism is also required, even

---

[4] A.A.S.I. (1909), 660.
[5] Canon 777.

when a lay person has administered the sacrament. If a private Baptism is followed by the supplying of the omitted ceremonies, the name of the priest who presided in the second instance as well as the minister of private Baptism must be recorded.

If someone other than the proper pastor of the subject administers the Baptism, he must notify the pastor as soon as possible, either personally or by mail, together with the same information as the latter would secure.[6] In the event that the Baptism took place outside the proper parish of the subject, it is probably sufficient to notify the pastor of the place where the Baptism took place, who, in turn, is required to convey the information to the subject's pastor. This notification must be in the form of an official document with signature of the pastor and parochial seal. If one has been delegated to perform a Baptism, he may also be permitted to make the entry in the register; but the pastor must confirm this with his own signature.

The name of the person baptized occupies first place in the baptismal register. Normally a Christian name is given. If the parents are unwilling to give a Christian name, the priest adds a Christian name to the given name and surname in the register.[7]

The names and address of the parents are also to be included. Although the Code does not require recording of the family residence, this information is important. As a matter of prudence, all pertinent information should be secured prior to performing the ceremony, so as to be certain that this Baptism comes within one's jurisdiction and that all special circumstances have been taken into consideration.

Under the heading of special circumstances, the legislation of the Church urges special precaution when dealing with the names of parents, to avoid the possiblity of ill fame or embarrassment. This is to be considered specifically (1) in the case of illegitimate progeny or (2) in the issue of "marriages of conscience."

Where the first case is verified, the Code stipulates that the name of the mother is to be inscribed in the registry if her

---

[6] Canon 778.
[7] Canon 761.

maternity is publicly known or she freely requests this registration in writing or in the presence of two witnesses. Likewise the name of the father is to be included if he freely requests it, in the same manner, or if he is known as the parent from an authentic public document.

In the case of the father, it should be noted that a private acknowledgment is not sufficient. A legal bond of paternity must be established, by authentic public document, whether ecclesiastical or civil. An example of a civil document fulfilling this requirement would be a civil court order requiring the reputed father to contribute to the support of the child. Such evidence should be preserved in connection with the register.

In cases where the names of both the father and mother are to be entered, the status of the progeny should be noted, not by the word "illegitimate," because of possible civil effects, but by an expression, preferably in Latin, indicating civil marriage or birth outside matrimony.

In other cases, the name of the child is to be inscribed as of an unknown father or unknown parents.[8] This inscription should be made in Latin to reduce as far as possible its becoming public property. Obviously, this matter requires prudent and conservative judgment.

When the child to be baptized is a foundling, the name is generally given by the protective organization, which will also supply the other information, including the date of finding, the place, by whom found, and the probable age.

Special precautions are to be taken in registering the baptisms of adulterine or incestuous progeny, even when maternal request has been made in the form stated above. The Code lays down the principle that the father of a child is indicated by recognized marriage, unless the contrary is demonstrated by convincing proof.[9] Therefore, the child is to be inscribed as legitimate, even though the married mother declares it to be extramarital and the father denies his paternity, unless evident arguments to the

---

[8] Canon 777, § 2.
[9] Canon 1115, § 1.

contrary are presented. In some cases, it may appear that no scandal will result by notation of illegitimacy, as for the child of a civil but adulterous marriage; but procedure in these cases should be governed by advice of the Ordinary.

The second special circumstance considered here involves children born in so-called "marriages of conscience" or marriages in which the ceremony has been contracted validly and licitly but secretly for special reasons.[10] The real name of the child must be given, but the names of the parents are to be withheld, or fictitious names are to be registered. In these cases the father or the mother is required, under penalty, to report to the Ordinary where the marriage was celebrated, within thirty days, including the fact, the place, and the date of the Baptism, stating whether names of the parents or aliases were registered. This report must be made by letter or a trusted person, such as the minister of Baptism or of the marriage. The minister of the marriage is required to inform the parties of this regulation and of the penalty, which is publication of the marriage and birth.[11]

A special book is to be maintained, as a secret archive, distinct from the ordinary register of marriages, for the inscription of the information which is forwarded to the Ordinary, including the parents' true names.

In addition to its regulations governing the inscription of the names of parents, the Code requires the entry of the names of the godparents in the Baptismal Registry.[12] According to Canon Law, there must be at least one witness and at most two, for solemn Baptism, with stated qualifications to act in the capacity of godparents. The same is desired even for private Baptisms, if available.[13] Their inscription is necessary principally because of the matrimonial impediment of spiritual relationship which arises between the person baptized and the godparents.

If different persons are used in a conditional Baptism from the previous Baptism, the godparents do not contract this im-

---

[10] Canons 1104–1107.
[11] Ep. encycl., *Satis Vobis*, Nos. 12, 13.
[12] Canon 777, § 1.
[13] Canon 762.

pediment. The same is true for a godparent who acts only in the supplying of ceremonies after a private Baptism.[14] Nevertheless, it is advisable to inscribe these names in the record, with a notation that the impediment has not been contracted.

In addition to the facts relating directly to Baptism, this same register must serve for later annotations relating to the status of the member of the Church. Specifically, it is to be noted if the baptized person receives Confirmation, contracts marriage (apart from secret marriage as governed by Canon 1107), receives the Holy Order of subdiaconate, or makes a profession of solemn vows.[15]

With respect to Confirmation, the Confirmation name, place, and date of reception are sufficient, although the name of the minister of the sacrament is of interest. The obligation for this inscription falls upon the pastor. If Confirmation has been received in a parish other than that of Baptism, the minister of Confirmation has the first obligation of notifying the pastor. Ordinarily, however, this duty will be performed by authentic documentary notification from the pastor where the Confirmation has taken place.[16]

The practical purpose of matrimonial notation in the Baptismal Register is that reference to or request for a certificate of this record immediately reveals the existence of an impediment to the bond or the freedom of the party or parties to contract marriage. The Code makes it clear that the pastor is required to note in this register, as well as in the Matrimonial Register, the fact and date of the marriage of persons baptized in the parish.

If the marriage takes place in the church where one or both parties have been baptized, the pastor inserts in the Baptismal Register adjoining the baptismal record the date and place of the nuptial ceremony and the name of the other spouse. It further orders that if the married person was baptized elsewhere, he must notify the pastor where the Baptism took place, of the

---

[14] Canon 763, § 2.
[15] Canon 470, § 2.
[16] Canon 799.

fact of the marriage so that proper notation can be made in the Baptismal Register. He may do this himself or through the Episcopal Curia, as circumstances may indicate.[17]

When this information is transmitted, it should include the names and surnames of the married parties and their parents, the ages of the couple, the place and date of marriage, and the names and surnames of the witnesses. If the place of Baptism is unknown, when transmitting this information, the document should be sent to the Ordinary of the presumed place of birth or origin. It must be transmitted even when the marriage has taken place in extraordinary form.[18] If a priest has witnessed such marriage, he is held responsible for conveying the necessary information to the appropriate parishes; otherwise, the parties and the witnesses carry a common responsibility for this transmission. In both cases, the pastor having matrimonial jurisdiction as well as the pastor or pastors of Baptism must be notified.

Extraordinary cases are also visualized in Canons 1043 and 1044, in which marriages may be performed under urgent danger of death to one or the other parties. Only those marriages need be inscribed where a public impediment exists. Marriages performed with these powers but similar to marriages of conscience and secretly convalidated marriages are to be treated with the same secrecy and in the same manner as marriages of conscience already touched upon.

The same general principle applies to the convalidation of marriages. If the nullity arose from a public impediment, record of the convalidation is made in the Marriage Register. If the marriage was never properly recorded, it should be entered in both the Marriage and Baptismal Registers. If the nullity arose from occult cause, it should be referred directly to the secret book of the Episcopal Curia without any reference to the Baptismal Register.

Other changes relative to marital status may also have to be noted in the record of Baptisms. If, for example, a registered

---

[17] Canon 1103, § 2.
[18] Canon 1098.

marriage has been declared null, the Baptismal as well as the Matrimonial Register must be amended accordingly.[19] Such notice is to be transmitted by the Ordinary or his delegate to the respective pastor or pastors. Subsequent marriages are also to be noted. If a marriage has been entered through the Pauline Privilege, this likewise should be recorded.

As already stated, the reception of the subdiaconate is to be noted in the Baptismal Record, as this act renders any attempt at marriage invalid. Higher Sacred Orders than the subdiaconate are not included, as they add nothing substantial to the impediment. The notation carries the name of the ordained, that of the bishop who performed the ordination, the place, and the date of ordination. The responsibility for transmitting this information to the pastor of the parish where the respective baptismal record is kept devolves upon the Ordinary of the place, whether he performed the ordination or authorized another to do so.[20]

Similar notation and for the same reason is required for persons who have made solemn religious profession, or simple perpetual profession in the Jesuit Order.[21] This information should include the name of the professed person, the order, the person who received the subject into the profession, the place (province or abbey), and the date of profession. The obligation for furnishing this information pertains to the major superiors of religious orders, in the case of religious ordained with dimissorials for the reception of Sacred Orders.[22] In the case of religious who receive major orders by what is called *jure saecularium,* this responsibility belongs to the Ordinary of the place where the religious house of the ordained is situated.

If solemn reception is received besides the subdiaconate, both must be recorded.[23] If a dispensation in the external forum is later granted, this must be recorded in the Baptismal Register, as the effect is to restore freedom to marry.

---

[19] Canons 1988, 1119.
[20] Canon 1011.
[21] Canon 1073.
[22] Canon 964, 2°.
[23] Canons 1011; 576, § 2.

3

The second of the parish registers is the Matrimonial Register. According to the prescriptions of Canon Law, this record must include the names of the party to the marriage, the minister, the ordinary witnesses, the place, and the date enumerating the year, month, and day written out.[24] As this date must coincide with the record made on the return portion of the civil license, one is warned against antedating the record.

In addition to this information, the Roman Ritual notes other information for the record.[25] This includes the publishing or the omission of one or more of the banns. The names of the parents, age and parish of those contracting marriage, and the parochial address of the witnesses are also demanded. If one of the persons being married is a widow or widower, the name of the deceased spouse is to be recorded. The status of the priest presiding at the marriage is to be given, whether he assisted by ordinary faculties or express permission.

The canon places the obligation of making this record upon the pastor of those being married. Inasmuch as any pastor can validly assist within the limits of his parish at the marriage even of nonsubjects, he is required to record all such marriages in his Matrimonial Register.[26] This rule applies even though he assisted without due permission or just cause. On the other hand, any priest who is delegated to assist at a marriage outside his territory is not held to this obligation. The pastor of the place is still the one required to record the marriage.

The same canon, however, imposes the same obligation as that of the pastor upon the priest who acts in his place (*qui ejus vices gerit*) in the matter of marriage. Such power might be conferred by episcopal designation or by delegation of the pastor. Thus the assistant pastor who is regularly authorized to perform marriages has the obligation of recording those at which he has

---

[24] Canon 1103, § 1.
[25] Title XII, Chap. IV.
[26] Cf. Canon 1097.

been the qualified witness. In this specific case it is not necessary for his inscription to be subsigned by the pastor.

As already observed, the pastor is required to make a notation in the Baptismal Register of the marriage if he is the pastor of the place where one of the persons was baptized.[27] He is bound to notify the pastor or pastors if the Baptism of one or both took place elsewhere. He may convey this information directly or through the diocesan Curia, depending upon custom.

The obligation of recording marriage exists also in the case where matrimony has been contracted in the extraordinary form. This situation arises in the case of a deathbed marriage or one which is celebrated in a place where it is reasonably foreseen that it will be at least one month before the Ordinary, the pastor, or a delegated priest is available. Under these circumstances, Canon Law declares that a valid and licit marriage can be entered, providing there are witnesses.[28] If a priest, although not duly delegated, is present, it is his obligation to have the marriage recorded; otherwise, the married couple and witnesses have a common obligation to do so.[29] This information may be transmitted to the pastor of the place where the marriage took place, or to the Ordinary of the place, or to the pastor of the domicile of the contracting parties.

If special circumstances are involved, requiring secrecy, the Ordinary should be notified for inscription in the secret Matrimonial Register of the Curial Archives.[30] The same regulation is to be followed in recording so-called "marriages of conscience" which are permitted only for the most exceptional reasons and are never to be noted in the parochial records.[31]

In addition to the information listed above, the *Roman Ritual* requires that a record be made of dispensations obtained from a *de facto* public impediment. This obtains also where the Pauline Privilege has been used. If the dispensation has been obtained in the external forum, the inscription is to be made in the parochial

---

[27] Canon 1103, § 2.
[28] Canon 1098, 1°, 2°.
[29] Canon 1103, § 3.
[30] Canon 1047.
[31] Canons 1104, 1107.

Matrimonial Register. If it has been given in the internal non-sacramental forum for a secret impediment, it is to be recorded in the Episcopal Archives.[32] Notation must be made also of dispensation from the banns and dispensations given after marriage, such as from a *ratum et non consummatum* marriage, as noted in Canon 1119.

Record must be made also of the convalidation of marriages in the external forum and of marriages contracted conditionally. Those convalidated in the internal nonsacramental forum are confided to the register of secret archives. Declarations of nullity are also inscribed in accordance with the same principles [33]

4

A special book or parochial register is to be maintained also for the sacrament of Confirmation.[34] This record is limited to the name of the person confirmed, the minister who is at the same time the qualified witness, the parents, and sponsors, and the date and place of the reception of the sacrament. The same procedure regarding the inscription of the names of parents as obtains in Baptism is to be followed when there is question of legitimacy or actual parentage.

As previously stated, a record of Confirmation must also be made in the Baptismal Register. If Confirmation is administered in a church other than the parish of the individuals concerned or other than the parish where they were baptized, the pastors are to be notified respectively, so that due record may be made. The obligation of this notification pertains to the minister of Confirmation, either personally or through another, such as the pastor of the parish where the sacrament was conferred.[35]

The Book of the Dead is likewise to be kept as a special register apart from the other parochial books and distinct from the sick-call register.[36] The inscription is to be made by the minister of the funeral ceremonies; but, as the responsibility for keeping

---

[32] Canon 379.
[33] Canons 1988, 1990.
[34] Canon 798.

[35] Canon 799.
[36] Canon 1238.

the parish registers devolves primarily upon the pastor, the latter must subsign his name to the record to make it authentic.

The full name, baptismal and family, of the deceased is to be noted, the age by notation of the date of birth or number of years, and the names of parents or spouse as the case may indicate. If the deceased was married more than once, the name of only the last spouse need be entered. The day, month, and year of death, and the cause of death if known, are to be set forth, and the spiritual status of the deceased at the time of death is to be noted by indicating the sacraments received before death, with the name of the minister, if possible, or the reason for their omission. The place and date of burial, including the church and cemetery, conclude this record.

The last of the five parochial books is reserved for a report on the spiritual status of the members of the parish.[37] This book, however, is specifically exempted from the annual transmission by the pastor to the Episcopal Curia, required by law.[38] The *Roman Ritual* outlines various procedures, all of which are obviously dependent upon a census-taking or visitation of the parish.[39] It has been suggested that, before actual visitation of the families and individuals concerned, the pastor send out a questionnaire to be filled in and returned. This information may then be transferred to the book or to a system of index cards.

The importance and methods of taking the census have been described in another chapter of this book. As already noted, the accuracy and value of the census material depend upon the personal action and planned, yearly, and current inventory taken by the pastor and his assistants of the souls under his care.

Enough has been said to indicate the importance, not only of keeping the parish records, but also of making them promptly and keeping them accurate. If considerations of justice and fairness to those under one's spiritual care are not sufficient motives

---

[37] Canon 470, § 1.

[38] Canon 470, § 3.

[39] XII, VI, 513. Cf. William Francis Fitzgerald, *The Parish Census and the Liber Status Animarum* (Washington, D. C.: The Catholic University of America Press, 1954).

to insure the fulfillment of one's obligations in this respect, the
Code of Canon Law states that a pastor who fails to keep or
preserve the parochial records diligently, according to the norms
of law, shall be punished by his Ordinary in proportion to the
gravity of his guilt.[40] This warning is further enlarged by Canon
2406, which declares that "any person who is bound by his office
to draft, write, or preserve . . . parochial books, and who presumes
to falsify, mutilate, destroy, or hide them, is to be deprived of
his office or punished by other grave penalties by the Ordinary
in charge of such records or books, and those who maliciously
refuse, when legitimately requested, to transcribe, transmit, or
exhibit those books, or who in any other way abuse their office,
are likewise to be punished."[41]

5

The general principles underlying the necessity and prescriptions
for keeping the parish registers stipulated by Canon Law are
pertinent also to the keeping of financial records and reports,
whether of a parish, school, institution, or any activity of an
ecclesiastical nature where funds are involved. As a trustee of
parochial, institutional, or organizational money, the priest has
the same accountability as if he were in a private business enterprise, responsible to investors, stockholders, or contributors. He
should never interpret the generosity of the faithful as an authorization to use their offerings as if they were his personal
property. Nor should he delude himself with the false idea that
the spiritual purpose of Church funds exempts him from strict
accounting or an audit of accounts.

The administration of ecclesiastical funds and properties is
governed by definite laws, set forth in the Code of Canon Law,
leaving no doubt on this matter. Thus Canon 1523, after stating
that the administrators of ecclesiastical possessions are required
to fulfill diligently their responsibilities, outlines certain principles
of justice and good business. For example, they are required

---

[40] Canon 2383.
[41] Canon 2406.

to see that the properties and funds entrusted to their care do not suffer loss or harm. They are required to fulfill the prescriptions of both canon and civil law and the terms imposed by founders, donors, and legitimate authority. They must see to the collection of interest and give an accurate accounting of the goods entrusted to them, in accordance with the intention of donors and the norms of the law. They must keep books of income and expense. They must keep all documents and papers pertaining to church funds and properties in secure and convenient custody.

There are three general types of financial reports in parish accounting: (1) annual or monthly reports to the Chancery Office; (2) annual reports to the parishioners; (3) annual or monthly reports made by officers of church societies to the pastor. The form of financial report which the pastor must submit to the Chancery Office is left to the discretion of the bishop. The form of the annual report to the parish is determined by the pastor in conjunction with his trustees; and organizational reports to the pastor usually follow the pattern which he may require. In all instances, however, the priest in charge ought to familiarize himself with at least elementary accounting and to the extent necessary engage professional accounting assistance.[42]

The establishment of a systematic procedure for the segregation of accounts by classification and for a record of receipts and disbursements is essential, not only for the proper sustaining of resources but also for the rendering of correct reports. While it may not be necessary or even advisable to open one's books to the general public, they should be in such condition that the administrator knows at all times exactly how his church, plant, organizations, and securities stand and can render to his legitimate superiors a full and honest statement of financial position.

In view of the high spiritual calling of the priest, these considerations may appear as heavily pedestrian. "Let a man so account of us," writes St. Paul, "as the ministers of Christ and

---

[42] Cf. Dumas Leon McCleary, C.S.V., *Parish Accounting, loc. cit.*

the dispensers of the mysteries of God. Here now it is required among the dispensers that a man be found faithful."[43] But the ministry of the priest extends to details as well as to generalities and to the true and faithful recording of facts, as well as to the dispensing of the mysteries of God, particularly when the rights of others are concerned. "For they that have ministered well," the same Apostle observes of temporal matters, "shall purchase to themselves a good degree and much confidence in the faith which is in Christ Jesus."[44]

What has been noted here in reference to the duty of keeping parochial records correctly, intact, and in security, may well be broadened to include the keeping of all records pertaining to the history of Church, whether they relate to parishes, institutions, or communities. The Church has suffered much from the false and libelous writing of history by its enemies and those whose partial or slanted views leave a distorted impression. The Church can profit much by the positive recording of facts and the keeping of records which redound to its credit and glory, and by the authentic interpretation of its history from true documentary evidence and the pens of qualified writers. The systematic keeping of parish histories, for example, may be a work of the greatest importance, for which future generations will be deeply grateful.

The priest who views his responsibility in this full light, conscientiously fulfilling his duties down to the last detail and viewing his ministry against the backgrounds of both time and eternity, can certainly regard himself as sharing an important part in the historic work of the Church. For him the injunction of St. Paul has a real and applied meaning: "Labor in all things: do the work of an evangelist: fulfill thy ministry."[45] And he may reasonably, with God's grace, expect to hear the words of Christ. "Well done, good and faithful servant, because thou hast been faithful over a few things, I will place thee over many things. Enter thou into the joy of the Lord."[46]

---

[43] 1 Cor. 4:1, 2.
[44] 1 Tim. 3:13.
[45] 2 Tim. 4:5.
[46] Mt. 25:21.

INDEX